Decision-Making in The New Reality

Complexity, Knowledge and Knowing

by
Dr. Alex Bennet
Dr. David Bennet
Mountain Quest Institute

MQIPress (2018)
Frost, West Virginia
ISBN 978-1-949829-25-9

The New Reality Series

MQIPress
Frost, West Virginia
303 Mountain Quest Lane, Marlinton, WV 24954
United States of America
Telephone: 304-799-7267

eMail: alex@mountainquestinstitute.com
www.mountainquestinstitute.com
www.mountainquestinn.com
www.MQIPress.com

ISBN 978-1-949829-25-9

Table of Contents

Table and Figures iv
Appreciation v
Preface vi

Section I: BUILDING A FOUNDATION 11
Chapter 1: The New Reality 12
Chapter 2: Systems and Complexity 19
      Systems Principles
Chapter 3: An Introduction to Knowledge 33

Section II: COMPLEX DECISION-MAKING IN A COMPLEX ENVIRONMENT 41
Chapter 4: The Complexity of Situations 42
Chapter 5: The Complexity of Decisions 49
Chapter 6: The Complexity of Actions 60
      Guiding Principles
Chapter 7: Complex Decision-Making 65
Chapter 8: Dealing with Complex Adaptive Organizations 73

Section III: DECISION-MAKING FROM THE INSIDE-OUT 79
Chapter 9: The View from the Inside Out 80
Chapter 10: Hierarchy as a Basic Property of the Decision-Making System 84
Chapter 11: Advanced Decision-Making: The Cortex 87

Section IV: ENGAGING TACIT KNOWLEDGE 91
Chapter 12: Differentiating Tacit Knowledge 92
Chapter 13: The Aspects of Tacit Knowledge 96
Chapter 14: Building Extraordinary Consciousness 103
Chapter 15: Decision-Making and Tacit Knowledge 111

Section V: THE NEW WORLD OF KNOWLEDGE AND KNOWING 115
Chapter 16: The Art of Knowing 116
      Principles of Knowing
Chapter 17: The New Decision-Makers 134
Chapter 18: A Guess about the Future 145

Appendix A: From Knowledge to Wisdom 149
Appendix B: Parable of the Watchmakers 155
References 156
Subject Index 165
About Mountain Quest 168

Table and Figures

Table 1: Systems in terms of complexity 22

Figure 1: The systems space 25
Figure 2: Cone of acceptable outcomes 34
Figure 3: Brief descriptions of systems 40
Figure 4: Organizational knowledge needs 51
Figure 5: The decision-making strategy 65
Figure 6: Neurons in the mind/brain 81
Figure 7: Continuum of awareness 94
Figure 8: Embodied tacit knowledge 97
Figure 9: Intuitive tacit knowledge 98
Figure 10: Affective tacit knowledge 99
Figure 11: Spiritual tacit knowledge 101
Figure 12: Building extraordinary consciousness 104
Figure 13: Eternal loop of knowledge and knowing 117
Figure 14: New ways of thinking 141
Figure 15: Old and new paradigms 142
Figure 16: Knowledge and consciousness 154

In Appreciation

Life is so amazing. Along the way we meet so many people who change our lives. As we were finishing this book, we took the time to reflect on our journey. There was one person who kept leaping to the top of our thoughts, our mentor, Dr. Charles Seashore, or, to all those who have learned from him and loved him, *Charlie*. Among so many other things, Charlie was a systems man, taking every opportunity to lead students at Fielding Graduate University through the Systems Knowledge Area, giving them an experience that was one of a kind. Several of these sessions were held here at Mountain Quest, during which we had the good fortune to participate in unforgettable experiences. Charlie has moved on to greater fields now; no doubt he is applauding our efforts from afar. *Charlie, we honor you, we thank you, we love you. This book is dedicated to you.*

There are many to thank for helping to bring this book into Reality. First, our sincere thanks to those who gave so freely of their time to read and comment on parts of this text, especially Bob Turner, Jonathan Lakes, and Dr. Boyd Smith; and to Dr. Joyce Avedisian, whose work contributed to our discussion of values.

Second, as always, we could not think the thoughts we think and act on them without the day-to-day support of Andrew Dean, the Manager of the Inn at Mountain Quest, and our son. And finally, our deep appreciation for all those whose lives we have touched along the journey, and from whom we have learned as we moved through our professional careers in the government and private sectors. We hope you enjoy reading this book as much as we enjoyed writing it!

Preface

Through the past 20 years we have engaged in a great deal of research—much of it experiential in nature—which has led us to break through life-long perceived limits and shift and expand our beliefs about Life and the world of which we are a part. The advent of self-publishing virtual books has opened the door to share this learning with the public at large. Right up front we offer the following assumptions:

Assumption 1: Knowledge is the capacity (potential or actual) to take effective action.

As a functional definition, knowledge is considered *the capacity (potential or actual) to take effective action in varied and uncertain situations* (Bennet and Bennet, 2004), and consists of understanding, insights, meaning, intuition, creativity, judgment, and the ability to anticipate the outcome of our actions. Knowledge itself is neither true nor false, and its value in terms of good or poor is difficult to measure other than by the outcomes of its actions. Hence, good knowledge would have a high probability of producing the desired (anticipated) outcome, and poor knowledge would have a low probability of producing the expected result. For complex situations the quality of knowledge (from good to poor) may be hard to estimate before the action is taken because of the system's unpredictability. After the outcome has occurred, the quality of knowledge can be assessed by comparing the actual outcome to the expected outcome. See Section I for an in-depth treatment of knowledge and its role in decision-making. Chapter 3 will introduce you to the core knowledge concepts and language used throughout this book.

Assumption 2: Human beings and the organizations they create are complex adaptive systems.

A complex adaptive system (CAS) contains many parts (in the case of an organization, people, etc.) that interact with each other. Complex adaptive systems are partially ordered systems that unfold and evolve through time. They are mostly self-organizing, learning and adaptive (thus their name). To survive they are always creating new ideas, scanning the environment, trying new approaches, observing the results, and changing the way they operate. To continuously adapt they must operate in perpetual disequilibrium, which results in some unpredictable behavior. Having nonlinear relationships, the CAS creates global properties that are called emergent because they seem to emerge from the multitude of elements within the system and their relationships. They typically cannot be understood through analysis and logic because of the large number of elements and relationships. Examples are life, ecosystems, economies, organizations and cultures. Further discussion of complex systems is included in Section II of this book.

Assumption 3: The human mind is an associative patterner that is continuously re-creating knowledge for the situation at hand.

Knowledge exists in the human brain in the form of stored or expressed neural patterns that may be selected, activated, mixed and/or reflected upon through thought. Incoming information is associated with stored information. From this mixing process new patterns are created that may represent understanding, meaning and the capacity to anticipate (to various degrees) the results of potential actions. Thus, knowledge is context sensitive and situation dependent, with the mind continuously growing, restructuring and creating increased organization (information) and knowledge for the moment at hand. Further discussion of these concepts is included in Chapter 3 and Section III of this book.

Assumption 4: Every decision-maker has a self-organizing, hierarchical set of theories (and consistent relationships among those theories) that guide their decision-making process.

Theories, beliefs and assumptions are the core essence of thoughts and experiences that are repeated over and over again. Theories that are invariant forms at the highest hierarchal level of the prefrontal cortex significantly influence decision-making. These invariant theories are continuously integrated across complementary sensing modes (visual, auditory, somatic, etc.) and through a downward feedback loop provide the decision-maker with the capacity to anticipate the outcome of actions. The larger the number of, and connections among, invariant forms developed through experience and learning, the more robust the spectrum of theories available to the decision-maker. Thus, the workings of our mind/brain provide a model for decision-making in a complex situation. Further discussion of these concepts is included in Section III of this book.

Assumption 5: The unconscious mind is multidimensional and, given a healthy mind and body, has a vast store of tacit knowledge available to us.

It has only been in the past few decades that cognitive psychology and neuroscience have begun to seriously explore unconscious mental life. Polanyi felt that tacit knowledge consisted of *a range* of conceptual and sensory information and images that could be used to make sense of a situation or event (Hodgkin, 1991; Smith, 2003). He was right. The unconscious mind is incredibly powerful, on the order of a million times more powerful than the conscious stream of thought. The challenge is to make better use of our tacit knowledge through creating greater connections with the unconscious, building and expanding the resources stored in the unconscious, deepening areas of resonance, and sharing tacit resources among individuals. Further discussion of these concepts is included in Section IV of this book.

Assumption 6: There are still vast workings of the human mind and its connections to higher-order energies that we do not understand.

The limitations we as humans place on our decision-making capacities and capabilities are created from past reference points, that which has been developed primarily through the rationale and logical workings of the mechanical functioning of our mind/brain, an understanding that has come through extensive intellectual effort. Yet we now recognize that knowledge is a living form of information, tailored by our minds specifically for a situation at hand. The totality of knowledge can no easier be codified and stored than our feelings, nor would it be highly beneficial to do so in a changing and uncertain environment. Thus, in this book—understanding the limitations of our own perceptions and understanding—we consider and explore areas and phenomena that are beyond old paradigms of decision-making. This does not mean that we ignore all that we have learned. Hardly! Rather, we recognize that there are many approaches to living, that knowledge takes many forms, and that the way we decide and act is a choice ... an extremely important choice, especially in a CUCA world!

Building on these assumptions, the focus of this book is decision-making. Decision-making has been around as long as management and leadership—and probably longer. In the full throes of bureaucracy, decisions lay fully in the domain of managers and leaders. In 1971, with decision-making still residing in the upper layers of the bureaucratic hierarchy, Chris Argyris described the introduction of "rational" management. This new management approach substituted formal calculation for judgment and instinct, what was then considered personally threatening to the traditional, control-oriented executives. (Argyris, 1971, p. 13) Some authors went so far as to state, "Don't waste an executive's time on decision-making ... when it comes to putting data together and making a decision, machines can do a better job than men." (Edwards, 1971, p. 63)

By the 1990's, decision-makers were well-versed in mathematical and statistical techniques such as utility analysis, operations research, decision matrices and probabilistic decision trees, and had begun to explore the human "qualitative" side of decision-making dealing with probabilities, preferences and propensities. (Sashkin, 1990, p. 17) As our environment continues to become more complex in the increasingly inter-connected world of the 21st century, decision-making has come full cycle. Decision-makers at the point of action (residing at all levels throughout the organization) must **increasingly rely on their intuition and judgment**. The impact of complexity has not been fully understood, or assessed. Research in complexity science is a relatively young field that has recently become of serious interest to scholars, decision-makers and organizational leaders.

This research, broadly connected with complexity science, has gathered attention in the business world ... as executives and scholars recognized that conventional theories of management, forged in the era of industrialization, vertically integrated companies, and relatively impermeable institution boarders, could no longer cope with the immensely complex organizations that have emerged during two decades of rising globalization and decentralization. (Buchanan, 2004, p. 71)

The first section of this book lays the groundwork for building an understanding of (1) the changing, uncertain and complex environment, (2) systems and complexity, and (3) knowledge and its role in the decision-making process.

The second section of this book explores decision-making in a complex environment. We begin by looking at the complexity of situations, exploring **the decision-making process for complex situations in a complex environment**—what we call complex adaptive messes, or CAMs—in terms of: (1) laying the groundwork for decision-making, (2) understanding and exploring complex situations, (3) discussing human additive factors, (4) preparing for the decision process, and (5) mechanisms for influencing complex situations. When the language of complexity thinking is used, it is defined in terms of its usefulness in considering the decision-making process. We then focus on the complexity of decisions, taking into account the human factor before turning our focus to the complexity of actions. Armed with the language of systems and complexity, we then address complex decision-making more directly. Finally, we focus on dealing with complex adaptive organizations.

The third section of this book looks at **decision-making from the inside-out**. We specifically focus on (1) the development of invariant hierarchical patterns removed from the context and content of a specific situation; (2) the connections among values, beliefs, assumptions and those patterns (a personal theory); and (3) the robustness of those patterns and connections in a complex decision situation. We believe that the decision-making process within the mind/brain can serve as a model for conscious decision-making when dealing with complex situations in a complex world.

The fourth section of this book moves further into the realms of tacit knowledge. As the importance of tacit knowledge grows in support of organizational performance, so must our depth of understanding and the articulation of that understanding. In this section we lay the groundwork for understanding the full scope of that which is available to the decision-maker in the **unconscious realms** of the mind/brain. This section includes: (1) differentiating tacit knowledge, (2) exploring individual learning through the aspects of tacit knowledge, (3) building extraordinary consciousness, and (4) accessing tacit knowledge.

The fifth and final section introduces a Knowing Framework developed for the U.S. Department of the Navy. Knowing is defined as a sense that emerges from our collective tacit knowledge, and more poetically described as: *seeing beyond images, hearing beyond words, sensing beyond appearances and feeling beyond emotions.* We then turn our focus to the Net Generation. Birthed within and growing up in a technologically-advantaged dynamic environment, these new decision-makers are Internet savvy and social media addicted, living a moment-by-moment existence globally connected and culturally conversant. We forward that this is a generation growing up *knowing*, and explore how this shifting frame of reference impacts the future of decision-making.

We do not even begin to suggest that this book provides the answers for the future. That future is emerging even as we complete the writing of this preface. What we do propose is that **fully developing an appreciation of the power of knowledge** in both the context of complexity and knowing can *shift our historic paradigms* and, as decision-makers, serve each of us well as we move into an unknown and exciting future.

Yours in learning, Alex and David Bennet

The Drs. Bennet live at the Mountain Quest Institute, situated on a 450-acre farm in the Allegheny Mountains of West Virginia. See www.mountainquestinstitute.com They may be reached at alex@mountainquestinstitute.com

Section I
Building a Foundation

(Chapters 1-3)

We live in a world that offers many possible futures depending on the choices we make. The ever-expanding complexity of information and knowledge provide increasing choices for decision-makers, and we are all making a myriad of decisions every single day! How do we make the best decisions in a changing, uncertain and complex environment?

To lay the groundwork for addressing this question, we first take a close look at the decision-making environment today and in the foreseeable future. We then offer a brief review of systems and complexity thinking, including defining key terms, looking at the differences between simple, complicated and complex systems, and providing some useful guiding principles. At the end of this section we provide an introduction to knowledge, tying in foundational concepts with systems thinking and decision-making.

Knowledge is considered the capacity (potential or actual) to take effective action, and is context-sensitive and situation dependent. The mind/brain is continuously creating new knowledge for the moment at hand. Thus developing knowledge about knowledge, or metaknowledge, is critical for decision-makers as we navigate a changing, uncertain and complex environment.

Section I includes the following Chapters: The New Reality (Chapter 1); Systems and Complexity (Chapter 2); and An Introduction to Knowledge (Chapter 3).

Chapter 1
The New Reality

[CUCA = increasing Change, Uncertainty, Complexity and Anxiety]

Our world has changed and it **will continue to change faster in even more unexpected ways** as we move into the near and distant future. Most of us have been lulled into believing that the world has always changed, so what's new? Our lives have seen continuous change, yet we are still here, we have jobs and families, our affluence level has up until the last few years been increasing, and we have many more conveniences than our parents. So why should we worry about change? Well, while it's true that change has always been with us—there is change and there is Ch-*AN*-*Ge*! Some change makes sense and other change creates confusion, overload, turbulence, paradox, anxiety and fear.

Today there's a lot that is new, different, challenging, and hard to understand. There is the change of the pace of change and there are ever-changing ideas, products, processes, desires and needs of customers, rules, laws and regulations. There is change in the way we communicate and the speed of communication, change in our jobs and careers, and what we need to know and do. There is the change in weather patterns, travel processes, speed of products to market, expectations of workers, and the complexity of the problems we are asked to solve daily. There is change as we grow older, move our household, and see our children grow up and get married, all occurring in the fog of a changing threat and reality of global terrorism and weapons of mass destruction.

> There is change, and there is Ch-*AN-Ge*! Today, there's a lot that is new, different, challenging, and hard to understand.

And then there is **uncertainty**. With all of the economic, social, political and technological change there comes a creeping uncertainty about what to expect in the future. We say "creeping" because we easily create explanations of history and then, using our analytical insights, extrapolate the past into the future. This sometimes works, and when it is wrong, we shrug it off by saying "well no one can predict what is going to happen." *Then we repeat the same process the next time we make a decision, with the same results.*

In our organizations when there is a very important decision to make, we may use the Delphi technique or go for advice to futurists, experts who spend their lives studying the future. While these approaches can certainly provide some answers and good ideas to think about, there are no warrants on future predictions. *As our society speeds up, there is less time to make decisions, often more information available than we want, and so many choices and possibilities* that we either simplify by fiat or con ourselves into thinking that we are smart enough to make the right decision based on our past record (as we remember it).

Besides, if things don't turn out as we plan, we can always justify our decisions to our boss (or wife, partner, kids, etc.), making up a tale of logic and reason that sounds great. Or, we can blame a bad result on bad luck rather than poor or inadequate judgment or incompetent decision-making. People have done this for centuries, and isn't necessarily wrong. Anyone who has worked in the government and has been tasked to write a "white" paper to explain and justify a particular decision knows that justifications can often be a gross oversimplification of reality.

Fortunately, things often *do* work out, and we achieve what was intended. Why? You may have been able to adequately influence the process and create the desired outcome, or our logic and approach may have been right, that is, the desired movement into the future is consistent with what is happening in the decision environment as the future unfolds. Note that if environmental change is relatively smooth and consistent over time, there are certainly some areas where we can continue to make decisions and produce the desired results. Sometimes our plans are less than accurate and we adjust them with money, people, schedules, or by changing objectives so our decisions and actions will at least partially succeed.

However—and it is a major however—if the decision environment is changing in a substantial way that is unpredictable and unforeseeable, all of the planning and forecasting in the world will never allow us to consistently set and achieve clear targets and objectives, or to create a successful strategic path to continue from here to there. The entire world is becoming more tightly connected and smaller; technology provides instant communication and our symbols (money, data, information, and timing triggers for coordinated actions) move with the speed of light.

And, as our systems continue to increase in **complexity** with the Internet, world GPS tracking, products, power grids, medical support, water supply, big data, distribution, etc., they *become more vulnerable to failure*, either from natural causes or from intentional sabotage. First, as systems become more complex, they have more internal connections and networks, making them more susceptible to possible failures. Second, these same complex systems are—or can easily become—unpredictable

> As our systems increase in complexity, they become more vulnerable to failure, either from natural causes or from intentional sabotage.

because they no longer operate via identifiable cause-and-effect relationships. While each connection may or may not be causal, the number of connections, the possible feedback loops (or sneak circuits), the time delays and nonlinear relationships, plus the sensitivity to input values and the effect of their local environment, create a situation of non-predictability. See Chapter 2 on complexity.

Thus, as our society becomes more complex, we are less and less able to understand the outcome of many of our decisions so long as we rely on Newtonian deterministic assumptions, and the application of Aristotelian logic to understand our world. In other words, we may become victims of our past successes unless we admit the tremendous ability of Homo sapiens for self-delusion. Both unfortunately and fortunately, determined mostly by our own actions, we have entered a time in evolution where our reality has transformed itself from simplicity and slow change (hunter gatherer era) to medium change and complexity (farming, rise of civilizations, the Renaissance and the age of Reason) to an exponential rise in change and complexity starting with the industrial revolution to the unknown future of 2020-2050.

Our world is now *accelerating toward complexity and greater and greater levels of entanglement*, leaving confusion, uncertainty and anxiety in its wake. This depth and breadth of change is leaving the Industrial Age in the dust. Note that until the end of the 20th century we did not have email, the Internet, computer viruses or spam killers. Revolutionary technologies such as nanotechnology, biotechnology, quantum computers and neuroscientific instruments, coupled with dynamic economic shifts and culture clashes are all interacting to produce a new emergent phenomenon—The New Reality (**TNR**). Unless some terrible disaster such as a nuclear holocaust puts the world on a different timeline, this is the world in which we must live and survive. Evolution has clearly shown that complexity begets more complexity; this is how we have arrived as a species from a simple single celled amoeba to where we are now.

> Our world is now accelerating toward complexity and greater and greater levels of entanglement, leaving confusion, uncertainty and anxiety in its wake.

Let's pause a minute in this diatribe. We as a species have several things going for us. We are adaptive and *we thrive on uncertainty*! As Skoyles and Sagan (2002) tell us, roughly 100,000 years ago we were the same as the great apes. *They* are still what they were, but *we* have developed language, civilizations and an incomparable level of knowing and comprehension. Neuroscientists say this comes from the plasticity of our mind/brain's ability to bootstrap ourselves into new skills and the creation of symbols and language. We are now facing the next big evolutionary challenge, a change in consciousness enabled by a global world, new ways of being that will test our capacity to learn, and forever change how we see, think about, interpret and act upon our world.

If we are to live successfully in The New Reality, we will have to expand our approaches to solving the challenges facing us every day. Because of the greater number of decisions, the speed with which they must be made, and the possible consequences of making poor choices, we are being forced to develop—and rely on more heavily—our intuitive right-brain abilities, and our powerful (but not always right) unconscious mind.

A good analogy to help understand this shift in uncertainty and complexity is the difference between living in the country and driving on back roads far away from the congestion of the cities versus living in an urban area finding ourselves driving in rush hour traffic. On the back roads, there are few cars and—except for the possibility of a deer jumping right into our path—we can use logic to determine how to navigate the curves, and plan when and where to pass safely. However, when driving in rush hour traffic on the freeway, speeding along with so many people in a hurry to get where they are going, we are forced to not only use our logical mind to process all the various information coming in from the road ahead and the mirrors all around us, we are forced to develop and use our intuition, second guessing what anxious drivers operating at all levels of experience are doing or about to do. If we don't take this intuitive approach, we may decide to move to the open spot in the lane beside us at the very same moment as another driver decides to move to that very same spot. Next thing we know, what seemed like a logical move, creates an accident that ties up traffic for hours, and sends one or more people to the hospital.

While the future is not predictable, the decisions we make today can—and do—have the potential to create or perhaps influence many possible futures. As you can see from our analogy, a world with ever greater levels of change, uncertainty and complexity requires us to move to an inclusive decision-making approach that honors the logical processing of information while also embracing the development and integration of our intuitive nature. This approach requires lifelong learning and adaptation, changing our focus from seeking conclusions to asking questions and developing open channels and continuous feedback loops between our knowledge and knowing. (Knowledge is introduced in Chapter 3; knowing is detailed in Chapter 16.)

Albert Einstein once said that we cannot solve today's problems from the same level of consciousness that created them. As we move to new levels of consciousness, we will be shifting from attempts at simplifying to the nurturing of the emergence of new understandings, from individualism and attempts at control to networking and realization of *the power of our ability to co-create in a field of collaborative entanglement*, from a single viewpoint to multiple perspectives, allowing answers to spawn new and intriguing questions that enable the emergence of new ideas and innovation.

The Era of Knowledge

This new weltanschauung or world view brings forth a whole different set of conditions, characteristics, problems and questions that have immense implications for organizations, communities, families, and decision-makers at all levels (individuals, managers and leaders). In the past two decades we have begun the move from a product-driven, relatively stable, bureaucratically-oriented society toward a knowledge-driven, dynamic complex adaptive society. A higher percentage of us use our brains instead of muscles to get work done. This transition *places knowledge at center stage as the primary resource to deal with complexity* and knowledge is the greatest source of value in the marketplace. Many organizations now produce their value from intellectual capital via products or services. The source of this value comes from knowledge workers.

Creativity comes exclusively from people. The development of true understanding, meaning and vision **require a human mind**, one that has the confidence, competence, freedom and support to venture into the unknown and comprehend ambiguity, uncertainty and complexity. But to do this requires a supportive environment, structure,

> Every living system (organism) must be flexible and adapt to its environment if it is to succeed and survive.

culture and leadership style that is not static. As the markets and customers in the environment change, so must the organization adapt and change. Every living system (organism) must be flexible and adapt to its environment if it is to succeed and survive. This holds true for a human cell, a fish, an individual, an organization, a society or a nation. In a stable world adaptation may be small, perhaps unnoticeable. But in a dynamic world, only the adaptive will survive and be around for the future.

This new role is placing many burdens on organizations that still believe in a deterministic, predictable, mechanistic world in which there is a direct relationship between decisions, actions and the results of those actions. Managers have historically held knowledge close and equated it with power. If knowledge is to be effective, we must recognize this new reality for what it is and learn how to deal with this reality on its own terms, not ours. In other words, we have to become aware of the dynamic, uncertain and complex nature of ourselves and the environment in which we live, and re-look at our beliefs, assumptions and ways of comprehending and creating knowledge. Because the central source of performance is learning that produces knowledge and takes effective action via creativity, problem solving, decision-making and effective implementation, we all need to become well acquainted with the term meta-knowledge. Meta-knowledge is data, information, knowledge and how they play together with our experience, feelings, intuition and thought to create understanding and meaning in our lives and actions (see Chapter 3).

> If knowledge is to be effective, we must recognize this new reality for what it is and learn how to deal with this reality on its own terms, not ours.

The Bottom Line

What is the bottom line? From both an individual and organizational perspective, CUCA and The New Reality will continue to become more difficult to live in and deal with as we move into the future. Before making decisions and taking action with respect to CUCA and The New Reality, consider the questions and possibilities addressed in the following five paragraphs. As explicated below, before we are willing to change our past beliefs and future behavior, we must first be **aware** (attention) of the new situation (reality), **understand** (knowledge) what it means, **believe** (truth) that it is true, **feel** good about changing past believes (emotion), knowing that our new **actions** are worthwhile (will make a difference), AND **know** what to do and have the courage to act (Bennet and Bennet, 2008b).

AWARENESS:

Are you aware of the changes in our world and society relevant to you? Have you seen other indicators that were triggered by the above discussion of The New Reality? What does *your* New Reality look like? Are your colleagues aware of what is happening? Should they be aware? Where can you get more information to help you better understand your current environment? If you are comfortable with the above discussion, then *do you believe that it is true?*

UNDERSTANDING:

If you believe CUCA or some variant thereof is true, then will its impact and implications be as outlined above? How well do you need to understand it? Is it important enough to take the time to learn more for yourself? Do you think complexity will get worse? Is it possible to predict the future of a complex adaptive system? (See Chapter 2.) Does expanding the way we see, think, behave and act make sense? Can we survive using our current cognitive problem-solving and decision processes? Why are these major shifts in our way of seeing and acting in the world so important?

You may understand what was said, but may not agree with the implications ... or you may not think that the environment will be as extreme as suggested ... or, even if it is, you may not think it will affect *you* (your job, future or family) to the extent implied above. So, *how do you feel about all this?*

BELIEF:

Why should you believe it? Are the changes described above real and are they moving in the direction suggested? Will *The New Reality* affect you, your professional responsibilities, your family and your children's future? Are the implications discussed above reasonable? Are they outlandish? If you disagree, are you sure? Can you objectively test the hypothesis of CUCA in your personal world for local validity?

Can you seriously and honestly question yourself to see if you are self-delusional (as we all are sometimes)? Do you really see the new world as it is or do you see it from your past experiences; through your old, comfortable lenses that worked so well when you were moving up in your organizations? Have you tried to take multiple views of reality to make sure that you understand what the true reality is?

How do you know change will continue to speed up, or that complexity begets complexity? Where is the proof? Is it worth your effort to look into this further? If you are not sure, then make a point of looking for indicators of The New Reality over the next few weeks. Check to see if the quality media provides validation, or invalidation, of CUCA. If you think the description is misleading then what is a better viewpoint? If you believe that it is a reasonable description of what is happening in the world today, do you understand it? *How well do/should you understand it?* Whatever your beliefs are, make sure they can carry you through the next two or three decades!

FEELINGS:

Does the above description *feel* right to you? Forget about facts, logic or details, does it agree with your *gut feelings* about the world and what is going on around you? Very often, our instincts, intuition and unconscious signals will tell us a lot about the external world. If you feel uneasy about The New Reality, you might consider looking inward and questioning your own feelings to make sure that you are not in denial. If you do not feel that The New Reality is valid, then you will not be willing to take action. Much of **our energy and drive comes from how we feel about something, not just what we think about it**. So, if The New Reality is to mean anything to you, it must be important enough for you to prepare to take the necessary actions, to learn more about it and get comfortable with its existence ... and to *think about what actions need to be taken to prepare for your future*.

ACTIONS:

(Ownership and Empowerment): If you are aware of The New Reality, understand what it means, believe that it is even close to being correct and therefore worthy of your attention, then is there something you should be doing about it? If so, *what* should you do about it? Do you have what you need to take action? And, do you have the courage to act?

Perhaps as a minimum you can continue monitoring, learning, and discussing with others what changes are occurring in your local surroundings as well as on a global scale. So many aspects of the individual decision-maker come into the decision-making process. What is your approach to problems and decisions? How do you see the world?

How well do you deal with ambiguity, complexity, uncertainty and paradox? Is there anything that you can/should be doing that will help improve your individual decision-making or your organization's performance? Are you doing what you should be doing with respect to your colleagues and helping others prepare for and deal with this new environment? How ready is your organization to live and perform in a dynamic, uncertain and complex world? Is your organization already an *intelligent* complex adaptive organization, or some variant thereof? Are you operating in an *intelligent* complex adaptive environment? What learning, knowledge, actions, values and wisdom do you need to be prepared for the future? (Appendix A offers a short literature review on the concept of wisdom.)

The possibilities are endless, and *there are no absolute answers*! The factors and pressures on you can be tremendous, arising from work, family, economies, media broadcasting, transportation, wars, epidemics, health needs, communication methods to demands on your time and knowledge. YOU, as the decision-maker, will have some tough calls to make. The important question becomes: What actions should/do I take and when?

We begin.

Chapter 2
Systems and Complexity

It would be very difficult to fully explore a problem, issue or opportunity in a CUCA environment without a basic understanding of systems and complexity. If you are already comfortable with these concepts, just scan this chapter for review.

For purposes of this book, a system is *a group of elements or objects, their attributes, the relationships among them, and some boundary that allows one to distinguish whether an element is inside or outside the system*. Elements of a system may be almost anything: parts of a television set, computers connected to a network, people within an organization, neurons within a brain, patterns of mind, ideas within a system of thought, etc. The nature and number of elements and their relationships to each other are very important in determining a given system's behavior.

As long as one part is interacting with—affecting the behavior of—another part, almost everything can be viewed as a system. The following examples are all systems because they have many parts and many relationships: automobiles, ER teams in a hospital, cities, organizations, engines on a submarine, ant colonies, and individuals. We often find systems within systems within systems. This can easily be seen in the typical hierarchy of organizations: department, division, branch, section, and individual worker. Some modern organizations are also structured to have teams within teams within teams.

Assuming that all situations have boundaries, then we can consider situations to be systems. Given this, then the environment external to the situation/system may, and probably is, influencing the situation in some manner. This needs to be taken into account when creating and implementing a potential solution to achieve the desired/intended outcomes.

Systems can evolve over time and they can change size, shape and space. Processes are often seen as systems moving through time. Several experts have noted that "everything is a system," it just depends on where you define the boundaries and from which perspective you are looking.

While additional terms are defined later in this chapter, it is important to define complexity and chaos up front. We consider complexity as the *condition of a system, situation, or organization that is integrated with some degree of order, but has too many elements and relationships to understand in simple analytic or logical ways* (Bennet and Bennet, 2004). Chaos is the *condition of a system exhibiting disorganized behavior with little or no predictability*; a system that appears to behave randomly, with little or no underlying coherence in its local interactions. Typically, chaos is a state of bounded instability, where highly nonlinear feedback exists but is not so high as to create explosions or implosions. Examples are turbulent streams, the weather, and some organizations or organizational subsystems.

Background of Systems Thinking

Systems thinking is a conceptual framework—a body of information, knowledge and tools that have been developed over the past 50 years—to clarify the structure of systems and their patterns of change in order to better understand and influence their behavior and more effectively solve problems that develop within them.

The term is often used to describe a new way of interpreting the world and our place in it. This new way of thinking began in the late 1950s and was originally known as General Systems Theory (GST). A seminal book published by the biologist Ludwig von Bertalanffy (1968) introduced readers to the theoretical and methodological reorientations of systems thinking as they could be applied to the physical, biological and social sciences. General Systems theorists studied many types of systems in search of their underlying principles of operation. In the mid- seventies Weinberg (1975) and Sutherland (1975) wrote basic texts that introduce students to general systems and systems analysis, respectively.

Other aspects of systems theory included management systems, hierarchies, world systems and even social systems and the quality of life (von Bertalanffy, 1964) (Pattee, 1973) (Laszlo, 1972, 1973, 1999; Laszlo and Keys, 1981) (van Gigch, 1978). While only moderately successful, they were able to identify many insights and observations that help to recognize major system parameters and understand overall system behaviors. For an excellent review of holistic thinking of some of the greatest systems thinkers of the time, see Koestler and Smythies (1969).

A significant methodology for understanding systems was provided by J. W. Forrester (1971) at MIT through his modeling approach called System Dynamics. Forrester was able to analyze systems by identifying their influence elements and modeling their feedback loops and time delays on early computers to simulate a systems behavior. Forrester's work has been built upon by many workers in the systems dynamic field until today it is used extensively in business and academia (Morrison, 1991) (Hannon and Ruth, 1997). With the advancement in the power of computers and greater sophistication of computer software programs, improvements in modeling systems and using the models to aid teams in understanding and solving complicated organizational problems have yielded highly effective results (Morecroft and Sterman, 1994) (Vennix, 1996).

Miller's works in the late seventies provided an extensive analysis of living systems in terms of the overall systems perspective, hierarchies and system interfaces and structures. In early 1991, MIT's Peter Senge published his seminal book *The Fifth Discipline* that made systems thinking, as a conceptual approach, a popular subject with managers throughout the world (Senge, 1990). Senge's approach, formally called "Systems Thinking," is now widely used in management and organizations to visually and qualitatively understand how elements of systems interact and affect each other, and to provide a comprehensive perspective of the role of work in organizations. It is a conceptual process of analyzing organizations using what are called system archetypes. These 12 patterns of relationships that occur over and over in organizations provide individuals with a powerful conceptual and problem-solving tool (Kim, 1995; Anderson and Johnson, 1997). O'Connor and McDermott (1997) provide many specific examples of systems properties such as emergent phenomena, feedback loops, system metaphors, causal loop analysis and mental models.

> Senge's Systems Thinking approach—a powerful conceptual and problem-solving tool—identifies system archetypes, patterns of relationships that occur over and over in organizations.

With the recent interest in—and explosion of—information, several books have addressed information from a systems perspective (Checkland and Holwell, 1998) (Stonier, 1992, 1997). In a book entitled *The Systems View of the World*, Laszlo (1999) introduced a modern systems perspective. The relatively new fields of ecology and biocosmology wholeheartedly embrace the systems perspective, with considerable gain in understanding how those systems work (Volk, 1997) (Myers, 1984) (Gardner, 2003). The relationship between social analysis and systems is addressed by Luhmann (1995).

Two final comments are noteworthy. Physics, historically a reductionist science, became more of a systems science as it moved into the domains of particle physics, field theory, quantum mechanics and cosmology (Smolin, 1997) (Leslie, 1998) (Callender and Huggett, 2001) (Harrison, 2003) (Omnes, 1999). An interesting use of systems thinking in the intersection of physics and Buddhism is provided in *The Quantum and the Lotus* by Ricard and Thuan (2001). Applying systems thinking to thought, the physicist David Bohm (1992) explored the ways in which thought actively assists in forming our perceptions, sense of meaning and daily actions. The extent of the penetration of systems thinking into modern areas of thinking can best be appreciated by noticing how often its methods and perspectives are used without ever mentioning the words systems or systems thinking.

As decision-makers, we all strive to become knowledgeable and competent in specific fields of inquiry to better meet our responsibilities. In schooling, training, and on-the-job experience we typically concentrate on fulfilling the immediate task in a specific domain of knowledge and on seeing the world as a never-ending sequence of problems and challenges that demand immediate attention and resolution. Understanding these tasks as elements or parts of systems that are holistic entities containing elements, relationships and feedback loops suggests a better way to view our work and its place in the world. Such thinking leads to comprehension and intuition which greatly enhances the capacity to work with systems.

This is true for a number of reasons. First, it helps broaden our perspectives to see how our work fits into a larger scheme and purpose. Second, we learn to understand and appreciate what systems are and how they work. Third, we have some tools that help us model systems to better understand and perhaps influence the key forces and the effect of major relationships within the system. It has often been said that everything is a system and that all systems are connected, it is only a matter of how closely they are connected.

Systems in Terms of Complexity

Systems range on a continuum from simple to chaotic, with complicated, complex and complex adaptive systems in between. There is increasing complexity as you move along the continuum from simple to chaotic systems. See Table 1 below. Recognize that these categories are a convenience of language. Nature does not separate systems into different types. So, the description of each type represents an ideal state to facilitate differentiation.

Simple	*Complicated*	*Complex*	*Complex Adaptive*	*Chaotic*
• Little change over time • Few elements • Simple relationships • Non-organic • No emergent properties	• Large number of interrelated parts • Connections between parts are fixed • Non-organic • Whole equal to sum of its parts • No emergent properties	• Large number of interrelated parts • Nonlinear relationships and feedback loops • Emergent properties different than sum of parts • May be organic or non-organic	• Large number of semi-autonomous agents that interact • Co-evolves with environment through adaptation • Varying levels of self-organization • Partially ordered systems that evolve over time • Operates in perpetual disequilibrium • Observable aggregate behavior • Creates new emergent properties	• Large number of parts that interact • Behavior independent of environment • Minimal coherence • Emergent behavior dependent on chance
Knowable and predictable patterns of behavior	Knowable and predictable patterns of behavior	Patterns of behavior difficult to understand and predict	Patterns of behavior may be unknowable but possibly not unfathomable	Random patterns of behavior

Table 1: *System types in terms of complexity.*

As shown in Table 1, **simple systems** remain the same or change very little over time. There is very little or no change in the elements, relationships, or their attributes.

They have few states, are typically non-organic and exhibit predictable behavior. Examples are a swing, a light switch, and a pulley.

Complicated systems contain a large number of interrelated parts and the connections between the parts are fixed. They are non-organic systems in which the whole is equal to the sum of its parts; that is, they do not create emergent properties. Examples are a Boeing 777 (without humans), an automobile (without a driver), a computer (without a user), and an electrical power system (without a technician).

As distinguished from complicated systems, **complex systems** consist of a large number of interrelated elements that may or may not have nonlinear relationships, feedback loops, and dynamic uncertainties very difficult to understand and predict. Complex systems have the ability to create global emergent properties that come from their elements and interactions yet these characteristics cannot be traced back to the connections because of the nonlinearity and unpredictability of the elements and relationships. These emergent properties make the whole of the system very different than just the sum of the parts. Examples of complex systems include organizations (with culture being an emergent property), teams (with *esprit-de-corps* being an emergent property) and a dialogue relationship between two knowledge workers (with an increase in knowledge and understanding being an emergent result).

A **complex adaptive system** (what is called a "CAS") contains many agents (people) that interact with each other. In organizations the people are semi-autonomous and have varying levels of self-organization. They operate and direct their own behavior based on rules and a common vision of the organization's direction, working in small groups to take advantage of the local knowledge and experience of coworkers. The aggregate behavior over time of all knowledge workers is a top-level characteristic commonly referred to as organizational performance. The interactions and activities that create this performance are numerous, complex, and often nonlinear, making it impossible to determine global behavior from local actions.

In complex adaptive organizations, where the attributes, experiences, attitudes, personalities, and goals of leaders and knowledge workers significantly impact their relationships with each other, the global emergent characteristics such as trust and intelligent behavior, etc. will arise if—and only if—many employees seek to create them. The variety and diversity of individuals also contributes to the creation and characteristics of the aggregate behavior. If one person leaves, a complex adaptive organization can immediately reorganize to fill the vacuum and the firm internally adapts to its new structure, often with some stress and learning. As people move in and out of the organization, its global behavior may shift and change, adapting to its new internal structure as well as its external environment. This continuous flexing of complex adaptive systems keeps them alive and gives them the capacity to quickly change pace and redirect focus.

Many modern organizations work in dynamic, uncertain, and complex environments. In order to survive and excel they must continually reinvent themselves, creating and acting on new ideas and knowledge while taking risks. They tend to operate (or oscillate) between stability and chaos. It is that narrow region just before chaos in which creativity, dialogue, and innovation serve to accelerate learning and facilitate adaptation and high performance. Complex adaptive systems, compared to complicated or complex systems, have the best chance of surviving in environments of rapid change, high uncertainty, and increasing complexity. They have the potential to create new emergent properties that provide people the intelligent behavior needed to adapt to such environments. Examples of complex adaptive organizations can be seen in successful start-up companies, surviving Internet businesses, and government organizations that have recently changed policies, created teams and are empowering employees.

Complex adaptive systems are partially ordered systems that unfold and evolve through time. They are mostly self-organizing, while continuously learning and adapting. To survive they are always creating new ideas, scanning the environment, trying new approaches, observing the results, and

> Complex adaptive systems are partially ordered systems that unfold and evolve through time.

changing the way they operate. In order to continuously adapt they must operate in perpetual disequilibrium, which results in some unpredictable behavior. Having nonlinear relationships, complex adaptive systems create global properties that are called emergent because they seem to emerge from the multitude of elements and their relationships. They typically cannot be understood through logic and analysis alone because of the large number of elements and relationships. Examples are life, ecosystems, economies, organizations, and cultures (Axelrod and Cohen, 1999).

It is not just the number of agents involved that creates complexity. For example, a closed bottle full of oxygen contains billions and billions of oxygen molecules, but their interactions are simple and predictable in principle, and the system is not complex—although it is complicated. Although its agents (molecules) are independent, they cannot take individual actions and make individual decisions. The interaction of the molecules will not create emergent properties.

On the other hand, two individuals interacting to solve a problem may exhibit a high variety of behavior and thoughts during their conversation. This variety will depend, among other things on how they feel about each other as well as their own experience and need to solve the problem. In solving their problem they will have created an emergent phenomenon—the solution—something that came into being from the two individuals *and* their interactions. The result is often different and usually better than either person could have developed alone. Neither person alone knew the solution. The solution is more than what each person could have developed independently. Clearly this is a complex adaptive system, yet there are only two agents. When two people share their information and knowledge, more knowledge is created, but only if their relationship is up to the task.

Chaotic systems, or more to the point, chaotic organizations, rarely survive because they are unpredictable and independent of their environment. They are complex organizations that have lost much of their coherence and can no longer solve their problems through communication and collaboration between people. There is often continual disagreement, poor communication, infighting, and a lack of leadership. Sometimes the chaos can be hard to observe. As Stacey (1992) has pointed out, "... chaos is a state of limited or bounded instability ... Chaotic behavior is random and hence unpredictable at the specific or individual level ... The particular behavior that emerges is highly sensitive to small changes and therefore depends to some extent upon chance." For example, chaos may exist when firms are going bankrupt or undergoing a merger, when a government office is closed, or when an organization suffers from a repeated change of divergent leadership over a short time. More subtle forms may occur when managers create and use conflict to meet their own agendas, or where small changes escalate and become reinforcing loops, creating a great deal of conflict and misunderstanding.

Figure 1 below, entitled *The Systems Space*, shows the five categories of systems laid out roughly in terms of their difficulty of understanding and hence their predictability. The curve provides a nominal indication of the knowledge required to understand each type of system. In fact, highly complex systems may never be understood by humans; although that remains to be seen as research continues to hunt for theories, laws, and underlying principles that would help explain their behavior. The dashed curve at the top demonstrates that the required knowledge increases as you move toward more complex systems.

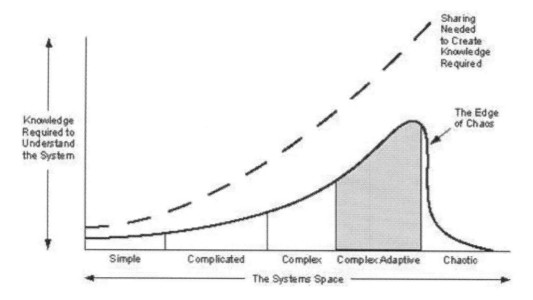

Figure 1: *The systems space.*

The concept and definition of knowledge, and its role in decision-making, is discussed in more detail in Chapter 3.

Terms and Definitions

With a new way of perceiving the world comes a new way of talking about it. While the language of systems thinking uses many familiar words, these words may have new meanings or nuances when applied to systems, and complexity comes with its own language. Thus, the definition of terms is a good place to start the exploration of systems and complexity. NOTE: These definitions are consistent with those provided in Bennet and Bennet (2004). Presented in alphabetical order the following terms are defined below:

Adaptation: Adaptation is the process by which a system such as an organization has and applies the knowledge to improve its ability to survive and grow through internal adjustments. Adaptation may be responsive, internally adjusting to external forces, or it may be proactive, internally changing so that it can influence the external environment.

Agent: In the literature the term refers to a semi-autonomous decision-making unit of a complex system that determines its own behavior within general guidelines. We consider individuals to be the agents in complex adaptive organizations. Examples of agents would be ants in an ant colony, individuals, or groups in organizations, and cities in a metropolitan area.

Equifinality: A system that tends to reach the same final state almost independent of its initial starting point is called an equifinal system. Most systems are not equifinal, although all living systems age and eventually dissolve. A common example would be highly successful organizations that become so self-centered, complacent and perhaps arrogant that they refuse to listen and change, resulting in decline or dissolution.

Environment: The region outside the boundary of a system is referred to as its environment. Since the environment may also be considered as a system, it is sometimes referred to as the supra-system. All open systems have inputs and outputs consisting of material, energy, or information. In essence they transform their inputs into outputs that satisfy internal purpose and environmental needs.

Feedback and regulation: Systems, particularly organizations, contain many elements with causal relationships among them. Some of these may be positive, reinforcing feedback loops and some will be negative, balancing feedback loops. Such feedback loops are needed to perform their mission during stable times and provide internal change and adaptation during time of change. Positive feedback loops create new ideas, products, and energy to try new ways of getting the job done---all needed during times of uncertainty and change. Sometimes, of course, positive loops can lead to disasters, such as when large funds are invested in new technology without a full understanding of the limitations of the technology. Often the idea of having the latest and greatest technology, the wonderful promises of venders and the need to improve organizational performance form a positive, reinforcing loop that can be very costly to an organization (yet sometimes very successful).

Inputs and outputs: Every system has inputs (energy, information, people, or material) from the environment and provides outputs (energy, information, people, or material) to its environment. To continue existing, organizations, particularly companies, must transform their inputs into outputs that add value to their environment. Without this value added, no company can stay in business and no government organization can justify its existence. In our world of information and knowledge, many organizations add value through the creation or leveraging of information and knowledge. Life forms are both open and closed systems. They are open in that they take in energy and information and extrude energy. They are closed systems in that they maintain internal patterns of organizations that create their identity and implement their replication capability (Capra, 1996).

Internal complexity: Internal Complexity is the complexity of a system that exists within the system. It is measured by its variety, the number of possible states that the system can have (a state is a specific configuration of the system). An organization of high variety has a large number of options and choices of actions it can take to adjust itself internally or when responding to or influencing its environment. If its variety becomes too high, the organization may become chaotic, with little or no coherence of thought or action.

Nonlinearity: A system possesses nonlinearity when actions within the system generate responses or outcomes that are not proportional to the action. A small action may generate a very large outcome---or a large action may have very little effect on the system. Examples are: a program office with a budget squeeze eliminates travel budgets causing increases in contractor costs due to lack of program office oversight; a key individual leaves the organization, resulting in many future expensive mistakes; a new leader comes in and redirects programs, thus raising costs and slowing down past investments; an influential low-level employee supports a management change effort and by doing so significantly moves the entire organization towards a better future; and a butterfly flaps its wings in South America and causes a severe snowstorm in New York (a well-known story from chaos theory).

Patterns: Sets of elements (people, events, and objects) their attributes and relationships in space and time that are stable or slow to change over time. Patterns are usually observed within some situation or background, i.e., there is some context associated with the pattern.

Purpose: There are two uses/meanings of the idea of purpose in systems theory. The first is the stated intention of the organization, its official goal or purpose. For technological systems purpose would be the use of the system intended by the system designers. The second interpretation of purpose is the set of interactions between the system and its environment. In other words, what the system does through its interaction with the environment, not necessarily what is officially stated, or what is intended. Where a system has a mission or purpose, the individuals within that system work to adjust their relationships and individual actions so that the sum of those actions achieves the desired purpose.

Self-organization: Self-organization is a complex system in which the agents (individuals) have a high degree of freedom to organize themselves to better achieve their local objectives. They also determine how to accomplish their objectives. Most complex systems found in nature are self-organizing, though human organizations are often the exception due to a human tendency to control. Current organizations exhibit a range of self-organization, from little or no control at the top to autocratic leadership. Self-organization provides the organization with robustness and resiliency. According to Wheatley (1994), Prigogine's work on the evolution of dynamic systems demonstrated that disequilibrium is a necessary condition for a system's growth. Prigogine called these systems dissipative structures because they give up their form (dissipate) in order to recreate themselves into new forms which could better deal with new information or external activities. Thus these self-organizing structures are adaptive and resilient rather than rigid and stable.

Sinks: Sinks are individuals, groups, processes, etc. that seem to absorb energy, time money and/or perhaps even morale. For example, some new projects have a budget that during implementation seem to demand more and more financial support. In other words, they represent a financial sink to the organization. People who continually need to be "mothered" (closely guided) represent sinks of time and energy on someone's part. One of the most famous phrases in organizations that have sponsored a project and poured more money into it is "the project is just about to make it." This "just about to make it" can continue for several years. Another example of a sink in organizations is an individual who continually asks questions, listens, and is learning but never seems to improve performance, nor do they help others by sharing what they are learning.

Sources: These are individuals, groups or even products which, in a complex organization (for example) obtain, create and provide (or share) information, knowledge, tools and processes with others in the organization. Particularly creative people are considered sources of ideas, and senior experts in organizations that know a tremendous amount related to a specific area of interest are extremely valuable sources of information, knowledge and action to help others in the organization meet their responsibilities. A senior executive or a chief financial officer in an organization often has responsibility for managing the financial needs of the organization and, as such, they represent the source of capital within the organization.

Structure: As noted earlier, systems that survive over time usually have some form of hierarchical structure. The reason that hierarchies and systems within systems are so prevalent is that systems, with their boundaries, are more stable than groups of elements without boundaries. This is because subsystems within a hierarchy tend to be more stable and able to withstand shocks from outside. When these subsystems are people, they get to know each other, establish trusting relationships and develop an environment that fosters effective actions. By sharing knowledge, processes and behaviors they create an efficient and effective organization. Thus, even if a subsystem fails, the rest of the system may maintain its integrity, permitting the entire organization to survive. The Noble Laureate Herbert Simon (1969) demonstrates this in his famous parable of the watchmakers. (This parable is included as Appendix B.) This being said, there are also detrimental side effects of too strict a hierarchy. Flexibility, adaptation, empowerment of individuals, creativity and innovation are all essential when the external environment is rapidly changing and threatens or offers opportunities to the system. Most organizations today have structures that combine hierarchies and teams, self-organizing groups, and somewhat flexible structures.

System boundaries: All systems have boundaries that separate them in some way from the environment or other systems. Organizations have people and facilities that are in the organization and there are customers, etc. that are outside the organization. Typically, lines of authority, policies, technology, and many processes and functions lie within the organization, but not always. The boundary may be highly permeable or low leakage. Completely closed systems are rare; gas in a closed bottle would be an example. Completely open systems are just as rare because there may be no way to define the system. There are degrees of openness in systems, some have boundaries that are very open to interaction with the outside world, others very controlling, the historic Berlin Wall being an example of the latter.

Useful Systems Principles

There are some useful principles for thinking about systems and applying systems theory. These principles, or rules, are primarily applicable to living systems such as organizations (or individuals) and should be considered more like guidelines that are useful but not always appropriate for a given situation.

Principle 1: Structure is a key to system behavior.

In addition to observing and reacting to events and patterns in the system, a useful insight and understanding of how organizations, i.e., systems, behave is found in their structure. The nature of the elements of a system and their function is derived from their position in the whole and their behavior is influenced by the whole to part relation. In other words, recognize that relationships and structure play a large role in driving individual and team behavior, that is, their causal interactions. Thus while it is normal to watch for and react to events that impact our organization, we should be wary of reacting to events without being conscious of the context and subsystem within which these events occur.

We often react to events when "patterns of events" are more important. When we observe patterns of events, we should look at the underlying structure of the system for root causes and possible leverage points for problem resolution. Systems thinking would suggest that when we understand the structure of a system, we are in a much better position to understand and predict the behavior of the individual elements (people) and their relationships and can therefore make better decisions and take more effective actions. Also, recognizing the importance of structure, we are less tempted to make one change to fix a problem, since the complex set of relationships will often require multiple changes to have a lasting result.

Principle 2: Systems that survive tend to become more complex.

This usually is a result of the system's defense against the external environment becoming more complex. When this happens, the immediate reaction is to simplify the system, whereas in fact the best action may be to take advantage of the environment's increased complexity. For example, if you normally receive 30 e-mails a day and you start getting 300, the natural reaction would be to quickly scan and ignore all but 30. You have simplified your own system at the risk of overlooking something that might be very important. Another approach is to assign another person the responsibility for reviewing and responding to the e-mails. This has increased the complexity of your system (you and now the other person) but it also has given you more options and possibilities for expanding business, etc.

There is some danger in oversimplifying organizational complexity. For instance, it is easy to assume that people will work harder if they are paid more salary. With the modern workforce, individual needs vary drastically and are usually quite complex. Often it is the challenge of contributing to a worthwhile cause and of working with others whom they respect and can learn from that motivates them. These drivers— worthy causes, respect and learning, etc.—frequently come from the entire system, that is, they are a result of the culture, the structure, and the individuals involved and they cannot be decreed by any single manager. An understanding of the organization as a system of relationships and patterns helps managers to recognize that they do not control the system but rather must learn how to nurture and influence the organization to achieve desired ends. This is why some modern organizations operate through collaborative leadership, leaders who work with and nurture teams and colleagues rather than managing through command and control. In the final analysis, complexity drives more complexity, which results in an exponential rise in overall complexity in many advanced systems.

There are, of course some simple, stable, living systems that have withstood millions of years in an increasingly complex environment.

Principle 3: Boundaries can be barriers.

It generally takes more energy and time to send information or products through a boundary than within the system. Most organizations require some form of approval for formal letters, products, etc. that go out of the firm to another organization. In a dynamic environment such policies can slow down the organization's reaction time. While open-door policies, empowerment, e-mails, communities of practices, etc. are opening organization boundaries, boundary protection is a natural phenomenon of systems and must be recognized and managed carefully. Many world class organizations maintain their self-identity while minimizing boundary protection by combining a shared vision and purpose with trust, knowledge sharing, learning, empowerment, and self-organizing teams. All of these give knowledge workers at the boundary the freedom and competency to make good decisions both internally and through the organizations boundary. For a more detailed discussion of this balance see Bennet and Bennet, 2004.

Principle 4: Systems can have many structures.

Systems often exist within systems and each level usually has a different purpose or objective. Given the hierarchical structure of most organizations, senior leaders select and integrate the information and knowledge needed to make decisions that optimize the right system-level objectives. By recognizing the long-term consequences of those decisions, they can optimize the desired results over time. This is the classical control-type of management. However, system structures can vary from pure hierarchical, to flat, to matrix, to networks, or to any combination of these. The optimum structure will depend upon the nature and purpose of the system and especially the nature of its environment and particularly on the rate of change, predictability and complexity of that environment.

Principle 5: Be extra careful when intervening in a system, especially organizations.

To minimize the unintended consequences of intervening in a system, consider the impact of second-order and long-term effects and the power of the systems internal (and informal) networks. Where organizations are concerned, a common rule of management is to *do no harm.* This means thinking about the possible consequences of decisions from a systems perspective, not only first-order effects but second and third orders as well. Here is where knowledge of key causal paths, feedback loops, and how the organization will react to the decision implementation become significant. A corollary is to *beware of unintended consequences.* Here again systems thinking helps in recognizing potential results of actions and decisions. Sometimes small changes can create big results caused by leveraging phenomena or positive feedback loops, and more often seemingly big changes have very little impact on organizational performance due to damping or negative feedback loops. It is helpful to separate the formal rules, policies, and directives of the organization from how the work really gets done. The work usually gets done through the informal network, giving it a vital role in determining the organization's perspective and performance. This informal system should always be taken into account when making changes within the organization.

In both living and non-living systems there often exist many fine, overlaying (sometimes invisible) networks that serve as mechanisms for integrating the systems behavior. These networks are highly influential and can drive system behavior. Examples would be gravity's influence in a Galaxy and reentrant connections in the human brain. (Edelman and Tononi, 2000)

Reflective Questions

Explain why a Boeing 707 sitting in a hanger is a complicated system while the same airplane taking off on the runway is more like a complex system, and when flying at 30,000 feet is more like a complex adaptive system?

What kind of system best represents your family? Why? Where are the boundaries? What kind of "connections" exist within the system? How well can it adapt to opportunities or threats?

As you get promoted in an organization why does it becomes more and more important to study and comprehend the organization as a complex adaptive system

How do the five principles provided in this chapter relate to your organization?

Chapter 3
An Introduction to Knowledge

Embracing Stonier's description of information as a basic property of the Universe—as fundamental as matter and energy (Stonier, 1990; Stonier, 1997)—we take information to be a measure of the degree of organization expressed by any non-random pattern or set of patterns. The order within a system is a reflection of the information content of the system. Data (a form of information) would then be simple patterns, and while data and information are both patterns, they have no meaning until some organism recognizes and interprets the patterns (Stonier, 1997; Bennet and Bennet, 2008d). Thus, knowledge exists in the human brain in the form of stored or expressed neural patterns that may be selected, activated, mixed and/or reflected upon through thought. From this mixing process new patterns are created by the mind/brain that may represent understanding, meaning and the capacity to anticipate (to various degrees) the results of potential actions. Through these processes the mind is continuously growing, restructuring and creating increased organization (information) and knowledge. This is a high-level description of knowledge that is consistent with the operation of the brain and is applicable in varying degrees to all living organisms.

As a functional definition, and introduced in Chapter 1, knowledge is considered *the capacity (potential or actual) to take effective action in varied and uncertain situations* (Bennet and Bennet, 2007a), and consists of understanding, insights, meaning, creativity, intuition, judgment, and the ability to anticipate the outcome of our actions.   The innate ability to evoke meaning through understanding and comprehension—to evaluate, judge and decide—is what distinguishes the human mind from most other life forms. This ability enables us to discriminate and discern—to see similarities and differences, comprehend and form patterns from particulars, and purposefully create, store and apply knowledge.

In this human process of creating meaning and understanding from external stimuli, *context shapes content* (Bennet and Bennet, 2007c). The word "context" comes from the Latin stem of *contexere* which translates as "weave together."   Today we recognize that all knowledge, to varying degrees, is context-sensitive and situation

> In the human process of creating meaning and understanding from external stimuli, context shapes content.

dependent (there are no impenetrable boundaries). This means that while the content may be constant, when you change the context the meaning of the content in that new context can be entirely different. The greater the complexity of a situation, the greater the potential number of patterns and relationships of patterns that make knowledge relevant to that situation, and the less likely that same knowledge would apply to different situations.

Knowledge is neither true nor false and its value is difficult to measure other than by the results of its actions. Hence, good knowledge would have a high probability

(P=.9) of producing the desired (anticipated) outcome, and relatively poor knowledge would have a low probability (P=.1) of producing the expected result. It should also be understood that desired outcomes cannot usually be described with high precision. Rather, there is likely to be a cone of acceptable outcomes that have different measures of goodness (see Figure 2). For complex situations, before an action is taken the quality of knowledge (from good to poor) may be hard to estimate because of the system's unpredictability over even a short time. After the outcome has occurred, the quality of applied knowledge can be assessed by comparing the actual outcome to the expected outcome. While any attempt to measure the value of specific knowledge can be difficult due to its dependency on situational context, the actual outcome of the decision/actions generally provide a good indicator of the quality of the knowledge when the context of the situation is taken into account by the decision-maker. Even the factors that caused the original actions to result in less than expected behavior may be visible. This is why tying knowledge directly to action is so valuable for learning.

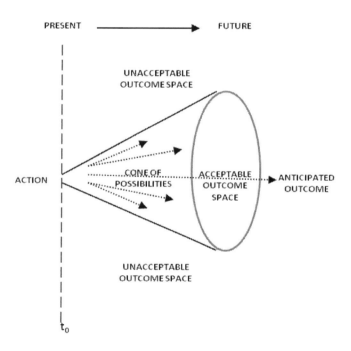

Figure 2: *Cone of acceptable outcomes with varying levels of goodness.*

Building on our definition of knowledge, learning is considered the creation or acquisition of the ability (potential and actual) for people to take effective action. From a neuroscientific perspective, this means that learning is the identification, selection and mixing of the relevant neural patterns (information) within the learner's brain with the information from the environment to comprehend the meaning, nature or importance of the results of selected actions.

Organizational learning is the sum of all learning processes within an organization. This includes not only individual learning, but also social learning from conversations such as team dialogues and community meetings. In other words, organizational learning represents the processes throughout the organization that create or acquire the knowledge necessary to survive, excel and grow in a changing environment. Learning is a dynamic process that manifests itself in the continuously changing nature of organizations, exemplified by innovation, collaboration, and culture shifts. For more information on neuroscience and adult learning see *Expanding the Self: The Intelligent Complex Adaptive Learning System* (A New Theory of Adult Learning) by David Bennet, Alex Bennet and Robert Turner (2018).

Knowledge (Informing) and Knowledge (Proceeding)

It is useful to consider knowledge as comprised of two parts: *Knowledge (Informing)* and *Knowledge (Proceeding)* (Bennet and Bennet, 2008d). This builds on the distinction made by Ryle (1949) between "knowing that" and "knowing how". Knowledge (Informing) is the *information (or content)* part of knowledge. While this information part of knowledge is still generically information (organized patterns), it is special because of its structure and relationships with other information. Knowledge (Informing) consists of information that may represent understanding, meaning, insights, intuition, expectations, theories and principles that support or lead to effective action. When viewed separately this is information even though it *may* lead to effective action. It is considered knowledge when used to *inform the knowledge process* that leads to effective action.

Consider Knowledge (Informing) as information that informs decision-makers. For example, if some situation occurs which is undesirable and needs to be changed, then Knowledge (Informing) could include the following: (1) a description of the situation and its context; (2) a meeting, nature and importance of the situation and its context; (3) a description of possible causes for the situation; (4) a description of the seriousness and the timing necessary to change a situation; (5) information addressing the question of who should take the action and why; (6) a description of what needs to be done, i.e., action A, B, C, etc.

Knowledge (Proceeding) represents the *process* and *action* part of knowledge. Knowledge (Proceeding) is the process of selecting and associating or applying the relevant information, Knowledge (Informing), from which specific actions can be identified and implemented, that is, actions that result in some level of anticipated effective outcome. There is considerable precedence for considering knowledge as information, or the product of a process versus an outcome of some action. For example, Kolb (1984) forwards in his theory of experiential learning that knowledge retrieval, creation and application requires engaging knowledge as a process, not a product. The process our minds use to find, create and semantically mix the information needed to take effective action is often unconscious and difficult to communicate to someone else (and thus could be described as tacit).

Continuing the example presented under Knowledge (Informing), Knowledge (Proceeding) is the unique way the decision-maker puts Knowledge (Informing) together in order to take effective action. This would include: (1) *knowing how* to do A, B, C, etc.; (2) actually doing A, B, C, etc.; (3) observing, evaluating and comprehending the results; (4) analyzing the results with respect to expected outcomes; (5) comparing actual and expected outcomes to determine the quality of the knowledge; and (6) studying the results and the process to enhance learning for future applications.

The Levels of Knowledge: Surface, Shallow and Deep

Acknowledging that any framework or model is an artificial construct, we nonetheless propose that it is helpful to consider knowledge in terms of three levels: surface knowledge, shallow knowledge and deep knowledge. The analogy built upon here is that of exploring the ocean. A pontoon or light sail boat catching the wind skims rapidly across the waters without concern for that which lies below in the water; as long as whatever lies below does not come to or affect the surface, it is of little concern to forward movement. For any boat moving in shallow waters, more attention (and some understanding) is required of what is beneath the surface, dependent on the ballast, to ensuring forward movement.

In deep waters—engaged over longer periods of time—safety and success require a proven vessel, an experienced captain, a thorough understanding of oceanography, a well-honed navigation system sensitive to current flows and dangers of the ocean, and a well-developed intuition, sensitive to deep water terrain, currents and so forth. Carrying the metaphor a bit further, whether surfing or moving through shallow or deep waters, a certain amount of skill is involved, although these also require somewhat *different* skill sets. The metaphor deals with the level of involvement with what is below the surface. Further, as a ship moves into deep waters there is increased reliance on experience and intuition as unforeseen perturbations move into the situation. Recall the idea of the iceberg, with the largest part submerged and unknown.

Surface knowledge is predominantly but not exclusively information. Answering the questions of what, when, where and who, it is primarily explicit, and represents visible choices that require minimum understanding. Further, little action is typically required; it is more of an awareness of *what is* on the part of the receiver.

Surface knowledge in the form of information can be stored in books, computers and the mind/brain. Much of our everyday life such as light conversations, descriptions and even self-reflection could be considered surface thinking and learning that creates surface knowledge. Perhaps too much of what is taught in schools is focused on awareness and memorization (surface knowledge) with inadequate focus on understanding or meaning. For example, at the turn of the century the National Research Council expressed concern that the U.S. education system teaches students science using a mile wide and inch deep approach (National Research Council, 2000; Oakes and Lipton, 1999). The emphasis is on surface learning, that is, learning that "relies primarily on short term memorization—cramming facts, data, concepts and information to pass quizzes and exams…deep learning asks that we create and re-create our own personal understanding" (Chickering et al., 2005, pp. 132-133). Chickering and his colleagues discovered that in Scotland, Canada and Australia 90 percent of student learning was surface learning, and felt this figure was similar to that in the United States. This suggests that many future adults may not be prepared to address problems that require deep learning. Further, surface knowledge is frequently difficult to remember and easy to forget because it has little meaning to improve recall, and few connections to other stored memories (Sousa, 2006).

Shallow knowledge is when you have information plus some understanding, meaning and sense-making. To understand is to make some level of meaning, with meaning typically relating to an individual or organization and implying some level of action. To make meaning requires context. For example, the statement "John's car hit a telephone pole" is descriptive. If you don't know John, it has minimal meaning (surface knowledge). On the other hand, if John was driving your car it has a deeper meaning to you. That meaning is added by you because the context of that statement has specific significance for you. Meaning is something the individual creates from the received information and their own internal information, a process of creating Knowledge (Proceeding).

Thus, shallow knowledge requires a level of understanding and meaning such that the knowledge maker can identify cohesion and integration of the information in a manner that makes sense. This meaning can be created via logic, analysis, observation, reflection, and even—to some extent—prediction. Using our example, if you know it's your car, you can predict you are going to have to fill out forms, get the car repaired, etc. You make sense of what happened in the situation via integrating it, making it cohesive or self-consistent, and creating the knowledge that gives you meaning and understanding in the sense-making process so that you can take effective action.

In an organizational setting shallow knowledge emerges (and expands) through interactions as employees move through the processes and practices of the organization. For example, organizations that embrace the use of teams and communities facilitate the mobilization of knowledge and the creation of new ideas as individuals interact in those groups. From an educational perspective, surface knowledge is roughly equal to knowledge learned in high school. Shallow knowledge would then be college level in terms of depth, complexity and comprehension.

In **deep knowledge** you have to develop understanding and meaning, integrate it, and be able to shift your frame of reference as the context and situation shift. Since Knowledge (Proceeding) must be created in order to know when and how to take effective action, the unconscious plays a large role in this area. The source of deep Knowledge (Proceeding) lies in your creativity, intuition, forecasting experience, pattern recognition, and use of theories (also important in shallow situations). Deep knowledge is the realm of the expert. The expert's unconscious has learned to detect patterns and evaluate their importance in anticipating the behavior of situations that are too complex for the conscious mind to understand. During the lengthy period of practice needed to develop deep knowledge, the expert has often developed an internal theory that guides his or her Knowledge (Proceeding).

The development of deep knowledge is not an easy task. It takes an intense and persistent interest and dedication to a specific area of learning, knowledge and action. An individual must "live" with their field of expertise and at the same time focus on the details and contexts of every specific experience, asking questions and analyzing what went right, what went wrong and why. Such an approach as this leads to uncovering relationships and patterns that over time become the unconscious bedrock of expertise, that is, deep knowledge. Gathering relevant information and combining it in chunks builds up a wide range of patterns to draw from when encountering a new or unusual situation. Gathered through what is called *effortful practice*, much of this knowledge resides within the unconscious and surfaces only when the individual takes an action or makes a decision based on "feel" or "intuition." Nevertheless, deep knowledge usually provides the best solution to a problem. This is more fully addressed in Section IV on "Engaging Tacit Knowledge."

Each learning experience builds on its predecessor by broadening the sources of knowledge creation and the capacity to create knowledge in different ways. When an individual has deep knowledge, more and more of their learning will continuously build up in the unconscious. In other words, in the area of focus, knowledge begets knowledge. The more that is understood, the more that can be created and understood.

Levels of Learning

Two of the four modes in Kolb's experiential learning cycle are referred to as internal reflection and comprehension (Kolb, 1984). Internal reflection is where understanding and meaning are created and includes some intuition based upon past experience of logic, analysis and causality. Comprehension includes creativity, insights, forecasting future results based upon specific actions, problem-solving, intuition, and logical analysis.

When you have internal reflection—when you look for understanding, meaning and sense-making—you look from a particular frame of reference. Underlying each frame of reference are specific, often unconscious assumptions and presuppositions that may need to be surfaced and evaluated from a critical thinking perspective. At the shallow knowledge level you might need to consciously shift reference frames. Shifting reference frames occurs most often at the shallow level of knowledge, where the individual stands back and says "maybe I'm using the wrong logic or analysis approach," and "I need to look at this situation from a different perspective." At the deep level this shifting would likely be automatic and occur without conscious awareness.

The value of shifting your frame of reference can be demonstrated by the monk on the mountain problem. One morning a monk decides to go for a walk up a mountain. He starts at 8 AM at the beginning of the path. He walks up the mountain at various speeds (always following the path), stops and has lunch, continues up the mountain and reaches the end of the path at the top of the mountain at 4 PM. He decides he's too tired to walk back down the mountain that evening, so he camps out at the top of the mountain. The next morning at exactly 8 AM he starts walking down the path, continues walking at various speed, stops and has lunch, continues on down the mountain and arrives at his original starting point at exactly 4 PM on the second day.

The problem is to provide a convincing explanation that there is *some point* on the monk's path that he will *cross at exactly the same time on each day*. Note that you do not have to know or state where that point is located on the path. This problem is quite difficult from the story's common frame of reference, that is, thinking of a single monk walking up and down the mountain on two different days. A different frame of reference is to recognize that the problem is the same as if there were two monks, one starting from the bottom and another starting from the top at exactly the same time on the same day. Then the question becomes will they ever meet on the path? From this different frame of reference, the answer is clearly yes, and wherever they cross is the answer to the question, since when and where they meet, it will be at exactly the same time and place.

Interestingly enough, in shallow knowledge there is some forecasting, problem-solving, logic and all of those other aspects found in the comprehension phase of Kolb's learning model. Note that although all four modes of Kolb's model (experience, internal reflection, comprehension and action) are experienced at every level, it is the amount of each mode that varies among the surface, shallow and deep levels of knowledge. Internal reflection is predominantly conscious. The comprehension part of deep knowledge is predominantly unconscious (tacit knowledge). We can take each of these two modes and look at what is surface, shallow and deep to get a perspective on the content. Figure 3 includes brief descriptors of experience, learning (internal reflection and comprehension), knowledge and action.

As the pieces begin to fall into place, let's take a closer look at complex decision-making in a complex environment.

LEVEL	SYSTEMS	EXPERIENCE	LEARNING	KNOWLEDGE	ACTIONS
SURFACE	SIMPLE SYSTEMS	• Immediate • Awareness • Sense-making	• Awareness • Memorizing • Understanding	• Knowledge (Informing) • Information • Conscious	• Remembering • Communicating • Acting
SHALLOW	COMPLICATED SYSTEMS	• Feeling • Relational • Intuitive	• Causality • Coherence • Meaning-making	• Knowledge (Proceeding) • Conscious • Causality	• Explaining • Anticipating • Problem-solving
DEEP	COMPLEX SYSTEMS	• Attuned • Embodied • Spiritual	• Effortful practice • Insights • Intuition • Lived experience	• Knowledge (Proceeding) • Mostly unconscious • Pattern detection	• Creating • Intuiting • Predicting

Figure 3: *Brief descriptors of systems, experience, learning (internal reflection and comprehension), knowledge, and actions in terms of surface, shallow and deep.*

Section II
Complex Decision-Making
in a Complex Environment

(Chapters 4-8)

Every decision has hidden within it a guess about the future. When solving a problem or working toward a goal, we anticipate that if we take a certain action (or series of actions) another situation will result that represents our desired objective. In anticipating the results of this decision/action we are in fact making a guess, howbeit educated or not, about what the consequences will be. This guess has many assumptions relative to the complex situation or its environment, and, as Axelrod and Cohen so succinctly summarize, "The hard reality is that the world in which we must act is beyond our understanding." (Axelrod, 1999, p. xvii) As the problems and messes of the world become more complex, our decision consequences are more and more difficult to anticipate. Our decision-making processes must change to keep up with this world complexification.

We will build on Ackoff's idea of a system of decisions as a set of actions in which the outcome of each action depends on earlier actions and the interactions of those earlier actions, this dependence and interdependence being created by the results of the previous actions and the situation's response (Ackoff, 1998). We call the anticipated set of decisions and their actions a decision strategy, an approach developed to convert a complex adaptive mess (CAM) into a desirable situation. Such a transformation usually requires a continuing process which must be built into a decision solution by planning a sequence of actions, some in parallel, others sequential, and building pivot points into the strategy to ensure surprise responsiveness. As introduced in this section, this can be thought of in terms of a journey, not a single intervention.

The five chapters in Section II are: The Complexity of Situations (Chapter 4); The Complexity of Decisions (Chapter 5); The Complexity of Actions (Chapter 6); Complex Decision-Making (Chapter 7); and Dealing with Complex Adaptive Organizations (Chapter 8).

Chapter 4
The Complexity of Situations

Recall that knowledge is defined as the ability (potential or actual) to take effective action. Clearly the effectiveness of action is highly dependent on the specific situation in which specific knowledge is applied. Thus, we now apply our analogy to decision-making and action after first building an understanding of the levels of the complexity of a situation. We use the term situation to mean any issue, problem, condition, opportunity or bounded system that the decision-maker believes needs to be changed, improved, transformed, etc. We interpret this situation to mean a complex adaptive system.

Simple to Complex

Something catches your attention. It could be something not quite right, a problem, or perhaps an opportunity requiring some decision and action. In order to understand the level of knowledge needed for decision-making and action, the first question to ask is what is the nature of the situation: Is it a simple situation? Is it complicated? Or is it complex, complex adaptive, or chaotic?

A simple situation is one that has knowable and predictable patterns of behavior. There are few elements involved in the situation and simple relationships exist among those elements. Easily fixed mistakes would fall into this category. If it's simple, and the solution is not apparent, that is, the information needed to solve the problem does not work, then either the wrong information is available and being used or perhaps the frame of reference needs to be shifted.

While a complicated situation also has knowable and predictable patterns of behavior, the number of interrelated parts and connections among the parts is so large that there may be some difficulty in identifying cause and effect relationships. A complicated situation requires information and shallow knowledge, implying that causality can be identified and understood. Good knowledge of the specific domain of causality related to the situation is needed. Then, by logical analysis, systematic investigation, and deductive processes the situation at hand can be corrected as desired. An example of a complicated system would be a television set or an automobile.

Again, however, the frame of reference and set of assumptions underlying the approach to a solution may significantly impact success. When a solution cannot be found to a complicated situation, it usually means that either insufficient or wrong information or inadequate knowledge is being used. Multiple perspectives may need to be considered as well as a review of implicit and explicit assumptions and

> The frame of reference and set of assumptions underlying the approach to a solution may significantly impact success.

presuppositions. Here also is where multiple individuals working collaboratively may find solutions more effectively and efficiently than a single individual. This is the concept upon which collaborative advantage is built. Given adequate information, complicated problems should be solvable, although deep knowledge may be required to do so. This is not the case for complex problems.

In a complex situation the patterns of behavior are difficult (and sometimes impossible) to understand and predict. The large number of interrelated parts may have nonlinear relationships, time delays, and feedback loops; thus, while the situation has some degree of order, it has too many elements and inter-relationships to understand in simple analytic or logical ways (Bennet and Bennet, 2004). In the extreme, the landscape of a complex situation is one with multiple and diverse connections with dynamic and interdependent relationships, events and processes.

These complex situations may be within an organization, a part of an organization, in an organization's external environment or at the boundaries of two complex systems. Such situations have been referred to as "messes." As Ackoff clarifies, "Managers are not confronted with problems that are independent of each other, but with dynamic situations that consist of complex systems of changing problems that interact with each other. I call such situations **messes**." (Ackoff, 1978) Messes produce conditions where one knows a problem exists, but it is not clear what the problem is.

Some examples of messes that have occurred throughout industry and government would include:

*Poor communication throughout most organizations.

*Isolation of individual departments within organizations—stovepipes.

*Cultures that perpetuate processes and beliefs rather than adapt to changing needs—organizational defense patterns. (Argyris, 1990)

*Retirees and departing employees who take critical knowledge with them—the brain-drain.

*The demands of the new economy, technology, and workforce versus the inertia and resistance to change experienced in many organizations and their employees.

*Rapidly changing leadership that prevents long-term consistent organizational improvements to meet ever-changing market needs.

*Emphasis on efficiency, productivity, and working harder and longer instead of working smarter and more effectively to achieve sustainable competitive advantage.

For purposes of this book, a complex situation in a complex environment will be referred to as a complex adaptive mess (CAM).

The Problem Setting

As early as 1983, Donald Schon couched the importance of understanding a problem setting in terms of the unknown. The problem setting is the process by which we define the decision to be made, the ends to be achieved and the means chosen to implement the decision. In this setting, the decision-maker "must make sense of an uncertain situation that initially makes no sense." (Schon, 1983, p. 40) Schon's example was professionals considering a road to build which dealt with a complex and ill-defined situation in which geographic, topological, financial, economic and political issues were entangled. This means that influencing any one of those areas may well initiate an unpredictable response from another area.

The varying needs of each creative situation will call for decision-makers to draw upon different types and qualities of awareness. In the extreme, the landscape of a complex situation is one with multiple and diverse connections with dynamic and interdependent relationships, events and processes.

> The varying needs of each creative situation call for different types and qualities of awareness.

While there are certainly trends and patterns, they may well be entangled in such a way as to make them indiscernible, and compounded by time-delays, non-linearity and a myriad of feedback loops. While sinks (absorbers) and sources (influencers) may be identifiable and aggregate behavior observable, the landscape is wrought with surprises and emergent phenomena, rumbling from perpetual disequilibrium. In this landscape, the problem or situation requiring a decision/decision strategy will likely be unique, dynamic, unprecedented, difficult to define or bound, and have no clear set of solutions.

For those unacquainted with the language of complexity, reading the above may sound like intelligent decision-making is a thing of the past. This, of course, is not true. As with any informed decision-making process, **we move into the complexity decision space with the best toolset and as deep an understanding of the situation as possible**. That toolset may include experience, education, relationship networks, knowledge of past successes and historic individual preferences, multiple frames of reference, cognitive insights, wellness (mental, emotional and physical) and knowledge of related external and internal environmental pressures. The *decision space* in which the CAM (complex adaptive mess) is to be considered—using relevant decision support processes such as the analytical hierarchy process, systems dynamic modeling, scenario development, etc., and information and technology systems—includes situation and decision characteristics, outcome scenarios, a potential solution set, resources, goals, limits, and a knowledge of political, sociological and economic conditions, i.e., ontology, the nature of the situation and its solution.

Analytical hierarchy process is a group process used to decompose a problem, issue or challenge into more easily understood subcomponents which can be independently analyzed. Then these various subcomponents are compared to determine their relative importance, providing numerical values and weights in which to compare the subcomponents (Saaty, 1988). System dynamics modeling—an approach from System Dynamics originated by Jay Forrester of the Massachusetts

Institute of Technology—uses feedback loops and stocks and flows to improve the understanding of system nonlinearity. Scenario development is an approach for exploring possible future states of the world which represent alternatives that are plausible under different assumptions.

Much like fact and logic-based decision processes, the *situation elements* to be considered in a CAM include perceived boundaries of the system; sets of relevant data and information; observable events, history, trends, and patterns of behavior; the underlying structure and dynamic characteristics of the system; and the identity and characteristics of the individuals/groups involved. Take your favorite decision-making process and add more elements if they appear pertinent. And by all means—always be aware of the role of judgment in this process—combine the virtually boundless information harvesting environment of mobile agents with the computational, pattern-matching and storage facilities of decision support systems to uncover as many connections and relationships as possible along with their probabilities of applicability to the situation at hand.

Behaviors of Complex Systems

Now, in your informed and reflective state, what is different about making a decision relative to a complex adaptive mess from traditional decision-making? First, the behavior of the system can be surprisingly different. Consider the following behaviors: correlations, the butterfly effect, emergence, feedback loops, nonlinearities, power laws, time delays, tipping points, and unpredictability. As you read the descriptions below reflect how your understanding of these behaviors might affect the decision-making process.

Correlations. The tendency for variation in one variable to be accompanied by linear variation in another variable. when two things are said to be correlated they seem to be related in some manner that is not direct cause and effect. Such correlations are often very difficult to explain even though the data clearly indicates a relationship. Correlations consider the causal, complementary, parallel, or reciprocal relationships, especially a structural, functional, or qualitative correspondence between two comparable entities. For example, there is a correlation between drug abuse and crime. As an organizational example, if an organization has a high-performing, well-liked manager over time many of the other managers may well start mimicking the high-performing manager's behaviors. Powerful correlations are emerging from the use of Big Data, using new tools to explore large amount of information to show the patterns within that information. This is addressed again in Chapter 18.

Butterfly Effect. The butterfly effect occurs when a very, very small change in one part of a complex adaptive system, (or CAM)—which may initially go unrecognized—results in a huge or massive change, disruption, surprise, or turbulence. These results may be impossible, or extremely difficult, to predict. For example, one small, misunderstood act by a single manager may escalate to a widespread distrust within an organization. A false and untraceable rumor can do great damage to a company's image, or a quiet speech by a president may change the emotional state of a nation.

Before taking action, study carefully the situation of concern and see if you can find any highly sensitive areas that could trigger a strong, or quick, reaction within the system. Some systems are extremely sensitive in specific areas and hence any strong action taken may create chaos and worsen the situation. Always observe, think and get other inputs before perturbing a tenuous situation. Attempt to put yourself in the middle of the situation and ask: How would I react to someone coming in and telling me how to change my organization/system? Now attempt to find the sensitive areas of the organization/situation and react accordingly.

Emergence. Emergence is a global/local (but not micro) property of a complex system that results from the interactions and relationships among its agents (people), and between the agents and their environment. These characteristics represent *stable or quasi-stable patterns*, often qualitative, within a system in disequilibrium that may exert a strong influence within the system. Examples are culture, trust, attitudes, organizational identity, and team spirit.

An emergent property is often said to be more than the sum of its parts, although it would be more accurate to say that the emergent property has different characteristics than the sum of its parts. For example, each individual can learn, and so can organizations. However, organizational learning is different than individual learning. Organizational learning requires individuals to work together to accomplish a task with the results created by combining each individual's own knowledge with the capability gained *through their mutual (and often interdependent) interactions*. The same results could not be obtained by adding the contributions of each individual together because the interactions change what each individual knows, learns, and does. It is this *interactive gain* that produces "synergy" or emergent characteristics of an organization. Thus, the sum of individual learning and organizational learning becomes the total learning of the organization. (Bennet and Bennet, 2003)

Reflective Question: Can you imagine a small organization which is having a difficult time surviving deciding to pull everyone together to have a serious discussion of the current situation, problems and opportunities? Frequently, but certainly not always, out of such a discussion will come several new ideas that suggest actions to boost the organization. While such emergence is usually unpredictable, in a situation where a leader supports and demonstrates positive thinking, serious listening, teamwork and unity, new ideas emerge. If these ideas are implemented, members will have a very different feeling and perspective of the organization.

Feedback Loops. Feedback loops can either be self-reinforcing or damping, improving a situation or making it worse. In a CAM these often take the form of excitement or an energy surge due to a successful event or perhaps a decrease in morale due to over-controlling management. In turn, management may interpret decreased morale as laziness and put more pressure on employees, creating a dangerous reinforcing loop. In cases such as these, it may be very difficult or impossible to identify the initial cause and effect; typically, there are a large number of symptoms, causes, and interactions.

Reflective Exercise: Take one day and observe carefully the communication and relationships that exist at home or at work. See if you can identify feedback loops. An example of a feedback loop would be hearing a good idea brought up in the morning staff meeting, and hearing the same idea that afternoon being shared by another individual in a casual exchange. Think about how you could come up with a good idea and tell it to specific individuals to see how it passes through the organization and comes back to you. Feedback systems typically amplify the major characteristics and can, in fact, motivate and move large groups or organizations into action, or nonaction. Negative feedback loops can, of course, minimize the initial idea action and may easily kill an idea action. If you know and understand your coworkers and you want to get an idea accepted by the organization, pick a small number of individuals whom you know will accept and like the idea, and who have a tendency to share their ideas with others. It is amazing how quickly an idea can spread in this manner. This process can be called "seeding" ideas to guide behavior.

Nonlinearities. When two parameters (or people) interact in a manner such that a small change in one part of the interaction frees up a larger change in the other part, a small change can create a large result. The power laws described below provide examples of such nonlinearities.

Power Laws. Closely related to tipping point theory are power laws. A power law, as used here, is a mathematical relationship that brings together two parameters (measures) within some complex system. For example, the number of earthquakes versus the magnitude of the earthquakes follows a simple power curve. "Double the energy of an earthquake and it becomes four times as rare." (Buchanan, 2001, p. 45).

Time Delays

Time delays occur when an action is taken in time T_1 but nothing happens until sometime later such as T_2. The system acted upon does not respond to the action until some later time; thus a time delay has occurred.

Time delays often occur between when an idea or action is initiated and when it gets implemented. While this is normal, sometimes the delays may prevent that idea or action from being implemented. Time delays also depend upon the particular part of the organization or group involved. Some organizations work efficiently and effectively with minimum time delays, while others may seem to take forever to get anything done. Become aware of your organization and choose a strategy which minimizes or bypasses the usual time delays.

Tipping Point

A tipping point occurs when a complex system changes slowly until all of a sudden it unpredictably hits a threshold which creates a large-scale change throughout the system. Examples of this are the stock market crashes in 1929 and 1984, the Cambrian explosion in which hundreds of new species were created in a relatively short time from an evolutionary viewpoint (this occurred about 500 million years ago), and perhaps closer to our focus, when a small company finds itself growing slowly in a niche market that all of a sudden takes off and propels the company to success. The important point about tipping points is that they are typically unpredictable and can significantly change decision outcomes, hence the need for decision strategy flexibility (Bak, 1996). The results of tipping points are similar to the results of contagious behavior, that is, "ideas and products and messages and behaviors [that] spread just like viruses do." (Gladwell, 2000, p. 7) Ideas, etc. that spread like viruses—taking on a life of their own—are called memes. (Blackmore, 1999)

Reflective Exercise: Closely observe those around you in your organization. See how ideas or actions move within the organization. Which ones move forward rapidly and which ones seem to die or fade away? Understanding tipping points can be very useful ... or dangerous, because when they occur, it is difficult to be sure of what direction they are going to fall. The goal is to get enough people behind the idea so that everyone, including senior management, jumps on the idea and immediately begins the implementation process.

Unpredictability. Unpredictability is the inability to predict the outcome of a decision or action. When a situation and/or its environment are so dynamic that it is impossible to anticipate the results of any action you might take, the situation is said to be unpredictable. When dealing with such situations, it is often best that you go slow, carefully deciding what actions to take, acting softly and watching carefully.

Reflective Exercise: Try to remember the last time you took action on some "hot topic" and it was immediately rejected by those around you; or, a fellow coworker offered a suggestion that seemed to explode within the organization, although you thought it was a poor idea. Before suggesting great ideas for new actions, it is a good idea to think carefully about the consequences once the idea becomes known to others within the community. Try to estimate how you think a group of your coworkers or your immediate boss would react to the idea or suggestion. If you're not sure of the reaction, it might be wise to talk quietly to other employees in a "roundabout" way in order to get a feel for their reactions or feelings.

Being familiar with some of the important concepts related to complexity in terms of situations, we are better prepared to specifically address the complexity of decisions.

Chapter 5
The Complexity of Decisions

There are strong relationships between the complexity of situations, the complexity of decisions and the complexity of actions. Since situations, decision and actions involve people, they are always complex. However, it is the *depth* of complexity that drives the need for varying levels of knowledge and learning: surface, shallow and deep. Chapter 4 introduced the complexity of CAMs (complex adaptive messes). This chapter will focus on the "complexity of decisions" and its unique relationship to knowledge. Chapter 6 will focus on the complexity of actions.

So how does understanding surface, shallow and deep knowledge help the decision-maker? Quite simply, recognizing the level of the situation (simple, complicated or complex) allows one to anticipate the level of experience, learning and knowledge needed to *take effective actions* (knowledge) in order to solve the problem. It also guides the decision-maker to ask the right questions and recognize which frames of reference may yield the desired payoff and which approaches are not too likely to work.

When a problem is highly complex, deep knowledge is needed to understand and deal with the situation, its complexities, its history, and, where possible, its patterns. Such knowledge can only be created by lived experience and intense, focused concentration of the unconscious to develop an appreciation for the patterns involved in the situation. This is needed to develop the insight and intuition needed to generate possible solutions and anticipate future pattern directions which will support and produce the desired results.

> Recognizing the level of the situation allows anticipation of the level of experience, learning and knowledge needed to take effective actions in order to solve the problem.

An example of a complex problem is knowledge conservation, an issue arising due to a large portion of the workforce reaching retirement age. What kind of knowledge needs to be retained? What level of knowledge is not available from other sources?

When dealing with surface level problems, information systems, common sense, guidance documents or a simple conversation with a colleague can typically provide the issue. When considering shallow knowledge, you need to look at what kind of decisions, actions and situations the departing individual dealt with: Were decisions causally determined? What processes were used? What information was needed? How did this individual go about making decisions? Logic, cause and effect, communication, mentoring, and coaching are all processes that work well when gathering surface knowledge. While the requisite knowledge may be implicit, it can usually be made explicit if you ask the right questions and know what to look for.

When sharing or conserving knowledge that is going out the door, it is critical to ensure that both parties are communicating at the same knowledge level. Finding the right questions to ask can help the transfer process. What questions can best elicit the knowledge that is needed at each level? What kinds of tools are appropriate to conserve knowledge at each level? How long does it take to develop each level of knowledge? How does the loss of each level of knowledge engaged by this departing individual affect the organization's mission? How many other individuals in the organization need this knowledge? The language, meaning, comprehension, level of intuition, frame of reference and presuppositions regarding a specific area of knowledge all come into play and can enhance, inhibit, or sabotage any attempt to share knowledge via the medium of information.

Deep knowledge is the most difficult knowledge to share. It takes two individuals who have similar backgrounds, who can develop a good relationship through dialogue, discussions, mentoring and/or coaching, and who ask the right questions. Sharing deep knowledge takes time, patience and dedicated effort. This means that such conversations need to be planned well before the retiring person leaves. Ron Dvir (2006 with the Futures Center in Tel-Aviv, Israel) uses the phrase *knowledge moments* to describe the intersection of people, places, processes and purpose. Knowledge moments can be facilitated and nurtured. For example, conversations, stories and dialogues can occur informally as we move through meetings and lunch-time training experiences, as well as through large socially-structured events such as knowledge fairs and town halls.

> Deep knowledge is the most difficult knowledge to share.

Ashby's law of requisite variety (Ashby, 1964) implies that any decision you make must allow more flexibility in implementation than the variability of the situation you are influencing. Thus a simple situation with few elements and relationships would require a simple decision solution set whereas a complicated situation would usually require a larger solution set, and a complex situation an even larger one. A simple decision might answer the questions: What days do we get off this month? Is my paycheck accurate? The answers to these questions require surface knowledge, routine knowledge based on what, when, where and how.

In exploring the hierarchy of product development decisions, Clausing indicates that most of these decisions are made on the basis of experience. That body of experience includes analyses, handbooks, computerized records and other depositories. Most of the decisions made in organizations are at this level (see Figure 4 below). As Clausing says, "In developing a complex product, there may be 10 million decisions; most of them are within the grasp of individuals equipped with these tools." (Clausing, 1994, p. 57) These decisions would be primarily at the surface and shallow level, that is, require those levels of knowledge. The more critical decisions, anywhere from 1,000 to 10,000 for what Clausing refers to as "complex products" (by our definition complicated) are undoubtedly at the shallow level.

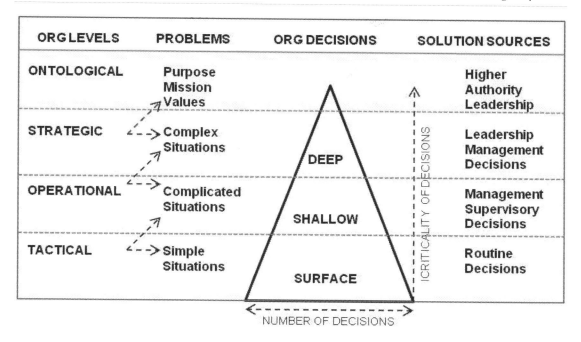

Figure 4: *Characterization of organizational knowledge needs. Routine decisions made in organizations are at the surface level. Decisions requiring deep knowledge are much fewer, and tend to be more critical to the organization's success.*

Finally, there is that small group of decisions that require even more attention. While most often these do not lie within the grasp of a single individual, "collective experience properly concentrated is sufficient. The right multifunctional team using a disciplined approach can make good decisions" (Clausing, 1994, p. 57). This level of decisions would likely require deep knowledge regarding the design, engineering, and production of complicated products. It would also require an understanding of the language and basics of systems as well as complexity theory in order to predict how the people and organization will react to system changes. For example, systems and complexity thinking can support leader and stakeholder understanding of demand, competition, product interrelationships, cultural changes, and market shifts. This understanding can also provide ideas for influencing complex situations. Three examples are boundary management, sense and respond, and seeding. (See below under Mechanisms for Influencing Complex Situations.)

Mechanisms for Influencing Complex Situations

A theory is a generalized statement about reality that describes how things relate to each other in a given domain of inquiry. Theory provides a foundation for understanding why things relate and what specific causality exists. Thus, in attempting to understand or generate a decision strategy for a specific CAM, one not only needs rules, patterns and relationships, but also the underlying theories, principles and guidelines (where available) to allow generalized knowledge creation from—and application to—the specific situation. This generalization may be quite challenging for complex problems, which may not repeat themselves within a semblance of coherence. However, before the mind can effectively observe, reflect and interpret a situation in the external world, the frame of reference of the decision-maker must be recognized since that frame will define and limit what is sensed, interpreted and understood. Multiple frames of reference serve as tools to observe and interpret the system from differing perspectives, providing the opportunity to find the best interpretations and explanations of the complex situation.

To find a frame of reference applicable to complexity requires an appropriate language, a set of concepts and ways to characterize the situation. For example, without an awareness and understanding of concepts such as the tipping point, butterfly effect, emergence, feedback loops, power laws, nonlinearity, etc., it is difficult to have a frame of reference which would adequately recognize and permit an integrated view of a complex situation.

> To find a frame of reference applicable to complexity requires an appropriate language, a set of concepts and ways to characterize the situation.

Thus, rather than intelligence or brilliance, it is more likely to be the homework, learning and experiences living with the situation that will ultimately guide the decision-maker through the landscape and subtle underlying patterns that adequately facilitate an interpretation of the future of any complex situation.

The following mechanisms for influencing complex situations are detailed below: Absorption, Amplification, Boundary Management, Ontology, Optimum Complexity, Seeding, Sense and Respond, Simplification, Structural Adaptation, and Trial and Error.

Absorption. Absorption is the act of bringing one complex situation into a larger complex system so that as the two slowly intermix, there is a resolving of the original problem by dissolving the problem system. This may happen during a merger or takeover. A related approach is for two organizations to swap people such that each learns from the other and brings back ideas, processes and insights. In this way, workers in a "problem" environment can experience and learn from a "desirable" environment.

Amplification. Closely coupled to the sense and respond approach is that of amplification, used where the problem is very complex and the situation's response is unknown. This is the evolutionary approach where a variety of actions are tried to determine which ones succeed. The successful actions are then used over and over again in similar situations (the process of amplification) as long as they yield the desired results. When actions fail, they are discarded and new actions are attempted; time is unlikely to help failed actions succeed because of the unpredictability of the future. Many trial actions will have a short half-life. This is not blind trial-and-error experimentation since decision-maker learning occurs continuously and judgment, experience, and deep knowledge can create understanding and knowing that result in more effective actions. In other words, sense and respond, trial and error, and amplification used both as part of a decision strategy and learning tools—coupled with knowledge of complex systems, the use of teams, and the deliberate development of intuition—suggest a valuable approach to dealing with complex systems.

Boundary Management. Boundary management is a technique for influencing complex situations by controlling/influencing their boundary conditions. For example, if a vendor is providing medium quality products to a manufacturing plant, the manufacturer's buyer may change the purchase price, delivery schedule, quantity, etc., to press the vendor to improve quality, forcing the problem into the vendor's system.

Changing the information, funding, people, material, or knowledge that goes into or out of a complex situation will impact its internal operation and behavior; for example, using the external media as a vehicle for effectively communicating the importance of internal organizational messages. Such indirect actions may prove more effective than direct intervention because complex system behavior is usually very sensitive to its boundary conditions; that is where the energy comes from that keeps it alive and in disequilibrium.

Ontology. The ontology of the decision process represents the schema or set of characteristics and conditions surrounding the decision strategy that potentially have an important influence on the desired outcome. To the extent that these factors may be identified, they can then be prioritized, rated as to significance, visualized through graphics, and then used to develop the optimum decision strategy. For example, if an organization is unable to perform well in a rapidly changing, uncertain environment, its senior leadership may decide that the Intelligent Complex Adaptive System (ICAS) organizational model may be the best solution. If so, the ontology would consist of the eight emergent characteristics of the ICAS model, namely: organizational intelligence, unity and shared purpose, optimum complexity, selectivity, knowledge centricity, permeable boundaries, flow and multidimensionality (Bennet and Bennet, 2004). The decision strategy would then be to change the current organization to encompass these eight emergent characteristics—ranked and weighted by their importance to the specific products, markets, mission, etc. of the organization—by building a set of actions that would move the organization toward the desired state.

Optimum Complexity. Another approach to dealing with a complex problem is embracing complexity. Consider the creation of optimum complexity as a tactic for the decision-maker. Ross Ashby's law of requisite variety states that for one organization or system to influence or control another, the variety of the first organization must be at least as great as—if not greater than—the variety of the controlled organization. (Ashby, 1964) This comes from Cybernetics, and is more of a rule than a law, but very useful when dealing with complex problems. What this means is that your decision strategy should have more options available than the CAM you are dealing with. By building more complexity into the decision strategy—finding more alternatives for action, pivot points, feedback networks, etc.—you are better able to deal with the unpredictable responses that may arise during implementation. See Axelrod and Cohen (1999) for an extensive treatment of the role of variation, interaction, and selection in dealing with external complexity.

Sense and Respond. Sense and respond is another strategy to deal with CAMs. This is a testing approach where the problem is observed, then perturbed, and the responses studied. This begins a learning process that helps the decision-maker better understand the behavior of the CAM. Using a variety of sensing and perturbations provides the opportunity to dig into the nature of the situation/problem before taking action. This tactic is often used by new managers and senior executives, who wait, watch and test the organization before starting any change management actions.

Seeding. Seeding is a process of nurturing emergence. Since emergent properties arise out of multiple nonlinear interactions among agents of the system (people), it is rarely possible to design a set of actions that will result in the desired solution. However, such actions may influence the system such that the desired emergent properties, outcomes, or something close to them, will emerge. An example of seeding is sponsoring several small pilot programs and giving them high visibility so other workers can observe their progress, learn from them, and appreciate their value to the entire organization. If the pilots are successful, application on a larger scale would be much more acceptable to organizational employees.

Emergence is not random. It is the result of the interaction of a variety of elements. If we cannot predetermine the exact emergent property, such as a specific culture, we may be able to create a culture that is acceptable—or perhaps better—than the one we believe is needed. If we can find the right *set of actions* to move a problem in the right direction, then we may be able to guide the situation to our intended outcome. Such a journey is the decision strategy.

Simplification. Simplification reduces our own uncertainty, makes decisions easier, and allows logical explanations of those decisions. Simplicity captivates the mind. Complexity confuses, and forces us to use intuition and judgment, both difficult to explain to others. As humans we tend to continuously simplify to avoid being overwhelmed, to hide our confusion, and to become more focused and efficient. In a simple, predictable world, this is rational and generally works well, although it is easy to ignore many incoming signals when we feel that they are not important. Unfortunately, in a complex situation and environment this approach can become dangerous, perhaps even disastrous. As Murray Gell-Mann (1995) states,

> *One of the most important characteristics of complex non-linear systems is that they cannot, in general, be successfully analyzed by determining in advance a set of properties or aspects that are studied separately and then combining those partial approaches in an attempt to form a picture of the whole. Instead, it is necessary to look at the whole system, even if that means taking a crude look, and then allowing possible simplifications to emerge from the work.* (Battram, 1996, p. 12)

Where complexity lives, it is hard to separate the unimportant from the critical information, events, or signals. The question becomes one of what aspects of this complex situation can be simplified, and how does that simplification benefit the overall solution set?

Structural Adaptation. When the complex situation/problem lies within the decision-makers own organization, special considerations come into play. It may become necessary to view the problem as part of the organization in the sense that both "systems" are complex and interconnected. As Stacey et al. describes, "Thinking in terms of interconnections and the consequent awareness of causal links that are distant in space and time alerts managers to the unintended and unexpected consequences of their action." (Stacey et al., 2000, p. 80) In other words, the organization may be *part of the problem* and any successful solution would include changes both inside the "problem" as well as in the surrounding organization. In a sense we have two coupled complex systems that are connected such that any change in one is likely to affect the other. Since such structural coupling or adaptation is common, the decision strategy may be to use this coupling to pull the problem situation along in the desired direction. In general, structural adaptation is a good way to influence complex organizations, although exactly where the system will end up cannot be predicted. For detailed analysis of structural adaptation see von Krogh and Roos (1995) and Maturana and Varela (1995).

Trial and Error. Where the system under study is highly complex and adaptive, it will be impossible to know how it will respond to some action. Evolutionary biology has dealt with this problem throughout the evolution of life. It appears that the standard solution is to create a variety of actions, try them, and use feedback to find out which ones succeed. The successful actions are then used over and over in similar situations as long as they yield the desired results: survival and reproduction. When they fail to work, they are stopped and new actions are rewarded.

It is important not to continue with an action that is not working. Time is unlikely to help the action work because in a highly complex environment the only future is the present; in a short time the environment will probably have a very different nature. This is not a pure trial-and-error procedure, since learning continuously occurs, judgment, experience, and deep knowledge may create a level of understanding that aids in moving into the future. As knowledge of the complex adaptive organization improves, better actions can be selected and used to change the system.

Introducing the Human Factor

People are complex adaptive systems who do not always operate intelligently when in stressful situations. For example, issues are not always clear to us because we're just too close to them. As we observe the external world and the events around us, we *think* that what we are doing is taking our observations, putting them into our minds and creating an accurate representation of the external world. Unfortunately, this is not the case. How we view a situation, what we look for and how we interpret what we see, depend heavily on our past experiences, expectations, concerns and goals.

As difficult as it might be to comprehend for many of us who have grown up professionally in a fear-based world where reason was king, *the four primary barriers to intelligent decision-making are fear, reason, social convention and tradition.* When we conform to a fear-based external code, we give up our unique individuality as a decision-maker. Fear as a primary motivational factor for decisions emotionally clouds the decision-makers awareness and ability to intelligently explore the situation from a systems perspective, limiting the scope of potential options. Fear can cause decision-makers to become so preoccupied with the projections of imagined outcomes that they become virtual prisoners to their own designs, unable to perceive beyond that

> Fear emotionally clouds the decision-maker's awareness and ability to intelligently explore the situation from a systems perspective.

singular interpretation. In the field of fear intelligence often takes a back seat. When fear dominates, we are unable to tap into our higher mental faculties and the expansive awareness available through our unconscious resources.

"Okay," you agree, "I understand that fear can be a barrier to intelligent decision-making, but how can reason be a barrier! Come on."

Let's do a role play. You are a limited-income farmer working hard to provide the necessities of life for your family, which includes three small children under five. As often occurs on farms, there is a rampant population of cats. One morning you discover a hand-full of newborn kittens near a dead mother cat just off the road. They are in pitiful shape. With a heart sigh, because you like animals of all kinds, you do what needs to be done. Now, picture yourself as that same farmer at the moment of his wife's death following the birth of premature twins. If reason were your only dictate, what decision would you make? "That's not a decision," you respond, "There is a big difference between motherless newborn kittens and motherless premature human babies." What is that difference? *It is the difference of values, of responsibility, of love, all of which trump reason in the decision-making process.*

While our role play might appear dramatic and somewhat absurd in our Western culture, this is not the case in other parts of the world where birth control is unavailable, overpopulation is rampant, and a premature multiple birth could threaten the family's survival. What decision would be made in this situation? What would reason dictate? What would your higher mental faculties dictate? Which brings us to the power of social convention.

The decision-making barrier of social convention is a bit easier to deal with in terms of understanding. Again, this is heavily influenced by culture. In some cultures breaking out of the social norm—no matter how unintelligent and unfair that norm—would have serious consequences for yourself and those in relationship with you, personally and professionally. Note that there is an element of fear that emerges in connection with not following social convention; the fear of social consequences. *The very attempt to hold onto patterns from the past destroys the **living nature of knowledge***.

Making an intellectual choice becomes more difficult for the decision-maker when the social convention appears to be harmless. We ask, "While I may not agree with it, what harm will come of it?" This is a choice that has to be made by the decision-maker in the situation at hand. Recall that all knowledge is situation dependent and context sensitive. The illusive "right" and "wrong" are also situation dependent and context sensitive.

> The illusive "right" and "wrong" are situation dependent and context sensitive.

The barrier of tradition can be based both on comfort and intellectual laziness as well as fear. If something has been done over and over again and has worked in the past, why not just keep doing things the way we have in the past? The answer, of course, is in the understanding of the change, uncertainty and complexity of our environment and our need to co-evolve with that environment as we move into the future. The answer is also within ourselves. Is this the best way to act? Is this how I choose to act?

In a culture of fear or where ego and saving face may trump perceived "rightness," it is far easier to do things the way they have been done in the past. Then, if the results do not turn out as desired, you can always blame the system. You can break this paradigm. Decisions are made by individuals, not the system. *There is a choice.* "The most destructive decision that an individual can make is to give away his or her decision-making authority." (Carey, 1995, p.43)

Before leaving this discussion of fear, reason, social convention and tradition as potentially destructive to intelligent decision-making, let us shift our frame of reference. These four areas are part of the human condition, elements that in some way touch a part of every human culture, in service to humanity, and they can also be in service to the decision-maker. For example, tradition can serve as a helpful behavioral guide as long as it is one context element in the context set. Fear, when intelligently considered and accompanied by intelligent choices, can serve as an agent of change, embedding a sense of urgency to accomplish some selected task. *But it cannot be the task master.* All emotions in the human emotion set are meant to serve as a guidance system, to ensure that we are in alignment with ourselves. Although we often perceive emotions as caused by external events or people, they emerge within ourselves. Thus, when we are feeling higher order emotions such as joy and love, we are in alignment with ourselves.

Another role play. Imagine yourself as a young woman who has the opportunity of a lifetime to interview with a large Public Relations firm in New York City. You meet with several executives, you provide writing samples, they look at some of your layouts, and somewhere in between they feed you. You get the job. Floating with happiness, you exit the office building and head toward your car, parked seven blocks away (assuming you were able to find a parking spot at all!) It is dark, and you notice two large men walking behind you. You speed up; they speed up. You turn the corner; they turn the corner. You start running; they start running. Catching up, one of them reaches out and grabs your elbow, saying, "Excuse me, miss. You dropped your wallet."

Any emotions of fear that were building within you were YOUR emotions, your imaginings of possibilities. Nothing bad or negative was going on other than your perception of the situation; quite to the contrary, something good was happening. While you cannot run away from your fears, acknowledging them in context as a signal that you are out of alignment puts them in another perspective. When you do make a decision, that decision along with the results of that decision become part of your Knowledge (Informing) set that you as a unique decision-maker will use as input for Knowledge (Proceeding).

In our earlier role play addressing reason, we insinuated that when we use our higher mental faculties, values trump reason. Values are an individual choice and, as knowledge, are situation dependent and context sensitive. For example, in our historic fear-based, reason-centered, scarcity-based economy it only made sense (in a general usage of the word sense) that societal values were highly materialistic. This frame of reference drove decisions and actions that proved highly destructive to both individuals and development of a global economy. The individual's perspective, knowledge and knowing, were hijacked by the allure of material goods and societal norms. This misappropriated influence of materialism and misalignment with self led to loss of confidence, confusion, and the inability to make intelligent decisions for the greater individual good or the greater good of humanity. (See the Appendix A discussion on wisdom.)

Group Decision-Making

The potential of the human mind can often be more fully engaged when working in teams, communities and networks. When addressing a complex situation, group decision-making can make a large difference. The use of teams develops multiple perspectives as they engage in dialogue and critical thinking, which can improve the overall understanding of a CAM, thereby improving the efficacy of a decision strategy. Of course, this must build on the availability and understanding of relevant facts, data, context information and past behaviors. Note that teams, communities and networks are cooperative associations of interconnected informational beings, bringing with them a great deal of individuated context.

The use of convergent thinking to develop a common team perception of the CAM, sets the stage for asking the right questions in order to identify underlying drivers, patterns and relationships that aid in developing decision strategies and anticipating consequences. Where possible, other approaches, such as the use of classic cognitive and operational research techniques (linear extrapolation, mind-mapping, fishbone diagrams, probability distribution functions, etc.), serve as excellent learning tools to develop and share an understanding of the CAM, and to encourage intuitive insights.

Complexity cannot be easily understood. Nevertheless, an organization, a team, or an individual must carefully think about, observe, study and become familiar with both the complexity *within the environment* and the complexity *inside the situation system* as preparation for any anticipated decision process. An example is the recognition that complexity in either (or both) the situation and the environment may have a high degree of *variety*. Much of this variety, i.e., the options, actions, choices, and number of possible states that may occur in the CAM, may be irrelevant to the problem at hand and yet require significant energy outlays. There can be too much information, too much variety for the decision-maker to make a decision; thus, the importance of a decision strategy with built-in learning and flexibility. This issue is similar to the information saturation problem which often leads to educated incapacity, that is, the inability to decide and act.

One solution is to ignore those aspects of the situation that are not directly related to the decision-making goals or objectives. While this sounds easy, it may be difficult unless the decision-makers involved have prepared themselves appropriately. For example, in order for a decision team to effectively eliminate some complex parts of a CAM within an organization, they must understand the values and purpose of the organization, the global vision and their own local objectives. They may also need some understanding of the present versus the future applicability of various events, actions, opportunities and threats in the environment, the organization and the situation. These are not obvious to decision-makers or knowledge workers because organizations rarely ensure that their people understand these facets well enough to make good decisions using simplification, i.e., by being able to judge *what to ignore* and *what not to ignore*. This takes time; it takes money; it takes learning on the part of managers and workers. It means developing a "feel" for the complex situation.

An approach proposed by Espejo et al., is to ascribe purpose in order to focus a complex problem.

> *If I am clear about the priorities that really matter to me as an individual and keep these few overriding priorities firmly in mind as I go about my day-to-day activities, this is perhaps the most effective 'complexity-reducer' I can employ. It means exercising the self-discipline required to continually hold my organizing priorities in view and refresh or update them regularly.* (Espejo, et al, 1996, p. 83)

Often, we may find ourselves in confusing situations, ambiguities or paradoxes where we don't know or understand what's happening. When this occurs, it is intelligent to recognize the limited mental capacity of a single individual. Confusion, paradoxes and riddles are not made by external reality or the situation, they are created by *our own limitations in thinking, language and perspective or viewpoint.* This is why networks and teams can frequently

> Confusion, paradoxes and riddles are not made by external reality, they are created by our own limitations in thinking, language and perspective or viewpoint.

improve understanding of complex systems. Multiple viewpoints, sharing of ideas and dialogue can often surface and clarify confusion, paradoxes and uncertainties to an extent far greater than any one individual mind can. Other techniques such as lucid dreaming, meditation, heuristics, chunking, gedanken experiments, creative thinking and exploration can improve our capacity to understand and interpret CAMs. See Rock (2004, pp. 152-171) for a discussion on lucid dreaming. See Christos (2003, pp. 149-157) and Tallis (2002) for an exposition of the history, role and power of the unconscious in our daily lives.

Chapter 6
The Complexity of Actions

Surface, shallow and deep can also be used to describe the complexity of actions. Surface actions would be common everyday actions such as opening a door, running, or turning on a light switch. Shallow actions would be where an individual deliberately sets about doing something that initially requires practice but becomes relatively easy as it is mastered over some period of time. Examples would be machining metal parts or driving a crowded four-lane highway during rush hour.

Deep action refers to actions based on deep knowledge and deep learning. A well-known example would be the transfer of the tacit knowledge involved with bread-making (Nonaka and Takeuchi, 1995). A similar example would be that of an apprentice learning to build a violin. In both cases, not only would the individual have to work with a mentor long enough to embed the same actionable movements as the expert, but that individual would have to develop an understanding of how and why these movements were applied. Karl Weick's study of expert firefighters fighting fires is another example of what is suggested by deep action (Weick, 1995). See Section IV for an in-depth treatment of tacit knowledge.

An example of a complex issue that would require complex actions is the desire to change an organization into a knowledge centric, adaptable, sustainable organization operating within a CUCA (changing, uncertain, complex) environment. This example is not an unusual challenge for large organizations struggling to survive in a global competitive environment. Deep knowledge is needed to understand and know how to deal with organizational culture, workers, managers and leaders. The environment (including the organization's customers) would need to be well understood. Initial actions might include supporting the growth of communities, integrating new social media, and setting up new information systems.

Patterns of change would need to be anticipated and integrated with new ideas, roles and structures to create the needed adaptability and sustainability. A deep sensitivity to the organizational history and management reactions to changes in their roles and responsibilities would need to be considered in order to construct an effective *change management program*. For example, you may want to initialize a "pass it down" strategy, with leaders directly inspiring their subordinates through hands-on training and action commitment. While this list goes on,

> Patterns of change need to be anticipated and integrated with new ideas, roles and structures to create the needed adaptability and sustainability.

it is clear that only a strong team of individuals with deep knowledge in a number of actionable areas and a large network of trusted relationships could successfully move an organization toward knowledge centricity.

Decide and Act

Armed with the realization that all of the information and knowledge gathered to this point lays the groundwork for understanding a CAM, the decision-maker tries to be in a position to *observe, study, reflect, experiment and use intuition* to develop a "feeling" for the key relationships and patterns of behavior within the system. Considering why and how something happens, not just what and when, the decision-maker looks for the structural sources (and the relationships among those structural sources) of multiple actions, interactions, events, and patterns. **Trial-and-error perturbations** coupled with effortful reflection over time will often provide a deeper knowledge and understanding of how the CAM functions and what actions it takes to resolve problems. (See Chapter 5 for an explanation of the trial-and-error approach.)

Where possible, **talking with people in the system** about how the work *really* gets done and who influences what goes on, asking questions and dialoguing to discover their insights, can provide a deeper level of knowledge and an invaluable sensing capability. The decision-maker is learning how to *feel* the system's pulse through close attention, listening, experience and reflection. This feel for the system is essential since analysis and logic produce useful answers only if their assumptions are correct, and all material causal relationships have been taken into account—an almost impossible task in a complex system. In a CAM understanding its non-adaptive behavior is inadequate.

Identifying emergent properties can be meaningful, qualitative, global and very informative. One approach to discovering what integrates and creates these emergent characteristics is reflecting on system behavior, history, patterns, properties, events and flows. Patterns are composed of relatively stable sets of relationships and events that occur throughout a system. Since properties are characteristics resulting from interactions within the system and can rarely be reduced to single sources, they must be observed and understood as broad, qualitative phenomena, patterns or underlying structures. An example would be the existence of stovepipes in an organization.

Events can result from single, multiple sequential, or simultaneous causes. Decision-makers can consider why they happen, what structural aspects are involved, and any related patterns that accompany the events. Questions to be asked include: Is this the problem or a symptom of a deeper situation? Is the formal or informal structure causing this result? What can be controlled? What can be influenced? What may be nurtured to emerge?

Another approach is to **extract patterns** and conceptually separate them from the CAM to see how much information they contain and how they influence, or can be used to influence, the complex system. Analyzing relationship networks can play a useful role in understanding the system and its behavior. *Social network analysis* (SNA) is an example of this, where you take a complex social system and identify through measurement the relative degree of influence of communication among individuals across the organization. Mapping this provides patterns of information flow and the sources and sinks of influence in the organization, allowing identification of those sources which can most effectively influence the system.

Another use of SNA is to map the interactions and relationships among individuals in the organization relative to the influence of individual A's work on individuals B, C and D, and vice versa. This is helpful where people work in relative isolation and yet their work significantly impacts other parts of the organization. That impact often goes unnoticed and individuals think they are doing their job effectively while, in fact, if viewed from a broader systems perspective there is a need for more cohesion, correlation and correspondence.

Developing a potential solution set to a CAM will require a diversity of mental resources. CAMs may need to be studied via both reductionist and holistic thinking, fully engaging decision-maker experience, intuition and judgment to solve problems. This competency to use intuition and judgment to solve problems without being able to explain how they know is a common characteristic of experts. These individuals actively learn through deliberate, investigative and knowledge-seeking experience, developing intuition and building judgment through play and intensive interaction with the system and its environment.

A recent study of chess players concluded that "effortful practice" was the difference between people who played chess for many years while maintaining an average skill and those who become master players in shorter periods of time. The master players, or experts, examined the patterns over and over again, studying them, looking at nuances, trying small changes to perturb the outcome (sense and respond), generally "playing with" and studying the patterns. A significant observation was that when these experts were observed outside their area of expertise, they were no more competent than everyone else. The report also noted that, "… the expert relies not so much on an intrinsically stronger power of analysis as on a store of structured knowledge." (Ross, 2006, p. 67)

In other words, they use long-term working memory, pattern recognition and chunking rather than logic as a means of understanding and analyzing. This indicates that by exerting mental effort and emotion while exploring complex situations knowledge becomes embedded in the unconscious. *By sorting, modifying, and generally playing with information—manipulating and understanding patterns and their relationships to other patterns in CAMs—a decision-maker can proactively develop intuition, insight and judgment relative to the domain of interest.* It is through such activities as these that our experience and intuition grow, becoming capable of recognizing the potential unfolding of patterns and the flow of activities in CAMs, leading to an intuitive understanding and a sense of the primary drivers.

Guiding Principles

The following principles for the decision-maker when dealing with a CAM is garnered from information that has been introduced in this book. Each principle must be treated as a rule-of-thumb that *may or may not* apply in any given situation. Remember, all knowledge is context sensitive and situation dependent. The decision-maker at the point of action, that is, with the best knowledge for a given situation, can best determine the application of a principle in that situation.

Guiding Principle 1. The future is truly unknowable and therefore we must learn to live and deal with uncertainty, surprise, paradox, and complexity. It may, however be fathomable in the sense of being able to comprehend certain probable future scenarios or trends (Stacy, 1992; McMaster, 1996).

Guiding Principle 2. Over time complexity increases in complex adaptive systems. Complex adaptive systems evolve and survive by learning, adapting, and influencing their environment, thereby increasing their own complexity. As a general rule, complexity begets complexity as systems strive for survival and growth through learning and adaptation with their concomitant increase in internal complexity (Capra, 1996) (Csikszentmihalyi, 2003).

Guiding Principle 3. Complex systems generate emergent characteristics through the rich and myriad relationships and interactions among their agents. These emergent properties may be volatile and hard to control because a few agents can make changes that may propagate through the structure via nonlinear reinforcing or damping feedback loops. Relatively stable emergent patterns such as cultures may also arise. One way to influence complex systems is to create, nurture, and modify their emergent phenomena by dealing with their structures, relationships and second order causal factors (Holland, 1998; Johnson, 2001; Morowitz, 2002; Battram, 1996).

Guiding Principle 4. Complex adaptive systems cannot be controlled, they can only be guided and nurtured. Control stifles creativity, minimizes interactions, and only works under stable situations. It is not possible to control a worker's thinking, feelings, creativity, trust, spirit or enthusiasm (Kelly,1994; Kelly and Allison, 1999; Csikszentmihalyi, 2003).

Guiding Principle 5. When two complex adaptive systems are interacting, the one with the greatest variety will usually dominate. However, too much variety may lead to chaos (Espejo et al., 1996; Ashby, 1964).

Guiding Principle 6. Diversity, innovation, selection, interaction, and self-organization are critical for the successful evolution and adaptation of complex systems (Axelrod and Cohen, 1999: Stacey, 1996).

Guiding Principle 7. Complex adaptive systems cannot be highly efficient and survive in a complex, dynamic environment. High efficiency leaves no room for creativity, learning, exploration or surge energy in response to threats. A certain level of noise is needed to maintain the system's ability to learn, change, and adapt since learning requires some level of error and instability (Bennet and Bennet, 2004; Davis and Meyer, 1998).

Guiding Principle 8. Effective structures are essential to a complex adaptive system which can survive in a complex environment. Structures influence relationships. Relationships drive interactions, patterns and actions. Actions create events. Events cause external changes that feedback to the originating complex adaptive system structures. This is how organizations and their environment co-evolve, with each affecting the other, resulting in iterative and recursive changes in both systems (Capra, 1996) (Meyer and Davis, 2003).

Guiding Principle 9. Self-organization encourages a diversity of patterns to develop, optimizing the interactions among people and creating more options for action, thereby supporting flexibility and adaptability (Kauffman, 1995; Stacey, 2000).

Chapter 7
Complex Decision-Making

When the traditional decision process is applied to a simple or complicated situation, the objective is to move the situation from the current state to some desired future state. As introduced above, when dealing with complex problems the decision process often requires a commitment to *embark on a journey toward an uncertain future*, creating a set of iterative actions whose consequences will cause a move from the current situation (A) *toward* a desired future situation (B) (see Figure 5).

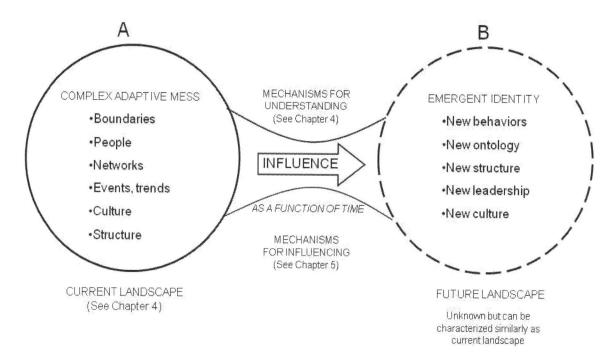

Figure 5: *The decision strategy is a sequence of actions to move the situation from A toward B.*

In Figure 5, the **current landscape** (and the future landscape) would encompass such characteristics of complex adaptive systems as surprise prone, multiple connections, relationships, and sinks and sources; and the behaviors of a complex adaptive system such as emergence, feedback loops, nonlinearities, time delays, butterfly effects, tipping points, power laws, correlations and unpredictability (see Chapter 4). **Mechanisms for understanding** CAMs would include observation, analysis, reasoning, critical thinking, synthesis, dialogue and effortful reflection (see Chapter 5). They would also include intuition and lucid dreaming (see Chapter 14 under "Surfacing Tacit Knowledge"). **Mechanisms for influencing** CAMs would include absorption, boundary management, sense and response, amplification and seeding (see Chapter 5).

Preparing for the Journey

Since there is no direct cause and effect relationship that is traceable from the decision to the desired future state, the journey may require extensive preparation. The decision strategy must have the capacity and internal support mechanisms needed for an implementation journey that cannot be predetermined.

The decision-making journey itself, then, could be thought of in terms of complexity. As Auyang describes,

> *I use complex and complexity intuitively to describe self-organized systems that have many components and many characteristic aspects, exhibit many structures in various scales, undergo many processes in various rates, and have the capabilities to change abruptly and adapt to external environments.* (Auyang, 1998, p. 13)

The success of this ability to change abruptly and adapt to external environments will be highly dependent on the self-organization and robustness of the adaptive elements built into the decision strategy.

The *preparation process* includes: understanding the domain of interest as well as possible; recognizing the level of uncertainty, surprise potential and nature of the landscape; preparing for the journey in terms of resources, flexibility, partners, expectations, goal shifting, etc.; making sure that individuals carrying out the decision strategy are ready (i.e., sustainability criteria are met); and ensuring that all relevant alternatives have been considered.

In preparing for making decisions that deal with complex adaptive messes, a number of broad competencies may prove helpful. These competencies are not typically part of professional discipline training and education, and therefore may be unfamiliar to many decision-makers. We use the term *integrative competencies* since they provide connective tissue, thereby creating knowledge, skills, abilities, and behaviors that support and enhance other competencies. They also help decision-makers deal with larger, more complex aspects of a CAM, either integrating data, information, knowledge or actions, or helping the decision-maker perceive and comprehend the complexity around them by clarifying events, patterns, and structures.

> Integrative competencies provide connective tissue, thereby creating knowledge, skills, abilities, and behaviors that support and enhance other competencies.

Managing risk is one such competency, that is, the risk of poor management, leadership or decision-making. Another is an understanding of the basic principles of systems and systems evolution, which provides the ability to look at complex problems from a systems perspective. Another is relationship network management to facilitate decision-makers developing networks to provide knowledge and cognitive support in building and implementing the decision strategy. Still another one is critical thinking, that is, ensuring that the decision-maker can ask the right questions, including questioning their own assumptions and beliefs, and can recognize when information is bogus or nonsensical, or simply doesn't fit. Information literacy, another integrative competency, is a set of skills that enable decision-makers to recognize when information is and is not needed, and how to locate, evaluate, integrate, use and effectively communicate information.

We mentioned earlier the importance of becoming comfortable with, understanding, and developing an intuition relative to specific complex systems and situations. As an example of the dangers of *not* understanding complex systems, consider an organization operating in a bureaucratic model where control, policies, and strong decision hierarchies ensure control over workers and a uniform, consistent way of making decisions. This organization is structured such that when a problem comes up, something fails, or someone does something that they shouldn't have done, management can quickly step in, make a decision, implement a policy or action, and create another rule which prevents re-occurrence. While this may work for routine, simple problems, it does not work for a CAM because there is no single cause of the problem and no single point of correction. As Battram explains, "Because complex systems have built-in unpredictability, the certainties of the 'command and control' approach to management no longer hold true. The implications of complexity theory for organizations are massive." (Battram, 1996, p. 11)

Influencing the System

The standard approach to problem-solving is to identify the cause of the problem, change it, and the problem goes away. As Sterman describes,

> ...*people generally adopt an event-based, open-loop view of causality, ignore feedback processes, fail to appreciate time delays between action and response and the reporting of information, do not understand stocks and flows, and are insensitive to nonlinearities that may alter the strengths of different feedback loops as a system evolves.* (Sterman, 1994, p. 304)

He cites several studies which indicate that when people tried to control a dynamically complex system their attempts were counterproductive. Often, their results were bested by a do-nothing rule. He concludes that, "Subsequent experiments show that the greater the dynamic complexity of the environment, the worse people do relative to potential." (Sterman, 1994, p. 304)

It is clear that *the simplistic approach to change does not work* if the problem is complex. When this approach is attempted for a CAM, the change often works for a short time, and then the complex adaptive system rejects the change (or works around it) and the problem returns, larger than before. J. W. Forrester, the originator of system dynamic modeling at the Massachusetts Institute of Technology, perhaps said it best when he noted that almost all single actions taken to change an organization result in an immediate response in the intended direction, but after a short time the organization returns to its natural state, sometimes overshooting with a vengeance (Bennet and Bennet, 1996, *a personal conversation with Forrester*). This is popularly known as *counter-intuitive behavior*.

As complex systems, organizations (no matter what their structure) have emergent properties such as culture that are created by individuals doing their work, developing habits, procedures, ways of thinking, ways of behaving and ways of interacting with others, all leading to a comfort level that usually facilitates getting the work done. Thus, culture emerges, created by a series of multiple, historical interactions and relationships which evolve over time and take on a life of their own. There is no single force or creator of culture, and there is no single action that will create a specific desired culture. *CAMs, while operating in a landscape of disequilibrium, are relatively stable because there is a balance of forces that have created some degree of equilibrium.*

When you influence part of the system there will be counter forces that try to neutralize the change. Therefore, it takes a set of events and the interactions among those events, far deeper and broader than just a single cause, to change a complex system. While multiple actions, carefully selected and orchestrated, may move the situation toward a desired state, there is no guarantee that the end state will be the one anticipated. However, multiple interventions via a decision strategy may create an environment which

> When you influence part of the system there will be counter forces that try to neutralize the change.

nurtures and gently pushes the system to readjust itself in a manner that results in the expected end state. Battram, referring to computer simulations at the Santa Fe Institute on changing a complex adaptive system from the outside, indicates that you have to:

> *Create a representation of the interactions in the system and enable the independent agents in the system to communicate about the representation. In the simulations without this representation, the 'agents' simply ignored the outside influences, treating them as mere perturbations. In human terms, you can't simply manipulate a team or a department from outside by telling them what to do. Humans are sense-making organisms: therefore you have to allow them to make sense of the task for themselves by giving them information about the combined results of their actions, and enabling them to talk about it. This is the nitty-gritty of 'holding up a mirror to the organisation'.* (Battram, 1996, pp. 254-255)

This approach makes sense in that it recognizes that change can only come from the inside and that people and their relationships, perceptions and beliefs are the major determinants of organizational effectiveness. (Bennet and Bennet, 2004)

Another very important consideration when dealing with complex systems is the ability to make maximum use of your past experience and cognitive capabilities. This means using your unconscious mind (with its memory and associative processing power) to help understand CAMs. For example, we all know much more than we think we know. We are often asked a question that we answer, and yet we didn't realize we knew the answer before the question was asked. (See Section III for a treatment of the decision-making process from the mind/brain perspective.)

We spend our lives soaking up data, information and knowledge, and through our experiences and internal thinking and contemplation, we develop understanding, insights and feelings about things of which we are often unaware. How does this happen? As Churchland observes,

> *On those occasions when a weighty decision involves conscious deliberations, we are sometimes aware of the inner struggles, describing ourselves as having conflicting or ambivalent feelings. Some processes in decision-making take longer to resolve than others, and hence the wisdom in the advice to "sleep on" consequential decision. Everyone knows that sleeping on a heavy decision tends to help us settle into the "decision minimum" we can best live with, though exactly how and why are not understood. Are these longer processes classically rational? Are they classically emotive? Probably they are not fittingly described by our existing vocabulary. They are the processes of a dynamical system setting into a stable attractor.* (Churchland, 2002, pp. 228-229)

Another aspect of dealing with complex situations is to prepare for unforeseen surprises and rapid jumps. These changes can be of a magnitude far larger than is expected. Some complex systems have the tendency to create surprises which follow a power law. For example, if you look at the sizes of cities in the United States, you'll find that there are many more small ones than large ones, while if you look at the distribution of heights of people in the world you will find a Gaussian distribution with some medium (average) and then some tails on each side of the distribution function. The population of cities in a given country varies according to a power law with the number of cities having N inhabitants is proportional to $1/N^2$. Thus, there will be four times as many cities with a population of 100K as those with a population of 200K. This distribution is quite different than the normal (or bell curve) Gaussian distribution.

> An aspect of dealing with complex situations is to prepare for unforeseen surprises and rapid jumps.

The reason this is important is because the left tail of the power law distribution is considerably stronger, sometimes by a factor as much as 100, i.e., they contain a higher probability of an event occurring than the same tail of the bell curve. A fundamental difference between the two is that the bell curve is based on *the independence of events* that are occurring, whereas the power law takes into account that there is some *relationship among those events*. By definition, complex systems are built with multiple interrelationships and therefore have an interdependence that may follow some source law, which has a much higher probability of extreme occurrences happening than does the bell curve. Since CAMs arise out of/within complex adaptive organizations, one might be very cautious in using Gaussian or any other measures within the organization.

Interdependence, connections, relationships, connectedness of choices and coherence of actions are mainstays of success in complex adaptive organizations.

Therefore, when problems arise, the focus is not just on individuals or policies, i.e., replacing individuals or issuing new policies is not likely to resolve a CAM. As to the significance of laws in complex systems, consider the case of stock market fluctuations.

The bell curve predicts a one-day drop of 10 percent in the valuation of a stock just about once every 500 years. The empirical power law gives a very different and more reliable estimate: about once every five years. Large disruptive events are not only more frequent than intuition might dictate, they are also disproportionate in their effect … most of the total movement in any stock over a single year is often attributable to abrupt changes on a few select days." (Buchanan, 2004, p. 73)

A Sample Decision-Making Process

The decision-making process begins with noticing a situation that is both context sensitive and situation dependent, and with four sets of information that start the learning process: (a) theories, values, beliefs, and assumptions internal to the decision-maker, (b) memories related to the situation at hand, (c) incoming information from the internal environment, and (d) incoming information from the external environment. The decision-maker creates knowledge by reflecting upon and comprehending the interactions among (a), (b) (c) and (d) above, complexed with knowledge related to potential actions available and applicable to the situation at hand. This represents a problem-solving aspect of decision-making. Out of this process emerges understanding, meaning, insights, perhaps creative ideas, and anticipation of the outcome of potential actions (that is, knowledge).

There may be several potential actions that could result in the desired outcome relative to the situation at hand. Assuming three potential actions and their forecasted outcomes, the decision-maker evaluates each decision option in terms of the science and the art of decision-making. The science of decision-making refers to the use of logic, reductionist thinking, analysis, cost-benefit investigations, linear extrapolation, and—where feasible—simulations, trade-off analysis, and probability analysis. The art of decision-making refers to the intuition, judgment, feelings, imagination, and heuristics which come mostly from the unconscious. (See Section IV and Chapter 16.)

Combining these two approaches to understanding the forecasted outcomes, the decision-maker selects the decision which either objectively or intuitively (or both) is expected to have the highest probability of success in achieving the desired goals and objectives. As can be seen, much thought is spent in anticipating the outcome of specific actions. This is discussed from the mind/brain perspective later in this chapter.

A "good" decision in a complex situation would result in an expected outcome that would fall within a cone of acceptable results. As part of the decision journey, implementation of such a decision requires continuous feedback loops to update the complex situation's response to management actions. It would most likely be necessary to guide the complex situation's movements by a series of corrective actions or nudges to keep the situation heading in the desired direction.

The Solution Team

A decision strategy may be to charter a team to work with the CAM, preparing the team to react quickly to surprises. Quick reactions on the part of the team in dealing with surprises or unknown, even unanticipated, opportunities can make a huge difference in the success of the effort. The ability to react quickly does not come automatically. It must be *deliberately infused* into the solution set and *supported* by managers and leaders such that the team has the experience, freedom, responsibility and accountability that allows them to react quickly to externally created opportunities and threats. This means, for example, that *self-organization and empowerment* may be important factors in the solution team's success. This means open communication so that team members who face a problem at the point of action understand the decision direction and intent, and have the ability and freedom to talk to anyone within the problem domain—and perhaps even external to that domain when needed—to quickly access information and expertise that can assist in handling surprise events or opportunities.

> The ability to react quickly must be deliberately infused into the solution set and supported by managers and leaders.

In addition to quick reactions, there's also the idea of team flexibility. Flexibility means the capacity to learn to maintain an open mind, not prejudiced by past success and bureaucratic traditions or rigorous thinking; the ability to assess an occurrence in the environment objectively; and the wherewithal to take whatever rational action makes sense—either on the basis of logic or intuition and judgment—to achieve decision-making goals. This flexibility means that decision-makers must be willing to try new approaches, moving beyond conservative solutions that have proven themselves in the past, and be willing to take risks in new areas where outcomes are uncertain (at best) and perhaps completely unknown (at worst). This also means that people must be capable and willing to work with each other, work with others they have not worked with before, work in new ways, and take unfamiliar actions. All of these aspects deal with flexibility, whether it's organizational, team, cognitive, social or resource flexibility.

A final item on the check-off list of team health needed to implement a decision strategy is adaptability. By this we mean the capacity of the team to significantly change its internal structure as needed to resolve the CAM. Adaptation may not be a small flexible change; it could be medium to large-scale internal structural changes resulting in more effective interfaces and interactions across multiple stakeholders. Solving a CAM may become a negotiated compromise with the result being a mutually beneficial co-evolution of the situation and the decision-makers organization. It becomes clear as we look at the corollary consequences of decision-making relative to CAMs that decision-making is directly tied to implementation, and that the organization and the complex situation may not be separable.

In summary, to prepare there are many things that individuals and teams can do to understand the complex environment more effectively, and there are actions and approaches that can improve the chance of success. In addition, there are actions that a team or an organization can take regarding its own structure and processes that will support decision-makers in dealing with CAMs. None of these actions or approaches can occur quickly since they are not naturally self-evident to workers who have not had experience in changing CAMs. Thus, a considerable amount of "new learning" may be involved in rethinking the perspectives of what the organization really is, what complexity means, and how to orchestrate a change in behavior. While learning and understanding are the first step, next comes changing behavior, changing modes of thinking, and changing how you approach problems, which are equally important, and often more difficult. The decision to put resources and time into creating a solution strategy and team which has the capability of quick reaction, flexibility, resilience, robustness, adaptability, etc., is a very tough question for leaders and managers who think predominantly in terms of the bottom line and are unfamiliar with the potential ramifications of complex problems.

Chapter 8
Dealing with Complex Adaptive Organizations

The following ideas are provided to suggest ways of looking, thinking, and evaluating complex adaptive systems that will help decision-makers understand and deal with the uncertainty and complexity in their environment. They are heuristic and suggestive rather than definitive. The following ideas and considerations also suggest an approach for applying complexity thinking to complex organizations. The following are not meant to be applied sequentially; and as always context is king:

1. Understand the complex adaptive organization of concern.

2. Review its history and context.

3. Look for the emergent characteristics of the organization.

4. Analyze the organizations networks, their functions and sources of influence.

5. Use more nurturing than control when intervening.

6. Use all available mental and physical resources in trying to understand the organization.

7. Beware of simplicity, organizational complexity may be immune to single and/or simple actions.

8. Self-organize your own learning. Let the complexity guide your path to its comprehension.

9. Expect mistakes, sense and response, feedback and learning may be the best approach.

These steps are explicated below.

1.   Understand the complex adaptive organization of concern.

Observe, study, reflect, and use your intuition to develop a "feeling" for the key relationships and patterns of behavior in the system. Think how, why and where something happened, not just what and when. Look for the structural sources of actions, events, and patterns. Talk to people in the system about how the work really gets done and who influences what goes on, asking questions and dialoguing with others. Learning to feel the organization's pulse comes only through intention, attention, listening, experience, and reflection. Trial-and-error and living with the organization over time can develop a deep knowledge and understanding of how the organization functions and what it takes to correct problems. Unfortunately, we frequently tend to simplify by finding what we believe is "the cause" of events or patterns and taking action to correct that cause. While sometimes this is right, often the action does not change the organization and the problem resurfaces at another location or time. The typical solution to a bad event is to create a policy that prohibits that event in the future. Over time this approach results in so many (often conflicting) policies and rules that the only way that work gets done is by ignoring or working around them. Another problem is that the "bad" event may be highly successful under different contexts or situations since knowledge is context-sensitive and situation-dependent.

Remember that analysis and logic produce useful answers *only if their assumptions are correct, and if every material causal relationship can be taken into account*---a difficult task at best in an organization. When in a position to manage or impact an organization that operates in a dynamic, complex environment, do not try to control its operation, rather nurture the people, networks, relationships, and processes so that they learn, work together when feasible, and take ownership for their actions and the outcomes. This approach encourages them to think for themselves, feel empowered, and create solutions at the local level. Encourage many simultaneous small changes if needed, just be sure that everyone in the organization knows where it is going and people know what values are important.

2. Review the organization's history and context.

History gives us a perspective on the past and on possibilities and probabilities for the future. It can provide context and highlight major forces that have influenced the complex organization in the past. Patterns are usually easier to identify in history than in the present, and they may extend into the future. The present context illuminates what the present situation looks like and what forces are currently in play. Context may indicate emergent characteristics that will extend into the future. Each of these perspectives provides insights into the workings of the organization, why it behaves as it does, and may provide indicators of where it is going.

3. Look for the emergent characteristics of the organization.

Emergent properties are meaningful, qualitative, global, and can be very informative. To find out what integrates and creates these emergent characteristics, reflect on the systems behavior, history, patterns, and flows. Patterns are composed of relatively stable sets of relationships and events that occur throughout the organization. Look for the properties created from the interrelation of all of the parts—the networks, teams, structure, hierarchy, technology, and individuals and their belief sets.

These properties can rarely be reduced to single causes and therefore must be observed and understood as broad, qualitative phenomena. Their source may be a particularly creative team, a disgruntled employee who is successfully spreading rumors and discontent, or from a source that can't be identified. Some events result from single causes and others come from multiple, sequential, or simultaneous causes throughout the organization. Try to understand how and why the event happened, any related patterns, and what structural aspects could be involved. Ask yourself the following: Am I looking at the problem or a broader situation? At a symptom, a cause or a complex causal network that spreads throughout the organization? Is the formal or informal structure causing this property? What can be controlled? What can be influenced? What may be nurtured to emerge?

4. Analyze the organization's networks, their functions and sources of influence.

Knowledge is created and embedded in individuals and their relationships. Networks—formal, informal, social, and technological—leverage the creation, sharing, and application of the ideas and knowledge of individuals and their relationships. Observe and study the networks in your organization. These networks, as an important part of the overall structure, play a significant role in creating the organization's culture and its other emergent properties. In addition, they can create ideas and new ways of getting the work done, thereby increasing the variety within the organization. Study your own internal networks and those in the external world; they may have a significant influence on the complexity of both the organization and its environment.

5. Use more nurturing than control when intervening.

Considering the management of a complex adaptive system operating in a complex environment, no one person is in control in the sense of setting goals *and* making employees follow a specific regime to achieve those goals. While leadership can set the goals, direction, vision, and structural form of the organization, it is the knowledge workers and their relationships that primarily drive how the work gets done and often even what gets done. What leaders and managers can do is make decisions and establish relationships that open the organization to change, and then guide and nurture that change to keep it moving in the desired direction. In complex adaptive organizations it is essential to bring employees into the decision-making process *whenever possible*. This gives them a context for their own work, adds value to the decision quality, and aids employees in better understanding and supporting implementation because of their involvement and "ownership". It also encourages more ideas and options for actions to respond to external demands.

In most organizations today, the certainties of command and control are myths. To the extent that current organizations are complex and adaptive, they exhibit various degrees of unpredictability and no one fully understands, nor can predict, their behavior. This observation says much about the future of autocratic leadership and the importance of nurturing and collaborative leadership, and of the positive effects of the growth, empowerment and flexibility/adaptability of employees. Leaders do not understand complex systems any more than workers, but if the environment is open and conducive to collaboration and inquiry, solutions can be found through leveraging the knowledge of the right people, wherever they are within the organization. This does not imply that hierarchical structures will go away, nor that they should. Chains of command, responsibility, and accountability are needed in all organizations; they just play a different role in complex adaptive systems. The hierarchy maintains the administrative oversight and its communication channels help ensure the coherence of direction of the subunits. It also supplies resources and knowledge support where needed. What it cannot do is dictate local tactics, schedules, and responses. By supporting employee learning and setting basic rules of operation and guidelines for decisions, leaders can free workers at the lower levels to empower and figure out for themselves how to work together and achieve their goals. Such freedom is, of course, situational and dependent on the task, the environment, the individuals, and the managers.

6. Use all available mental and physical resources in trying to understand the organization.

In complex systems there may be times when a small number of dominant causes drive the system. Under these circumstances logic and analysis can be used to identify, study, and understand how the system works. Causal feedback loops can be described and modeled to predict the system's behavior. MIT's systems thinking and J. W. Forrester's system dynamics are representative of this approach. Unfortunately, we are often unable to trace the cause-and-effect paths within the system because they are too numerous, nonlinear, and have too many connections. These complex systems unfold and evolve through multiple interactions and feedback loops; there is no small number of causes behind their movement. Because of this fundamental behavior, we may not be able to understand them by using logic, analysis, and the reductionist approach. Under these situations, complex systems can only be understood by holistic thinking.

Experts who understand certain complex systems use their experience, intuition, and judgment to solve problems. They know, but are often unable to explain how they know. When dealing with complexity, we need to actively learn from experience, deliberately develop our intuition, build our judgment, and play with the system in our minds and especially in-group dialogues (not debates). It is through these activities that our experience and intuition become capable of recognizing the unfolding of patterns and the flow of activities in the complex system or situation. Such recognition leads to intuitive understanding and a sense of what the primary drivers are in the system.

Sometimes a combination of analysis and educated intuition work best. For example, with practice a leader may learn to "sense" how well the structure, culture, processes, and customer relationships are going. To resolve problems or make changes in their organization, they can combine a systematic analysis with their intuition and emotion by looking for leverage points, patterns, and key relationships in all of the following: structure, culture, processes, customers, technology and knowledge systems, leadership, management, and knowledge workers. Asking how one feels about an event, pattern, or situation provides another perspective with attendant insights. In summary, complex systems can best be understood holistically; they take on a life of their own and often a speed of their own. To be prepared to deal with complexity we need to develop and use all of our mental capabilities: logic, analysis, intuition, judgment, and emotion. The key to living with a complex adaptive organization is learning and knowledge. These are the two things that result in effective action; everything else is guesswork.

7. Beware of simplicity, organizational complexity may be immune to single and/or simple actions.

Simplification reduces our own uncertainty, makes decisions appear easier, and allows logical explanations of those decisions. Simplicity captivates the mind; complexity confuses and forces the use of intuition and judgment. Both are difficult to explain to others. We continuously simplify to avoid being overwhelmed, to hide confusion, and to become focused and efficient. In a simple, predictable world this is rational and generally works well. It is easy to ignore many incoming signals, knowing that they are not important to our work. Unfortunately, in a complex world this can become dangerous, and even disastrous. Where complexity lives, it is hard to separate the unimportant from the critical information, events, or signals. It is under these latter conditions that teams, networking, contingency planning, experience, and deep knowledge become so essential. The hardest thing of all is for a leader to admit, "I don't understand this and need help in making this decision." Sometimes the hardest way is the only way!

8. Self-organize your own learning. Let the organization's complexity guide your path to its comprehension.

Accept full responsibility for your own learning and use problems and complex organizations as opportunities to learn how you learn while improving your judgment and intuition. Develop your listening capacity by thinking about the above ideas and practice in all conversations. Enter into dialogues more often than discussions. Spend time reflecting, asking yourself difficult questions, and deliberately shifting your perspective on topics of importance. Always strive for insight, understanding, and balanced decisions. Let the complex adaptive organization drive your learning path. It may lead the way better than you can. With complexity, logic and rational thought have their place and their limitations. Do not hesitate to ask unreasonable or irrational questions, make guesses, and speculate with metaphors when trying to comprehend a complex situation.

9. Expect mistakes, sense and response, feedback, and learning may be the best approach.

Mistakes are a necessary part of interacting with complex adaptive systems. Anyone attempting to change a complex adaptive organization from within, or trying to understand and deal with an external complex adaptive system (CAS), is bound to make mistakes during the process. Every CAS is unique and to deal effectively with them requires experience, intuition, insight, judgment, innovation, trial-and-error, testing, and feedback. Since no one has total control in a CAS, it is not possible to completely understand and predict its behavior. Complex adaptive systems are by their very nature unpredictable---recall that they operate close to the boundary between complexity and chaos, with their behavior contingent upon a large number of semi-autonomous individuals as well as a complex or perhaps even chaotic boundary. Thus, mistakes are to be anticipated as part of the learning, understanding, and the intervention process. However, prudent risk assessment should always be considered prior to any intervention. Clearly a good risk assessment of the unintended consequences is difficult for complex adaptive systems. Nevertheless, the first rule of management, "Do no harm," should always be considered before any significant intervention.

Where the system under study is highly complex and adaptive, it will be impossible to know how it will respond to some action. Evolutionary biology has dealt with this problem throughout the evolution of life. It appears that the standard solution is to create a variety of actions, attempt them, and use feedback to find out which ones succeed. The successful actions are then used over and over in similar situations as long as they yield the desired results: survival and reproduction. When they fail, they are stopped and new actions are rewarded. It is important not to continue with an action that is not working. Time is unlikely to help the action work because in a highly complex environment the only future is the present; in a short time, the environment will probably have a very different nature. This is not a pure trial-and-error procedure, since learning continuously occurs, and judgment, experience and deep knowledge may create a level of understanding that aids in moving into the future. As knowledge of the complex adaptive organization improves, better actions can be selected and used to change the system. See (Axelrod and Cohen, 1999) for an extensive treatment of the role of variation, interaction, and selection in dealing with external complexity by creating internal complexity within your own organization.

Section III
Decision-Making from the Inside Out

(Chapters 9-11)

Decision-makers have a self-organizing, hierarchical set of theories (and consistent relationships among those theories) that guide their decision-making process. A theory is considered a set of statements and/or principals that explain a group of facts or phenomena to guide action or assist in comprehension or judgment (American Heritage Dictionary, 2006). While a written theory could be considered information, when used by a decision-maker to guide action it would be considered knowledge. Further, while in its incoming form it is Knowledge (Informing) as it is complexed with other information in the mind of the decision-maker it may become part of the process that is Knowledge (Proceeding).

We believe that the decision-making process within the mind/brain can serve as a model for the conscious decision-making process in dealing with complex situations in a complex world. This discussion will be a high-level overview since there is much that is unknown about the neural details of decision-making.

For purposes of this discussion, we clarify the difference between the terms "brain" and "mind." The brain consists of an atomic and molecular structure and the fluids that flow through this structure. The mind is the totality of the patterns in the brain created by individual neurons, their firings and their connections. These patterns represent our thoughts, both conscious and unconscious. Neuronal (and the prefix neuro-) refers to any of the impulse-conducting cells that constitute the brain, spinal column, and nervous system.

Section III includes the following chapters: The View from the Inside (Chapter 9); Hierarchy as a Basic Property of the Decision-Making System (Chapter 10); and Advanced Decision-Making: The Cortex (Chapter 11).

Chapter 9
The View from Inside

The similarities between decision-making in a CAM introduced in Section II and the internal workings of the mind/brain are striking. In the brain of the decision-maker, thoughts are represented by patterns of neuronal firings. Recall that the brain stores information in the form of patterns of neurons, their connections, and the strength of those connections. These patterns represent thoughts, images, beliefs, theories, emotions, etc. Although the patterns themselves are nonphysical, their existence as represented by neurons and their connections *are* physical, that is, composed of atoms, molecules and cells.

If we consider the mind as the totality of neuronal patterns, then we can consider the mind and the brain to be connected in the sense that the neural patterns cannot exist without the brain, yet the brain would have no mind if it had no patterns. It may be helpful to consider the following metaphor: the mind is to the brain as waves of the ocean are to the water in the ocean (Bennet and Bennet, 2008d). Even this is simplified because surrounding the neurons are continuous flows of blood, hormones and other chemicals which have complex interactions within the brain and the body (Church, 2006; Pert, 1997).

The power of the metaphor derives from the relationship between the neuronal network patterns used to represent the external (and internal) world of concepts, thoughts, objects and their relationships, and the physical neurons and other material in the brain. To get some idea of the density and intricacies of the brain, consider the following: "A piece of brain tissue the size of a grain of sand contains a hundred thousand neurons and one billion synapses (connections), all talking to one another" (Amen, 2005, p. 20). A single thought might be represented in the brain by a network of a million neurons, with each neuron connected to 10,000 other neurons (Ratey, 2001). See Figure 6.

A decision is the result of recursive interactions between external information and internal information of relevance to the problem at hand, what we call the process of associative patterning (Bennet and Bennet, 2006, 2009; Byrnes, 2001; Stonier, 1997). Consider the following description of how the brain creates patterns of the mind. In the quote below, neuroscientist Antonio Damasio uses the term "movie" as a metaphor for the diverse sensory images and signals that create the show

> A decision is the result of recursive interactions between external information and internal information of relevance to the problem at hand, which is the process of associative patterning.

and flow (patterns) we call mind. The quote also brings out a few of the large number of semi-independent systems in the brain that work together to make sense of our external environment.

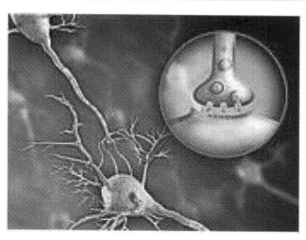

Figure 6: *Neurons in the mind/brain. The picture below shows a typical neuron and one of its synaptic connections to the neuron. It has been estimated that the average brain contains 10 billion neuron cells with each neuron connected to about 10,000 other neurons through synapses or small gaps through which neurotransmitters may flow. The pattern of neuron connections, the flow of small electrical impulses through the neuron axons and dendrites, together with the flow of molecules through the synaptic junctions, creates the patterns within the mind/brain.*

As Damasio (2007, pp. 63-64) contends:

> *Further remarkable progress involving aspects of the movie-in-the-brain has led to increased insights related to mechanisms for learning and memory. In rapid succession, research has revealed that the brain uses discrete systems for different types of learning. The basal ganglia and cerebellum are critical for the acquisition of skills—for example, learning to ride a bicycle or play a musical instrument. The hippocampus is integral to the learning of facts pertaining to such entities as people, places or events. And once facts are learned, the long-term memory of those facts relies on multi-component brain systems, whose key parts are located in the vast brain expanses known as cerebral cortices.*

We learn by changing incoming signals (images, sounds, smells, sensations of the body) into patterns (of the mind and within the brain) that we identify with specific external concepts or objects. These incoming neuronal patterns have internal associations with other internal patterns that represent (to varying degrees of fidelity) the corresponding associations in the external world. The intermixing of these sets of information (patterns), what is referred to as semantic mixing (Stonier, 1997) or complexing, creates new neural patterns that may represent understanding, meaning, and the anticipation of the consequences of actions, or, in other words, knowledge. We re-present external reality through the creation and association of internal patterns of neuron firings and connections. Thus associative patterning is the way the mind/brain creates knowledge.

The mind/brain is essentially a self-organizing, cybernetic, highly complex adaptive learning system that survives by converting incoming information from its environment into knowledge (the capacity to take effective action) and then using that knowledge. The mind, brain and body are replete with feedback loops, control systems, sensors, memories, and meaning-making systems made up of about 100 billion neurons and about 10^{15} interconnections. It is self-organizing because there is no central subsystem that "controls" the mind, brain or body.

Anticipating the Outcome of Actions

The process of storing sequences of patterns or memories is one way the mind/brain anticipates the outcome of actions. In 1949 the Canadian psychologist Donald Hebb explained learning and memory as a result of the strengthening of synapses (connections) between neurons in the brain. In other words, when connected neurons *fire simultaneously*, their synaptic connections become stronger (Begley, 2007). This has become known as Hebb's rule: learning takes place when pairs of neurons fire in coincidence. Although an oversimplification, the colloquial version is *neurons that fire together wire together*. One implication of Hebb's rule is the ease with which we can remember sequences of information. As Begley describes this process, "... traveling the same dirt road over and over leaves ruts that make it easier to stay in the track on subsequent trips" (Begley, 2007, p. 30). For example, we remember songs or stories (especially ones we sing or hear over and over again) much better than isolated or disconnected facts. This is

> The more often we recall what we have learned, the better we will recall it in the future.

also why memory of information can be improved by repeating the information over and over. In other words, the more often we recall what we have learned the better we will recall it in the future.

From another perspective, the rule is, "use it, or lose it" (Christos, 2003, p. 95). While the pattern may stay in memory if it is not repeated (used), it could prove very difficult to retrieve. Freud suggested that there are separate sets of neurons for perception and memory. The neural networks concerned with perception create fixed synaptic connections and by doing so ensure the accuracy of our perceptual capability. On the other hand, neuronal networks concerned with memory make connections that change in strength as we learn. This is the basis of memory and of higher cognitive functioning (Kandel, 2006a, 2006b).

We never see the same world twice; the brain (as distinct from a computer) does *not* store exact replicas of past events or memories. Rather, it stores invariant *representations*. These forms represent the basic source of recognition and meaning of the broader patterns (Hawkins, 2004). In an email titled "Very Interesting Stuff" that made its way across the Internet, landing on a lot of websites dedicated to humor, there is an anonymous entry that begins: "Don't delete this just because it looks weird. Believe it or not, you can read it." Reading the following text (from an anonymous source) begins to demonstrate the power of patterns stored as invariant forms.

I cdnuolt blveiee that I cluod aulaclty uesdnatnrd what I was rdanieg. The phaonmneal pweor of the hmuan mnid Aoccdrnig to rscheearch at Cmabrigde Uinervtisy, it deosn't mttaer in what oredr the ltteers in a word are, the olny iprmoatnt tihng is that the first and last ltteer be in the rghit pclae. The rset can be a taotl mses and you can still raed it wouthit a porbelm. This is bcuseae the huamn mnid deos not raed ervey lteter by istlef, but the word as a wlohe. Amzanig huh?

According to Hawkins, "…the problem of understanding *how* your cortex (a small part of your brain) forms invariant representations remains one of the biggest mysteries in all of science" (Hawkins, 2004, p. 78). This isn't for lack of trying; "no one, not even using the most powerful computers in the world, are able to solve it" (Hawkins, 2004, p. 78). Nobel laureate Eric Kandel describes this process:

By storing memories in invariant forms, individuals are able to apply memories to situations that are similar but not identical to previous experiences. Cognitive psychologists would describe this as developing an internal representation of the external world, a cognitive map that generates a meaningful image or interpretation of our experience. (Kandel, 2006b, p. 298)

In summary, the ability to anticipate the future stems from the brain remembering the patterns associated with past experiences and their outcomes. When a new experience or situation is encountered, the brain tries to match it with past experiences and then identifies the probable outcome based on those prior experiences. A series of these similar experience-outcome events generates a belief, frame of reference, or mind-set that is likely to drive the decision-makers choice of what action(s) to take. The brain also may try to put these past experiences together, coupled with new possibilities based on current data and the creation of new possibilities, to *generate possible new scenarios for the future.*

While this system is robust with a high level of trustworthiness, it is not perfect. Because of the uniqueness of context and content of a situation coupled with the complexity of a situation, there is always the danger of oversimplifying and relying on largely unconscious beliefs learned from past—no longer applicable—experiences. As the world changes more rapidly, old decision rules or theories may be inappropriate and outdated. Complexity creates many unique states, each of which may have to be independently explored from a decision-makers perspective. This foreshadows the need for each decision-maker to consciously create and apply a set of theories that respond to their decision space.

Chapter 10
Hierarchy as a Basic Property
of the Decision-Making System

The brain stores patterns in a hierarchical and nested fashion. Recall that thoughts are represented by patterns of neuronal firings, their synaptic connections and the strengths between the synaptic spaces. As introduced earlier, from the viewpoint of the mind/brain, any knowledge that is being "re-used" is actually being "re-created" and—especially in an area of continuing interest—most likely complexed over and over again as incoming information is associated with internal information (Stonier, 1997). Further, if Knowledge (Informing) is different, there is a good chance that Knowledge (Proceeding) will be different, that is, the *process* of pulling up, integrating and sequencing associated Knowledge (Informing) and semantically complexing it with incoming information to make it comprehensible (and usable and applicable) is going to vary. In essence, every time we apply

> Our thinking is unknowingly guided by the situation at hand and by our objectives.

knowledge (Informing and Proceeding) it is to some extent new knowledge because the human mind—unlike an information management system—unconsciously tailors what is emerging as knowledge to the situation at hand (Edelman and Tononi, 2000). In other words, *our thinking is unknowingly guided by the situation at hand and by our objectives.*

As Marchese points out, another characteristic of this process is that when you see a picture, only about 20 percent of what you are seeing is brought into your brain; the other 80 percent of that image comes from information, ideas and feelings *already in your brain* (Marchese, 1998). The point is that the mind/brain doesn't store memories like a computer; that is, storing an exact replica of everything coming in. The mind/brain stores the *core* of the picture, what was referred to above as an invariant form (Hawkins, 2004). This particular phenomenon of relating external and internal forms of experience is called "appresentation" (Marton and Booth, 1997), and is an example of the mind's search for meaning. As Moon explains, "Appresentation is the manner in which a part of something that is perceived as an external experience can stimulate a much more complete or richer internal experience of the 'whole' of that thing to be conjured up." (Moon, 2004, p. 23) The reader experienced this in our earlier example of "Very Interesting Stuff."

Exploring this further, if you see your friend from the side or back you can usually recognize who they are since your mind has stored an invariant core basic memory that includes major features of that person (Begley, 1996; Hawkins, 2004). When you see your friend, your mind is filling in the blanks and you recognize the incoming image as your friend. There is a robustness in the way the brain *stores* invariant core memories. If it takes a million neurons to create a specific pattern (the core part of incoming information), the brain may set aside 1.4 million neurons with their connections as space for that pattern, providing a looseness to account for future associative changes, or dying cells (Hawkins, 2004). Thus, for this particular pattern you could lose tens of thousands of brain cells and still have significant aspects of the invariant core memory available for future retrieval via re-creation. *The brain stores the meaning or essence of the incoming information*; it does not store every detail. If it did, it would be overwhelmed with data and information. This phenomenon also explains the resilience of beliefs, frames of reference and mental models since a memory cannot simply be erased by the desire to do so.

> The mind/brain stores the meaning or essence of the incoming information; it does not store every detail.

At the same time, you catch sight of your friend and are smiling, getting ready to call out and wave, you may be swatting gnats away from your eyes, shivering from a soft breeze, registering the dark clouds moving in from the west, feeling hunger pains in your stomach, and sensing a soreness in your little toe from tight shoes, etc. The brain is multidimensional, simultaneously processing visual, aural, olfactory and kinesthetic sensory inputs and, as discussed above, combining them with mental thoughts and emotional feelings to create an internal perception and feeling of external awareness (Bennet and Bennet, 2006). Thus, as introduced above, the brain is simultaneously identifying and storing core patterns from incoming information, with some more important to the situation at hand than others. In other words, there is a *hierarchy of information* where hierarchy represents "an order of some complexity, in which the elements are distributed along the gradient of importance" (Kuntz, 1968, p. 162). This hierarchy of information is analogous to the physical design of the neocortex, "a sheet of cells the size of a dinner napkin as thick as six business cards, where the connections between various regions give the whole thing a hierarchical structure" (Hawkins, 2004, p. 109).

In a hierarchy the dominant structural element may be a central point such as in a circular structure, or have an axial symmetry. Wherever the central point (dominant structure) is located, each part is determined by where it is located in relation to that central point. While it is true that in a radial version of hierarchy the entire pattern may depend directly on an open center, most hierarchies consist of groups of subordinate hierarchies who in turn have groups of subordinate hierarchies, with each group having its own particular relation to the dominant center point (Kuntz, 1968). The core pattern stored in the brain could be described as a pattern of patterns with the possibility of both hierarchical and associative relationships to other patterns.

The mind/brain develops robustness and deep understanding derived from its capacity to use past learning and memories to complete incoming information and, instead of storing all the details, *it stores only information meaningful to this individual mind/brain*. This provides the ability to create and store higher level patterns while simultaneously semantically complexing incoming information with internal memories, adapting the resulting patterns to the situation at hand. Through these processes—and many more that are not yet understood—the brain supports survival and sustainability in a complex and unpredictable world.

As a brief summary, our brain receives patterns from the outside world, stores them as memories, and makes predictions by combining what it has seen before and what is happening now. In particular, the cortex has a large memory capacity and is constantly predicting what we will see, hear, and feel, usually occurring in the unconscious. The reason this is possible is because our cortex has built a model of the world around us, a hierarchical and nested structure of the cortex that "stores a model of the hierarchical structure of the real world" (Hawkins, 2004, p. 125).

Chapter 11
Advanced Decision-Making:
The Cortex

There are six layers of hierarchical patterns in the architecture of the cortex. For a deeper discussion of these levels we draw on the extensive work of Hawkins (2004). Using what he describes as the memory-prediction model of the cortex, Hawkins has developed a framework for understanding intelligence. The cortex's core function is to make predictions. A comparison of what is happening and what was expected to happen is part of the prediction process. In order to do this, there are not only avenues of incoming patterns but feedback paths, that is, information flowing from the processing area of the brain (the highest levels of the hierarchy) back to the lowest levels of the hierarchy that first received the input from the external world.

While only documented for the sense of vision, it appears that the patterns at the lowest level of the cortex are fast changing and spatially specific (highly situation dependent and context sensitive) while the patterns at the highest level are slow changing and spatially invariant. For example, since the light receptors in the retina are unevenly distributed and the cells in the cortex are evenly distributed, the retinal image relayed to the primary visual area of the cortex is highly distorted. Through the use of probes, it has been discovered that at the lowest level of the cortex any particular cell responds only to a tiny part of the visual input coming into the retina. Each neuron at this level has a "so-called receptive field that is highly specific to a minute part of your total field of vision" (Hawkins, 2004, p. 112). Further, each cell at this level also appears to be fine-tuned to specific kinds of input patterns which change with every fixation. (A fixation occurs approximately three times a second as the eyes make a small, quick movement (a saccade) and then stops.)

In contrast, when probes are used at the higher fourth level of the cortex, some cells that become active *stay active*. As Hawkins explains,

> *... we might find a cell that fires robustly whenever a face is visible. This cell stays active as long as your eyes are looking at a face anywhere in your field of vision. It doesn't switch on and off with each saccade ... cells have changed from being rapidly changing, spatially specific, tiny-feature recognition cells, to being constantly firing, spatially nonspecific, object recognition cells.* (Hawkins, 2004, p. 113)

What this conveys is the presence of higher-order patterns as incoming sensory information flows up from the lowest level to the highest level of the cortex, and then back down in a continuous feedback loop. Further, our example represents only the visual sense, yet *all* the senses (visual, auditory, somatic, etc.) are interconnected, acting as one associated whole, part of a "single multi-branched hierarchy" (Hawkins, 2004, p. 119). This affirms that a decision-makers ability to anticipate expected outcomes is based on the patterns of his experience, that is, incoming sensory information is integrated with stored information in its invariant form as it moves up through the hierarchical structure of the cortex, with each level a representation (stored in invariant form) of the information patterns beneath it in the hierarchy. Now, add the presence of feedback loops from the higher-order patterns to the lower-order patterns and you have a continuously self-organizing system that relies heavily on its invariant forms that do not change easily.

Let us look at this process from the viewpoint of the four modes of Kolb's experiential learning model (concrete experience, reflective observation, abstract conceptualization and active experimentation) (Kolb, 1984). You have a situation. You experience the situation. Out of that experience you have a set of information (the first and lowest level pattern in the pre-frontal cortex), and all the details (in the form of information) that have come into your mind/brain. Then you reflect on the situation, and that reflection process is one of assembling and integrating all of the incoming information (thus creating second-level patterns). The third level of patterns is created in the comprehension phase and where not just understanding and meaning (started in the reflection process) are generated, but also insight, creative ideas, judgment and anticipating the outcome of various actions.

In your mind, you already have certain invariant patterns which represent past beliefs, experience, values and other previous assumptions that exist in the top level of the hierarchy in your cortex. Those patterns that already exist are matched with the patterns created at levels 1, 2 and 3, and through that learning process create high-level invariant forms. You've thrown away all of the excess information and are looking at the core meaning of the incoming information from the situation at hand. You have now generated neuro-knowledge that presents avenues for taking action to achieve the desired situation. Here is where the highest level of invariant forms—theories, beliefs and assumptions—are used to select the best action to take. This information is passed back down the hierarchical levels which then supplies the details of the solution that drive the actions that are anticipated will change the situation.

Learning from Ourselves

As can be seen, there is a great deal we can learn from ourselves. For example, the hierarchy is a powerful way to picture and understand system and subsystem relationships including organizational structures, personnel focus, and decision responsibility. The decision-maker is looking for relationships and patterns, and the mind/brain is very good at this.

As another example, in the external reality of a decision-maker addressing a complex issue there are many *visible* elements in the problem space and many sources of information informing those visible elements; and there are just as many, or more, *invisible* elements. In storing experiences and thoughts in invariant form, the mind/brain has already completed a selection process, that is, storing that which is "most important" to you and which will provide the best accessibility to thought when it is needed. A parallel practice in information systems storage is to provide various levels of summaries and key words, easily searchable, all with connections to related information for depth and context as needed for the situation at hand.

Further, in the mind/brain these invariant forms are weighted in terms of value. The more important a thought is to you and what you think and do, the more connections a thought has and the higher it is stored (in invariant form) in the frontal cortex. Thoughts and feelings that are repeated over and over again through a variety of experiences affect your core beliefs and values, or can become a core belief or value. As the decision-maker moves through the myriad of information associated with a problem at hand, that information is weighted in importance based on both external and internal criteria. External criteria would include relationship to, and potential impact on, the issue in terms of input and output variables, sinks and sources, feedback loops, etc. Internal criteria would include the decision-makers knowledge about the system, memory, rational judgment capability, and feelings—all of which are affected by the decision-makers past experiences and associations.

> Invariant forms are weighted in terms of value to you.

Finally, it is important to note that the lived experience of a decision-maker, especially a decision-maker who works *within* a specific domain of decision-making (deep knowledge) while also having related experiences and recognizing related patterns *outside* that domain (moving toward wisdom), has extensive *internal resources* that can be engaged ... the focus of our next section.

[Intentionally left blank]

Section IV
Engaging Tacit Knowledge

(Chapters 12-15)

Knowledge and its management continue to increase in importance throughout society. As CUCA accelerates and extended and global relationships multiply, making good decisions and taking effective actions become crucial elements in the survival and sustained performance of our organizations. Whether in corporations, not-for-profits or government entities, functioning well and meeting the demands of an unpredictable and precarious world are the major challenges to leaders and managers. The way ahead is one of learning, adapting, taking risks, collaborating and creating organizations where employees are willing and competent to deal with complexity and uncertainty. That means they have the knowledge and freedom to take both action and responsibility. This environment demands deep knowledge, which comes primarily from tacit knowledge (Goldberg, 2005), that is, knowledge that cannot be fully shared through communication and is not part of one's ordinary consciousness (Polanyi, 1958). How do we get the knowledge needed to deal with complex problems, dynamic systems or unpredictable events?

The deeper we go into the meaning and characteristics of the concept of tacit knowledge, the more complex it becomes. Nevertheless, as the importance of tacit knowledge grows in support of organizational performance, so must our depth of understanding and the articulation of that understanding. Taking a functional definition of knowledge as introduced in Chapter 3, that is, knowledge as the capacity (potential or actual) to take effective action, this section looks carefully at the four aspects of tacit knowledge: embodied, affective, intuitive and spiritual. Each of these has its own unique characteristics and plays a different role in learning and decision-making within individuals and organizations. As our understanding of these aspects grows, techniques for working with tacit knowledge emerge.

Section IV includes the following Chapters: Differentiating Tacit Knowledge (Chapter 12); The Aspects of Tacit Knowledge (Chapter 13); Building Extraordinary Consciousness (Chapter 14); and Decision-Making and Tacit Knowledge (Chapter 15).

Chapter 12
Differentiating Tacit Knowledge

By the latter part of the 20th century the push to understand knowledge and its value to organizations had spread across a number of disciplines with the result that concepts of explicit, implicit and tacit knowledge began to emerge in both the academic organizational literature and the popular press. In Chapter 3 we introduced characteristics of knowledge and levels of knowledge. In order to focus on tacit knowledge, we first develop a common understanding of what it is and what it isn't.

Explicit knowledge is the process of calling up information (patterns) and processes (patterns in time) from memory that can be described accurately in words and/or visuals (representations) such that another person can comprehend the knowledge that is expressed through this exchange of information. This has historically been called declarative knowledge (Anderson, 1983). Emotions can be expressed as explicit knowledge in terms of changes in body state. As Damasio notes, "Many of the changes in body state—those in skin color, body posture, and facial expression, for instance—are actually perceptible to an external observer" (Damasio, 1994, p. 139). Often these changes to the body state represent part of an explicit knowledge exchange (Bennet and Bennet, 2007c). Examples would be turning red with embarrassment or blushing in response to an insensitive remark.

Implicit knowledge is a more complicated concept, and a term not unanimously agreed-upon in the literature. This is understandable since even simple dictionary definitions—which are generally unbiased and powerful indicators of collective preference and understanding—show a considerable overlap between the terms "implicit" and "tacit," making it difficult to differentiate the two. We propose that a useful interpretation of *implicit knowledge* is knowledge stored in memory of which the individual is *not immediately aware*. While this information is *not readily accessible*, it may be pulled up when triggered (associated), although, "The words that trigger comprehension are no longer important once comprehension is accessed" (Carey, 1996, p. 84). Triggering might occur through questions, dialogue or reflective thought, or happen as a result of an external event. In other words, implicit knowledge is knowledge that the individual *does not know* they have, but is self-discoverable! However, once this knowledge is surfaced, the individual *may or may not* have the ability to adequately describe it such that another individual could create the same knowledge; and the "why and how" may remain tacit knowledge.

A number of published psychologists have used the term implicit interchangeably with our usage of tacit, that is, with implicit representing knowledge that once acquired can be shown to effect behavior but is not available for conscious retrieval (Reber, 1993; Kirsner et al., 1998). As described in our above discussion of implicit knowledge, what is forwarded here is that the concept of implicit knowledge serves a middle ground between that which can be made explicit and that which cannot easily (if at all) be made explicit. By moving beyond the dualistic approach of explicit and tacit—that which can be declared versus that which can't be declared, and that which can be remembered versus that which can't be remembered—*we posit implicit as representing the knowledge spectrum between explicit and tacit*. While explicit refers to easily available, some knowledge requires a higher stimulus for association to occur but is not buried so deeply as to prevent access. This understanding opens the domain of implicit knowledge.

Calling them interactive components of cooperative processes, Reber (1993, p. 23) agrees that there is no clear boundary between that which is explicit and that which is implicit (our tacit): "There is ... no reason for presuming that there exists a clean boundary between conscious and unconscious processes or a sharp division between implicit and explicit epistemic systems." Reber describes the urge to treat explicit and implicit (our tacit) as

> There is no clear boundary between that which is explicit and that which is tacit.

altogether different processes the "polarity fallacy." Similarly, Matthews says that the unconscious and conscious processes are engaged in what he likes to call a "synergistic" relationship (Matthews, 1991). What this means is that the boundary between the conscious and the unconscious is somewhat porous and flexible. Given that caveat, how do we describe tacit knowledge?

Tacit knowledge is the descriptive term for those connections among thoughts that cannot be pulled up in words, a knowing of *what* decision to make or *how* to do something that cannot be clearly voiced in a manner such that another person could extract and re-create that knowledge (understanding, meaning, etc.). An individual *may or may not* know they have tacit knowledge in relationship to something or someone. But even when it *is known*, the individual is unable to put it into words or visuals that can convey that knowledge. We all know things, or know what to do, yet may be unable to articulate *why* we know them, *why* they are true, or even exactly *what they are*. To "convey" is to cause something to be known or understood or, in this usage, to transfer information from which the receiver is able to create knowledge.

Knowledge starts as tacit knowledge, that is, the initial movement of knowledge is from its origins within individuals (in the unconscious) to an outward expression (howbeit driving effective action). What does that mean? Michael Polanyi, a professor of both chemistry and the social sciences, wrote in *The Tacit Dimension* that, "We start from the fact that we can know more than we can tell" (Polanyi, 1967, p. 108). He called this pre-logical phase of knowing tacit knowledge, that is, knowledge that cannot be articulated (Polanyi, 1958).

Tacit and explicit knowledge can be thought of as residing in "places," specifically, the unconscious and conscious, respectively, although both Knowledge (Informing) and Knowledge (Proceeding), whether tacit or explicit, are differentiated patterns spread throughout the neuronal system, that is, the volume of the brain and other parts of the central nervous system). On the other hand, implicit knowledge may reside in either the unconscious (prior to being triggered, or tacit) or the conscious (when triggered, or explicit). See Figure 7.

Level of Awareness of
Origins / Content of Knowledge

UNCONSCIOUS AWARENESS → CONSCIOUS AWARENESS

TACIT

SPIRITUAL
- Based on matters of the soul
- Represents animating principles of human life
- Focused on moral aspects, human nature, higher development of mental faculties
- Transcendent power
- Moves knowledge to wisdom
- Higher guidance with unknown origin

INTUITIVE
- Sense of knowing coming from within
- Linked to FOR
- Knowing that may be without explanation (outside expertise or past experience)
- 24/7 personal servant of human being
- Why (unknown)

AFFECTIVE
- Feelings
- Generally attached to other types or aspects of knowledge
- Why (evasive or unknown)

EMBODIED
- Expressed in bodily/material form
- Stored within the body (riding bike)
- Can be kinesthetic or sensory
- Learned by mimicry and behavioral skill training
- Why (evasive)

IMPLICIT
- Stored in memory but not in conscious awareness
- Not readily accessible but capable of being recalled when triggered
- Don't know you know, but self-discoverable
- Ability may or may not be present to facilitate social communication.
- Why (questionable)

EXPLICIT
- Information stored in brain that can be recalled at will
- In conscious awareness
- Can be shared through social communication
- Can be captured in terms of information (given context)
- Expressed emotions (visible changes in body state)
- Why (understood)

Figure 7: *Continuum of Awareness of Knowledge Source/Content*

Note that there is no clean break between these three types of knowledge.

Knowledge (Proceeding) may be explicit, implicit or tacit. For anything except the simplest knowledge, the process we use to find, create and mix the information needed to take effective action is difficult, if at all possible, to communicate to someone else. Thus, the expertise involved in deciding what actions to take in many situations is almost always tacit. Team discussions, problem solving and decision-making, while helpful and necessary, must address the emotional, intuitive and embodied aspects as well as relevant data, information, and explicit knowledge of the participants.

As another point of comparison, explicit, implicit and tacit knowledge appear to almost always include both Knowledge (Informing) and Knowledge (Proceeding). As an example of how these three aspects of knowledge can work together, consider the development that occurs as we learn to drive a car. When you first get behind the steering wheel of a car, each action comes slowly and is learned only through practice (trial and error). You are creating explicit knowledge, and able to talk about every action you take. As your experience increases, many things—such as how to brake evenly, how to turn corners in your lane, or how to accelerate smoothly—become automatic. Soon, with practice, many of the aspects of driving become natural, moving them into implicit knowledge. After driving to work for some length of time, you know the road, the car and the traffic patterns so well that you can think about other things and still drive safely. Much of your driving is now tacit knowledge, yet there is always an alert, implicit part a seasoned driver will immediately *know* when something ahead may become a problem. Implicit driving can quickly become explicit if someone in front of you slams on their brakes or a passing car swerves too close to you. Yet when nothing special happens during your trip, you may have no memory of driving the last ten miles!

Chapter 13
The Aspects of Tacit Knowledge

Tacit knowledge—the focus area of this section—can be thought of in terms of four aspects: embodied, intuitive, affective and spiritual. Each of these aspects represents different sources of tacit knowledge whose applicability, reliability and efficacy may vary greatly depending on the individual, the situation and the knowledge needed to take effective action. They are represented in Figure 7 along with explicit and implicit knowledge on the continuum of awareness. Remember, all knowledge is context sensitive and situation dependent. **Thus, intelligent decision-makers are not bound by the past, but continuously adjust their knowledge to the specific situation at hand in concert with the living nature of knowledge.**

Embodied tacit knowledge, also referred to as somatic knowledge, can be represented in neuronal patterns stored within the body. It is both kinesthetic and sensory. *Kinesthetic* is related to the movement of the body and, while important to every individual every single day of our lives, is a primary focus for athletes, artists, dancers, kids and assembly-line workers. A commonly used example is knowledge of riding a bicycle.

Sensory, by definition, is related to the five human senses through which information enters the body (sight, smell, hearing, touch and taste). An example is the smell of burning from your car brakes while driving or the smell of hay in a barn. These smells can convey knowledge of whether the car brakes need replacing (get them checked immediately), or whether the hay is mildewing (dangerous to feed horses, but fine for cows). These responses would be overt, bringing to conscious awareness the need to take effective action and driving that action to occur.

Because embodied learning is often linked to experiential learning (Merriam et al., 2006), embodied tacit knowledge can generally be learned by mimicry and behavior skill training. While deliberate learning through study, dialogue or practice occurs at the conscious level, when significant or repeated over time such learning often becomes tacit knowledge. Further, as individuals develop competence in a specific area, more of their knowledge in that area becomes tacit, making it difficult or impossible for them to explain how they know what they know. The neuronal patterns representing that knowledge become embedded within long-term working memory where they become automatic when needed, but lost to consciousness.

Embodied tacit knowledge can be both preventative and developmental. For example, a physical response can warn *not* to do something or move an individual *to do something*. Both of these responses constitute the capacity to take effective action since *not taking an action is an action choice*. Figure 8 provides examples of embodied tacit knowledge.

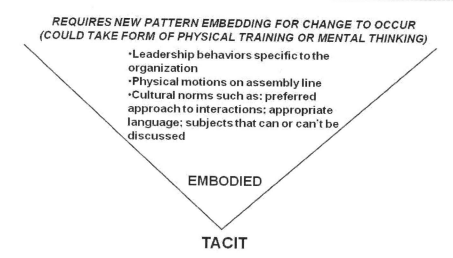

Figure 8: *Embodied tacit knowledge.*

Intuitive tacit knowledge is the sense of knowing coming from inside an individual that may influence decisions and actions; yet the decision-maker or actor cannot explain *how* or *why* the action taken is the right one. Damasio calls intuition, "the mysterious mechanism by which we arrive at the solution of a problem *without* reasoning toward it" (Damasio, 1994, p. 188). The unconscious works around the clock with a processing capability many times greater than that at the conscious level (on the order of a million times greater!). This is why as the world grows more complex, decision-makers must depend more and more on their intuitive tacit knowledge. But in order to use it, decision-makers must first *be able to tap into their unconscious.*

Intuitive tacit knowledge can be both Knowledge (Informing) and Knowledge (Proceeding), and it may reside in either the potential aspect of taking effective action (knowing how) or the actual aspect of taking effective action (acting). A form of knowing, deep tacit knowledge is created within our minds (or hearts or guts, which have neurons similar to the brain) over time through experience, contemplation, and unconscious processing such that it becomes a natural part of our being—not just something consciously learned, stored, and retrieved (Bennet and Bennet, 2008e). In other words, intuitive tacit knowledge is the result of continuous learning through experience. To develop intuitive skills requires making sure that your experiences are meaningful, that is, having specific objectives in mind such as how to size up situations quickly and develop a good sense of what will happen next (Klein, 2003). It is also important to get immediate and accurate feedback directly related to the context within which a decision was made, thus developing patterns in the unconscious (intuition). According to Klein, to build up expertise requires: (1) feedback on decisions and actions, (2) active engagement in getting and interpreting this feedback (not passively allowing someone else to judge them); and (3) repetitions, which provide the opportunity to practice making decisions and getting feedback (Klein, 2003). Figure 9 provides examples of intuitive tacit knowledge.

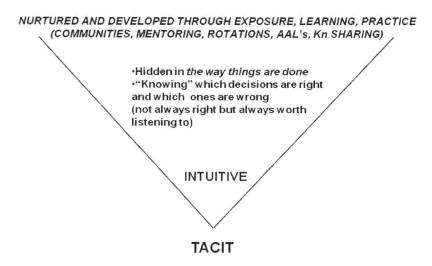

NURTURED AND DEVELOPED THROUGH EXPOSURE, LEARNING, PRACTICE
(COMMUNITIES, MENTORING, ROTATIONS, AAL's, Kn SHARING)

•Hidden in *the way things are done*
•"Knowing" which decisions are right
and which ones are wrong
(not always right but always worth
listening to)

INTUITIVE

TACIT

Figure 9: *Intuitive tacit knowledge.*

Affective tacit knowledge is connected to emotions and feelings, with emotions representing the external expression of some feelings. Feelings expressed as emotions become explicit (Damasio, 1994). Feelings that are not expressed—perhaps not even recognized—are those that fall into the area of affective tacit knowledge. From the viewpoint of neuroscience, information coming into the body moves through the amygdale, that part of the brain that is,

> ... *important both for the acquisition and for the on-line processing of emotional stimuli ... [with] Its processing encompassing both the elicitation of emotional responses in the body and changes in other cognitive processes, such as attention and memory.* (Adolphs, 2004, p. 1026)

It is as incoming information moves through the amygdale that an emotional "tag" is attached. If this information is perceived as life-threatening, then the amygdale takes control, making a decision and acting on that decision before conscious awareness of a threat! Haberlandt (1998) goes so far as to say that there is no such thing as a behavior or thought not impacted by emotions in some way. Even simple responses to information signals can be linked to multiple emotional neurotransmitters. Thus affective tacit knowledge is attached to other types or aspects of knowledge. For example, when an individual thinks about recent occurrences like an argument or a favorite sports team losing in the Rose Bowl, feelings are aroused. Or recall the internal responses to holding the hard copy of your first book, or your new born child. As Mulvihill states,

Because the neurotransmitters which carry messages of emotion are integrally linked with the information during both the initial processing and the linking with information from the different senses, it becomes clear that there is no thought, memory, or knowledge which is 'objective,' or 'detached' from the personal experience of knowing. (Mulvihill, 2003, p. 322)

Feelings as a form of knowledge have different characteristics than language or ideas, but they may lead to effective action because they can influence actions by their existence and connections with consciousness. When feelings come into conscious awareness, they can play an informing role in decision-making, providing insights in a non-linguistic manner and thereby influencing decisions and actions. For example, a feeling (such as fear or an upset stomach) may occur every time a particular action is started which could prevent the decision-maker from taking that action. Figure 10 provides examples of affective tacit knowledge.

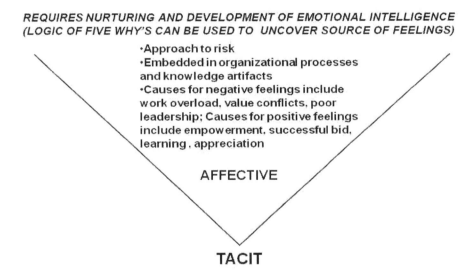

Figure 10: *Affective tacit knowledge.*

Spiritual tacit knowledge can be described in terms of *knowledge based on matters of the soul*. The soul represents the *animating principles of human life in terms of thought and action*, specifically focused on its moral aspects, the emotional part of human nature, and higher development of the mental faculties (Bennet and Bennet, 2007e). While there is a "knowing" related to spiritual knowledge similar to intuition, this knowing does not include the experiential base of intuition, and it may or may not have emotional tags. The current state of the evolution of our understanding of spiritual knowledge is such that there are insufficient words to relate its transcendent power, or to define the role it plays in relationship to other tacit knowledge. Nonetheless, this area represents a powerful influence on decision-making, a form of higher guidance with unknown origin.

In a research study in early 2007, representative human characteristics spiritual in nature were identified that contribute to learning (Bennet and Bennet, 2007b). These characteristics were grouped into five general areas: *shifting frames of reference* (represented by abundance, awareness, caring, compassion, connectedness, empathy, openness); *animating for learning* (represented by aliveness, grace, harmony, joy, love, presence, wonder); *enriching relationships* (represented by authenticity, consistency, morality, respect, tolerance, values); *priming for learning* (represented by awareness, eagerness, expectancy, openness, presence, sensitivity, unfoldment, willingness); and *moving toward wisdom* (represented by caring, connectedness, love, morality, respect, service). (Appendix A offers a short literature review of the concept of wisdom.)

The general area of *shifting frames of reference* was intertwined with learning, thinking and acting (Bennet, 2006), covering the external approach (looking from an outside frame of reference) and the internal approach (taking an empathetic perspective which moves the viewpoint from the objective to the subjective). Frames of reference can be focusing, allowing the mind to go deeper in a bounded direction, and/or limiting. Shifting frames of reference potentially offer the opportunity to take a multidimensional approach to exploring the world around us. *Animating for learning* speaks to the fundamental source of life—learning, the energy used for survival and growth. The area of *enriching relationships* is tied to competence theory (White, 1959), which assumes that it is natural for people to strive for effective interactions with their world. This brings in the two dimensions of spirituality that exist beyond ourselves (others and that which is beyond the human) with whom we can truly learn to grow in understanding (Nouwen, 1975). *Priming for learning* attributes are considered as those that actively prepare and move an individual toward learning.

Wisdom, the highest part of the knowledge spectrum (see Appendix A), is considered as forwarding the goal of achieving the common or greater good (Sternberg, 2003). Reflecting on this short study, it would appear that spiritual knowledge would provide a *transcendent frame of reference* that puts things in relationship to a larger perspective while promoting self-knowledge and learning.

Spiritual knowledge may be the guiding purpose, vision and values behind the creation and application of tacit knowledge. It may also be the road to moving information to knowledge and knowledge to wisdom, i.e., purpose, vision and values are excellent guidelines. Zohar and Marshall describe spiritual tacit knowledge as,

> *... the intelligence with which we address and solve problems of meaning and value, ... place our actions and our lives in a wider-richer meaning-giving context, [and] ... can assess that one course of action or one life-path is more meaningful than another.* (Zohar and Marshall, 2000, pp. 2-3)

In the context of this book, spiritual tacit knowledge would be the source of higher learning, helping decision-makers create and implement knowledge that has greater meaning and value for the common good—wisdom.

An example of spiritual tacit knowledge that is primarily Knowledge (Proceeding) is Csikszentmihalyi's concept of flow (Csikszentmihalyi, 1990). Spiritual tacit knowledge that is primarily Knowledge (Informing) is what is often referred to as streaming or channeling of information that is outside an individual's personal experience or awareness. An example would be the numerous recorded instances in times of warfare where *military personnel under fire have known what actions to take to save lives* without detailed knowledge of the terrain or enemy troop movement. Figure 11 provides examples of spiritual tacit knowledge.

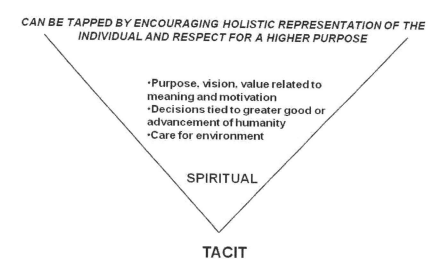

Figure 11: Spiritual tacit knowledge.

Note that Figures 8, 9, 10 and 11 can be printed and pieced together in a square for a memory guide.

Similar to the possible interactions among tacit, implicit and explicit knowledge, the four aspects of tacit knowledge can experience considerable interconnections and overlaps. For example, referring to a somatic learning model by Amann, Merriam says that "the spiritual aspect of somatic learning is meaning-making through music, art, imagery, symbols, and rituals and overlaps or intersects with the other three dimensions" (Merriam et al., 2006, p. 195), which are described as kinesthetic learning, sensory learning and affective learning. While organized differently than the knowledge model presented here, the Amann somatic learning model includes four elements—kinesthetic, sensory, affective and spiritual—as tacit knowledge (Amann, 2003).

As a second example of overlap, affective and embodied somatic states can operate both inside and outside an individual's awareness or consciousness; however, if overlap occurs in the unconscious the results may surface as intuition. Conversely, affective and embodied somatic states are often accompanied by overt somatic markers; for example, a "gut feel." In contrast, intuition comes from the neural network of the reticular activating system. Instead of producing a body-state change (semantic marker), it inhibits the regulatory neural circuits located in the brain core, which can influence behaviors (Damasio, 1994).

Chapter 14
Building Extraordinary Consciousness

It has only been in the past few decades that cognitive psychology and neuroscience have begun to seriously explore the unconscious mental life. This includes the recognition that conscious experience, thought, decisions and actions are influenced by unconscious concepts, memories and other mental constructs inaccessible to conscious awareness and somehow independent of voluntary control (Eich, et al., 2000). At the same time, research in neuroscience is also digging deeper into the understanding of the emotions, working memory and the unconscious processing that occur within the mind, and to some extent throughout the body.

Polanyi felt that tacit knowledge consisted of *a range* of conceptual and sensory information and images that could be used to make sense of a situation or event (Hodgkin, 1991). We agree. Two observations that have emerged in the discussion above are: (1) While the terms explicit, implicit and tacit may be useful in clarifying and understanding knowledge, these terms describe aspects of a fluctuating continuum (a range) rather than a rigid classification schema. (2) In the unconscious mind the association of incoming information with internal information is a powerful form of continuous learning. **Significant gains can be made in the effectiveness of problem solving and decision-making through understanding and stimulating this process**. *So how do we make best use of this process for our own and our organization's decision-making competence?* The search for an answer leads to thinking beyond what is described as ordinary consciousness towards what we will call extraordinary consciousness which can lead to extraordinary decision-making.

> Tacit knowledge consists of a range of conceptual and sensory information and images that can be used to make sense of a situation or event.

Ordinary consciousness represents the customary or typical state of consciousness, that which is common to everyday usage, or of the usual kind. Polanyi sees tacit knowledge as *not part* of one's ordinary consciousness (Polanyi, 1958); thus, tacit knowledge resides in the unconscious. To access tacit knowledge, an individual needs to move from ordinary consciousness to extraordinary consciousness, acquiring a greater sensitivity to information stored in the unconscious. Extraordinary consciousness would be considered special, exceptional, and outside of the usual or regular state of consciousness. This means a **heightened sensitivity to, awareness of and connection with our unconscious mind**, together with its memory and thought processes.

The *challenge* is to make better use of our tacit knowledge through creating greater connections with the unconscious, building and expanding the resources stored in the unconscious, deepening areas of resonance, and sharing tacit resources among individuals. We propose a four-fold action model with nominal curves for building extraordinary consciousness within individuals that includes surfacing tacit knowledge, embedding tacit knowledge, sharing tacit knowledge, and inducing resonance (see Figure 12).

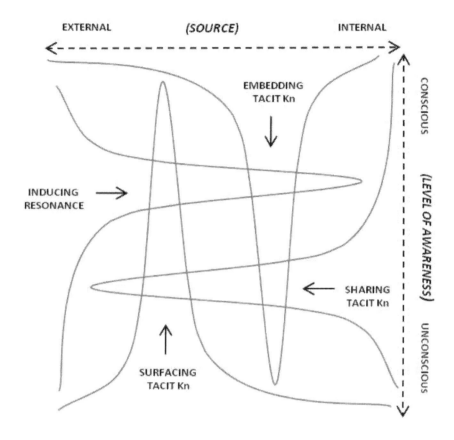

Figure 12: *Building extraordinary consciousness within the individual decision-maker.*

Surfacing Tacit Knowledge

The first approach toward building extraordinary consciousness is *surfacing tacit knowledge*. As individuals observe, experience, study and learn throughout life they generate a huge amount of information and knowledge that becomes stored in their unconscious mind. Even though an individual may have difficulty pulling it up when needed, learning how to access their unconscious—and listen to it—can become a valuable learning resource. Surfacing tacit knowledge is focused on accessing the benefit of that which is tacit by moving knowledge from the unconscious to conscious awareness. Three ways that tacit knowledge can be surfaced are through external triggering, self-collaboration and nurturing.

As represented in Figure 12, the process of triggering is primarily externally driven with internal participation. For example, conversation, dialogue, questions, or an external situation with specific incoming information may trigger the surfacing of tacit knowledge needed to respond. The unconscious is aware of the flow of consciousness, available to affect decisions as incoming information is associated with internal information. In these cases we would describe the knowledge surfaced from the unconscious as implicit, with externally-generated information mixing with tacit knowledge in order to create that surfaced implicit knowledge. (See the earlier discussion on implicit knowledge.) Triggering is often the phenomenon that occurs in "sink or swim" situations, where an immediate decision must be made that will have significant consequences.

Although collaboration is generally thought about as interactions among individuals and/or groups, there is another collaboration that is less understood. This is the process of individuals consciously collaborating with themselves. What this means is the conscious mind learning to communicate with, listen to, and trust its own unconscious. In order to build this trust, it is necessary for individuals to first recognize where their tacit knowledge is coming from. Recall that tacit knowledge is created from continuous mixing of external information with internal information. This means that when you trust your unconscious you trust yourself, and the semantic complexing of all the experiences, learning, thoughts and feelings throughout your life. Thus the process of associating (learning) in your unconscious is related to life-long conscious learning experiences (see the section below on embedding tacit knowledge).

One way to collaborate with your self is through creating an internal dialogue. For example, accepting the authenticity of, and listening deeply to, a continuous stream of conscious thought while following the tenets of dialogue. Those tenets would include: withholding quick judgment, not demanding quick answers, and exploring underlying assumptions (Ellinor and Gerard, 1998, p. 26), *then* looking for collaborative meaning between what you consciously think and what you feel. A second approach is to ask yourself a lot of questions related to the task at hand. Even if you don't think you know the answers, reflect carefully on the questions, and be patient. Sleeping on a question will often yield an answer the following morning. Your unconscious mind processes information 24/7 and exists to help you survive. It is not a figment of your imagination, or your enemy. To paraphrase the Nobel Laureate Neuroscientist Dr. Eric Kandel, you unconscious is a part of you. It works 24 hours a day processing incoming information on your behalf. So when it tells you something via intuition, lucid dreaming, etc., you should listen carefully (but it may not always be right) (Kandel, 2006a, 2006b).

Although requiring time, openness and commitment, there are a number of approaches readily available for those who choose to nurture their sensitivity to tacit knowledge. These include (among others) meditation, inner tasking, lucid dreaming, and hemispheric synchronization. Meditation practices have the ability to quiet the conscious mind, thus allowing greater access to the unconscious (Rock, 2004). Inner tasking is a wide-spread and often used approach to engaging your unconscious. Tell yourself, as you fall asleep at night, to work on a problem or question. The next morning when you wake up, but before you get up, lie in bed and listen to your own, quiet, passive thoughts. Frequently, but not always, the answer will appear, although it must be written down quickly before it is lost from the conscious mind. Like meditation, the efficacy of this approach takes time and practice to develop (Bennet and Bennet, 2008e).

Lucid dreaming is a particularly powerful way to access tacit knowledge. The psychotherapist Kenneth Kelzer wrote of one of his lucid dreams:

> *In this dream I experienced a lucidity that was so vastly different and beyond the range of anything I had previously encountered. At this point I prefer to apply the concept of the spectrum of consciousness to the lucid dream and assert that within the lucid state a person may have access to a spectrum or range of psychic energy that is so vast, so broad and so unique as to defy classification.* (Kelzer, 1987)

Another way to achieve sensitivity to the unconscious is through the use of sound. For example, listening to a special song in your life can draw out deep feelings and memories buried in your unconscious. Sound and its relationship to humans has been studied by philosophers throughout recorded history; extensive treatments appear in the work of Plato, Kant and Nietzsche. Through the last century scientists have delved into studies focused on acoustics (the science of sound), psychoacoustics (the study of how our minds perceive sound) and musical psychoacoustics (the discipline that involves every aspect of musical perception and performance). Sound (as do all patterns in the mind) has the ability to change and shape the physiological structure of the brain. Neuroscience has slowly begun to recognize the capability of both internal thoughts and external incoming information (including sound) to affect the physical structure of the brain—its synaptic connection strength, its neuronal connections and the growth of additional neurons (Pinker, 2007; Nelson et al., 2006; Gazzaniga, 2004). This phenomenon called plasticity is independent of an individual's age.

Hemispheric synchronization (bringing both hemispheres of the brain into coherence) can be accomplished through the use of sound coupled with a binaural beat. (See Bennet and Bennet, 2008g, and Bullard and Bennet, 2013, for in-depth treatment of hemispheric synchronization.) Inter-hemispheric communication is the setting for brain-wave coherence which facilitates whole-brain cognition, assuming an elevated status in subjective experience (Ritchey, 2003). What can occur during hemispheric synchronization is a physiologically reduced state of arousal, quieting the body *while maintaining conscious awareness* (Mavromatis, 1991; Atwater, 2004; Fischer, 1971; West, 1980; Delmonte, 1984; Goleman, 1988; Jevning et al., 1992), thus providing a doorway into the unconscious. It is difficult to imagine the amount of learning and insights that might reside therein—and the expanded mental capabilities such access may provide—much less the depth and breadth of experience and emotion that has been hidden there, perhaps making such access a mixed blessing. Nonetheless, for the decision-maker it is critical to have access to the flow of information that is possible by tapping into the unconscious, as well as the understanding of any affective tacit knowledge that may unknowingly be contributing to the decision-making process.

Embedding Tacit Knowledge

The second approach toward building extraordinary consciousness is *embedding tacit knowledge*. Although information is continuously going into our unconscious all of the time, only significant things stay in memory—often without our conscious awareness. Said another way, every experience and conversation is *embedding* potential knowledge (information) in the unconscious as it is associated with previously stored information to create new patterns. Thinking about embedding as a process for improving our tacit knowledge can lead to new approaches to learning. In Figure 12, we see that embedding is both externally and internally driven, with knowledge moving from the conscious to the unconscious. Embedding knowledge in the unconscious can occur through exposure or immersion, by accident or by choice. Examples would include travel, regularly attending church on Sunday, or listening to opera and imitating what you've heard in the shower every day. Practice moves beyond exposure to include repeated participation in some skill or process, thus strengthening the patterns in the mind. For example, after many years of imitation (practice) look at what Paul Potts, Britain's newest opera singer, accomplished! Paul Potts was the winner of the *Britain's Got Talent* competition. See *Paul Potts One Chance* music CD (SYCOmusic, 2007).

Creating tacit knowledge occurs naturally and quietly as an individual lives through diverse experiences and becomes more proficient at some activity (such as public speaking) or cognitive competency (such as problem solving). As their scope of experience widens, the number of relevant neuronal patterns increases. As an individual becomes more proficient in a specific area through effortful practice, the number of neurons needed to perform the task decreases and the remaining pattern gradually becomes embedded in the unconscious, ergo it becomes tacit knowledge. When this happens, the reasons and context within which the knowledge was created often lose their connections with consciousness.

Recognizing the differences among the four aspects of tacit knowledge suggests specific ways to embed knowledge. *Embodied tacit knowledge* requires new pattern embedding for change to occur. This might take the form of repetition in physical training or in mental thinking. For example, embodied tacit knowledge might be embedded through mimicry, practice, competence development or visual imagery coupled with practice. An example of this would be when an athlete training to become a pole vaulter reviews a video of his perfect pole vault to increase his athletic capability. This is a result of the fact that when the pole vaulter performs his perfect vault, the patterns going through his brain while he is doing it are the same patterns that go through his brain when he is watching himself do it. When he is watching the video, he is repeating the desired brain patterns and this repetition strengthens these patterns in unconscious memory. When "doing" the pole vault, he cannot think about his action, nor try to control them. Doing so would degrade his performance because his conscious thoughts would interfere with his tacit ability.

In the late 1990's, neuroscience research identified what are referred to as mirror neurons. As Dobb's explains,

These neurons are scattered throughout key parts of the brain—the premotor cortex and centers for language, empathy and pain—and fire not only as we perform a certain action, but also when we watch someone else perform that action. (Dobbs, 2006, p. 22)

Watching a video is a cognitive form of mimicry that transfers actions, behaviors and most likely other cultural norms. Thus, when we *see* something being enacted, our mind creates the same patterns that we would use to enact that "something" ourselves. As these patterns fade into long-term memory, they would represent tacit knowledge—both Knowledge (Informing) and Knowledge (Proceeding). While mirror neurons are a subject of current research, it would appear that they represent a mechanism for the transfer of tacit knowledge between individuals or throughout a culture. For more information on mirror neurons, see Gazzaniga, 2004.

Intuitive tacit knowledge can be nurtured and developed through exposure, learning, and practice. Knowledge (Informing) might be embedded through experience, contemplation, developing a case history for learning purposes, developing a sensitivity to your own intuition, and effortful practice. Effortful study moves beyond practice to include identifying challenges just beyond an individual's competence and focusing on meeting those challenges one at a time (Ericsson, 2006). The way people become experts involves the chunking of ideas and concepts and creating understanding through the development of significant patterns useful for solving problems and anticipating future behavior within their area of focus. In the study of chess players introduced earlier, it was concluded that "effortful practice" was the difference between people who played chess for many years while maintaining an average skill and those who became master players in shorter periods of time. The master players, or experts, examined the chessboard patterns over and over again, studying them, looking at nuances, trying small changes to perturb the outcome (sense and response), generally "playing with" and studying these *patterns* (Ross, 2006). In other words, they use *long-term working memory, pattern recognition and chunking* rather than logic as a means of understanding and decision-making. This indicates that by exerting mental effort and emotion while exploring complex situations, knowledge—often problem-solving expertise and what some call wisdom—becomes embedded in the unconscious mind. For additional information on the development of expertise see Ericsson (2006). An important insight from this discussion is the recognition that when facing complex problems which do not allow reasoning or cause and effect analysis because of their complexity, the solution will most likely lie in studying patterns and chunking those patterns to enable a tacit capacity to anticipate and develop solutions. For more on the reference to wisdom see Goldberg (2005).

Affective tacit knowledge requires nurturing and the development of emotional intelligence. Affective tacit knowledge might be embedded through digging deeply into a situation—building self-awareness and developing a sensitivity to your own emotions—and having intense emotional experiences. How much of an experience is kept as tacit knowledge depends upon the mode of incoming information and the emotional tag we (unconsciously) put on it. The stronger the emotion attached to the experience, the longer it will be remembered and the easier it will be to recall. Subtle patterns that occur during any experience may slip quietly into our unconscious and become affective tacit knowledge. For a good explanation of Emotional Intelligence see Goleman (1998).

Spiritual tacit knowledge can be facilitated by encouraging holistic representation of the individual and respect for a higher purpose. Spiritual tacit knowledge might be embedded through dialogue, learning from practice and reflection, and developing a sensitivity to your own spirit, living with it over time and exploring your feelings regarding the larger aspects of values, purpose and meaning. Any individual who, or organization which, demonstrates—and acts upon—their deep concerns for humanity and the planet is embedding spiritual tacit knowledge.

Sharing Tacit Knowledge

The third approach toward building extraordinary consciousness is *sharing tacit knowledge*. In our discussion above on surfacing tacit knowledge, it became clear that surfaced knowledge is new knowledge, a different shading of that which was in the unconscious. If knowledge can be described in words and visuals then this would be by definition explicit; understanding can only be symbolized and to some extent conveyed through words. Yet the subject of this paragraph is sharing tacit knowledge. The key is that **it is not necessary to make knowledge explicit in order to share it**.

In Figure 12, sharing tacit knowledge occurs both consciously and unconsciously, although the knowledge shared remains tacit in nature. *There is no substitute for experience.* The power of this process has been recognized in organizations for years, and tapped into through the use of mentoring and shadowing programs to facilitate imitation and mimicry. More recently, it has become the focus of group learning, where communities and teams engage in dialogue focused on specific issues and experiences mentally and, over time, develop a common frame of reference, language and understanding that can create solutions to complex problems. The words that are exchanged serve as a tool of creative expression rather than limiting the scope of exchange.

The solution set agreed upon may retain "tacitness" in terms of understanding the complexity of the issues (where it is impossible to identify all the contributing factors much less a cause and effect relationship among them). Hence these solutions in terms of understanding would not be explainable in words and visuals to individuals outside the team or community. When this occurs, the team (having arrived at the "tacit" decision) will often create a rational, but limited, explanation of why the decision makes sense to communicate to outside individuals.

Inducing Resonance

The fourth approach toward building extraordinary consciousness is *inducing resonance*. Through exposure to diverse, and specifically opposing, concepts that are well-grounded, it is possible to create a resonance within the receiver's mind that amplifies the meaning of the incoming information, increasing its emotional content and receptivity. In Figure 12, inducing resonance is a result of external stimuli resonating with internal information to bring into conscious awareness. While it is words that trigger this resonance, it is the current of truth flowing under that linguistically centered thought that brings about connections. When this resonance occurs, the incoming information is consistent with the frame of reference and belief systems within the receiving individual. This resonance amplifies feelings connected to the incoming information, bringing about the emergence of deeper perceptions and validating the re-creation of externally-triggered knowledge in the receiver.

Further, this process results in the amplification and transformation of internal affective, embodied, intuitive or spiritual knowledge from tacit to implicit (or explicit). Since deep knowledge is now accessible at the conscious level, this process also creates a sense of ownership within the listener. The speakers are not telling the listener what to believe; rather, when the tacit knowledge of the receiver resonates with what the speaker is saying (and how it is said), a natural reinforcement and expansion of understanding occurs within the listener. This accelerates the creation of deeper tacit knowledge and a stronger affection associated with this area of focus.

An example of inducing resonance can be seen in the movie, *The Debaters*. We would even go so far as to say that the purpose of a debate is to transfer tacit knowledge. Well-researched and well-grounded external information is communicated (explicit knowledge) tied to emotional tags (explicitly expressed). The beauty of this process is that this occurs on *both sides* of a question such that the active listener who has an interest in the area of the debate is pulled into one side or another. An eloquent speaker will try to speak from the audience's frame of reference to tap into their intuition. Such a speaker will come across as confident, likeable and positive to transfer embodied tacit knowledge, and may well refer to higher order purpose, etc. to connect with the listener's spiritual tacit knowledge. A strong example of this occurs in the U.S. Presidential debates. This also occurs in litigation, particularly in the closing arguments, where for opposing sides of an issue emotional tags are tied to a specific frame of reference regarding what has been presented.

Chapter 15
Decision-Making and Tacit Knowledge

Given the definitions, descriptions and characteristics of tacit knowledge presented in Chapters 13 and 14, and considering the value of tacit knowledge in organizations, we now turn to the role of leadership in managing the organizational environment for, and nurturing the creation and utilization of, tacit knowledge in support of sustainable high performance. Most organizations face a two-fold problem with tacit knowledge. First, it must be recognized and its value to organizations understood and appreciated. Once this occurs, tacit knowledge can then be managed to various degrees (depending on the knowledge, its context and the organization's culture and leadership). In this context, management does not mean control, rather it refers to taking actions and creating environments in which the best decisions will be made and most desirable results will be achieved.

The value of any specific tacit knowledge may be positive or negative. For example, where tacit knowledge is the capability to maintain a quick response—such as the flexible and high-quality assembly line Dell Computer had for a number of years, or Walmart's nation-wide distribution capacity—tacit knowledge is extremely valuable and very difficult to replicate. However, where certain *fixed beliefs and habits of decision-making have become so internalized that they are unrecognized by their owners and perpetuate decisions that no longer relate to a changing world*, such knowledge forecasts the decay and possible disappearance of the organization.

> The value of any specific tacit knowledge may be positive or negative.

Both possibilities must be recognized and understood to leverage decision-making capability. Armed with this understanding, leaders and managers can create an environment that maximizes the creation and contribution of employee tacit knowledge. This environment can facilitate the recognition and removal of outdated tacit knowledge while creating, modulating and adapting tacit knowledge that can respond to opportunities and demands of an unpredictable market. The role of leaders and managers begins with recognizing, respecting and rewarding the use of productive tacit knowledge, supporting the surfacing of this knowledge where it makes sense, and encouraging open communications among decision-makers.

A significant strength of tacit knowledge is in its efficiency and efficacy as internal patterns are combined with incoming information to *develop situation-focused responses that are context sensitive*. The costs are in the difficulty of sharing such knowledge with others. Since tacit knowledge is usually deeper than explicit knowledge, it can be more powerful; but when outdated it is much harder to change, usually requiring a transformational learning experience. See Mezirow (2000) for a thorough discussion of this phenomenon.

From a decision-maker perspective, techniques for ***surfacing tacit knowledge*** include observing and discussing the role of emotions in decision-making, actions and dialogue; and practicing reflection and self-questioning by individuals when they are using feelings, intuition, or gut feel as guides for decisions or actions. Where embodied sensations arise during an experience, the decision-maker can seek to understand this internal effect, and explore the situation in terms of their own history, frame of reference and the sources of their reactions. In addition, individuals who have developed tacit knowledge through experience can sometimes surface the thinking and understanding underlying that knowledge by getting in touch with their unconscious through self-reflection and inner tasking, questioning their own thinking and looking for underlying patterns in their actions (see Chapter 14).

Embedding tacit knowledge in an organizational setting serves a number of significant purposes for the organization. In a changing and surprise-prone environment, individuals with deep knowledge and wide experience related to an area of focus—rich sources of tacit knowledge—are able to quickly respond to a variety of emerging challenges. Another example is the embedding of tacit knowledge in complex areas vital to corporate survival; for instance, a series of highly efficient processes that give the organization competitive advantage. It is difficult if not impossible for competitors to copy or reproduce complex processes, particularly those that have tacit knowledge embedded within them. Such tacit knowledge is often the sum of the separate (and different) tacit knowledge of many individuals.

From a leader's perspective, ways to embed tacit knowledge include encouraging decision-makers at all levels to become aware of what tacit knowledge is and its importance to the organization; and encouraging all decision-makers to improve their competency through the techniques of effortful practice, repetition, and experience that develops a high level of expertise.

Sharing tacit knowledge may occur in communities of practice, interest and learning that have emerged over the last decade as the significance of knowledge to organizational survival was recognized. (See Bennet and Bennet, 2004, a new theory of the firm.) Communities provide an excellent environment for questions, dialogues and information exchanges which can bring out the nuances, feelings and insights related to the tacit knowledge of participants. Von Krogh et al. (2000) suggest that the best way to share tacit knowledge is through what is called micro communities of knowledge. These are small teams of five to seven members who are socialized through team projects and come to understand each other through a common language and purpose. This facilitates the surfacing and sharing of meaning and understanding, provided the participants are able to verbalize their unconscious knowledge.

Such communication can never be perfect because tacit knowledge comes with emotions, memories and deeper meanings that may not be known to its owner, and may be truly inaccessible. What can happen is that the listener may receive sufficient information to re-create a significant part of the speaker's knowledge within their own cognitive reality. When this occurs, the listener's perceptions, understanding, and meaning may be close enough for an approximate re-creation of the speaker's tacit knowledge. This learning process is contingent upon the listener being receptive to the information and finding the results compatible with their own knowledge, beliefs and assumptions (see the discussion on resonance above). If this does not occur, the listener may reject what is heard, misinterpret what was said, or have a "disorienting experience" that leads them to question their own beliefs and assumptions through critical analysis—perhaps leading to transformational learning. Clearly, the best transfer will occur if there is a compatible and reinforcing dialogue between the listener and the owner of tacit knowledge, with both parties coming from a common (or similar) frame of reference.

Other ways of sharing tacit knowledge include employees discussing and learning from their own and others experience, feelings and intuition. Decision-makers can facilitate deliberate learning in domains of their decision-making focus through conversations, dialogues, after-action reviews, reflection and continuous questioning of policies, practices, and historical ways of doing things.

The process of mentoring can stimulate the surfacing, embedding and sharing of tacit knowledge of both individuals involved. Mentoring is most effective when the individuals have similar backgrounds, vocabulary and outlooks on the organization, particularly in their areas of expertise. If the groundwork for understanding has not been developed, deeper aspects of knowledge cannot connect and grow. It is helpful to provide the mentee with a good set of questions that encourage the expert to reflect on his/her own thinking, feeling and unconscious proclivities. Recall the previous discussion on getting in touch with your own unconscious, and being very sensitive to emotions, hunches, gut feelings, body tenseness, etc. In a healthy mentoring relationship, it is important not to let the dialogue stay only on a logical, cognitive plane. While the rational approach is natural in a professional setting, it is the non-rational and non-vocal areas that may lie within the unconscious that are primary domains of interest. Each of us (through experience and expertise) develops an internal world that re-presents the history of our learning—although never precisely accurate. The map is not the territory. Nevertheless, it is just this *autobiographical history, plus the situational inputs* (as perceived by the mentor), that "wakes up" the non-vocal signs representing tacit knowledge.

For best understanding of a mentor's tacit knowledge, the mentee must try to "see" the same situation as the mentor. This is where good communication about the situation can become very helpful; but realize the mentor may not consciously know why he sees what he sees. Also, seeing the same situation differently may open the door to an understanding of differing frames of reference which can be the starting point for exploring why the mentor has the frame of reference she has. This in turn can lead to questions that help the mentee understand his frame of reference and an exploration of why certain feelings occur and why certain actions are chosen over others. Since the unconscious mind can detect patterns and influence actions without the conscious mind being aware of it, the mentor may be unconsciously detecting patterns in the situation, and acting on his tacit knowledge without being aware of doing so. An alert mentee who is aware of this phenomenon can consciously look for those subtle patterns that the mentor uses to make decisions but does not see.

To establish a base for ***inducing resonance*** in an organization, leaders need to create a culture that recognizes, understands, appreciates and is aligned with the purpose, mission, vision and values of the organization. Such a culture is open to resonance of information and knowledge generated by leaders, thought leaders or outside experts who can focus the meaning and intent of their knowledge such that it resonates with decision-makers at various levels of the organization. When this occurs individual understanding, acceptance and enthusiasm for the knowledge is significantly enhanced because it is consistent with, and greatly enhances, their personal competency and contribution to the organization. This relationship is the resonance phenomena.

Within the culture described above, ways of facilitating local resonances include setting up formal dialogues, conversations and brainstorming sessions. As a point of caution, too much resonance throughout the workplace may act as a narrow band filter causing the rejection of non-resonant or diverse ideas. This, of course, would stifle innovation, creativity and adaptability to changing world situations. The point made here is the importance of recognizing and honoring resonance on both sides of any issue or question.

A Quick Summary

The recognition that tacit knowledge resides beyond ordinary consciousness led to the search for approaches to identifying extraordinary consciousness, that is, developing a greater sensitivity to information stored in the unconscious in order to facilitate the management and use of tacit knowledge in decision-making. Surfacing, embedding and sharing tacit knowledge were discussed as approaches for mobilizing tacit knowledge in support of individual and organizational objectives. The importance of extraordinary consciousness became clear as we discussed these approaches. In addition, it was forwarded that participating in or exposing ourselves to situations that induce resonance engages our personal passion in developing deeper knowledge and expanded awareness of that knowledge. Chapter 16 on "The Art of Knowing" provides a framework to expand our understanding of—and access to—tacit knowledge resources.

Changing and uncertain times require new ways of thinking and new ways of acting. We can take good actions only if we can make good decisions. We can make good decisions only if we have good understanding. Good understanding comes from good knowledge. We can have good knowledge only if we know how to learn, from our external environment and our internal environment. Since much of our information and knowledge is tacit, engaging tacit knowledge is an important focus for decision-makers at all levels. Our understanding of tacit knowledge is crucial to our future. What better resource than our minds to co-evolve with and contribute to our world? This book offers a single drop in an ocean of possibilities.

Section V
The New World of Knowledge and Knowing

(Chapters 16-18)

As we learn to tap into our unconscious, increasingly relying more on our sense of knowing and acting accordingly, we are expanding our knowledge base. That which was once tacit begins to emerge and the continuous feedback loops, as we see the results of our actions, enables more knowledge.

While tacit knowledge was covered in Section IV, we choose to explore knowing from a more pragmatic viewpoint inclusive of brief exercises to expand our external sensing capabilities. To this end, a Knowing Framework developed for the U.S. Department of the Navy is utilized. For purposes of this discussion, knowing is poetically defined as seeing beyond images, hearing beyond words, sensing beyond appearances, and feeling beyond emotions. It is a sense that emerges from our collective tacit knowledge.

We then turn our focus to the Net Generation. Birthed within the dynamic environment of CUCA, pulsing with challenges and opportunities, a new kind of decision-maker is moving into the workplace. This decision-maker is Internet savvy and social media addicted, living a moment-by-moment existence globally connected and culturally conversant. Accompanying this virtual social addiction are characteristics that will forever shift historical concepts of leadership, management and decision-making in the work place. Blessed with the availability of ever-increasing stores of surface and shallow knowledge, these decision-makers are simultaneously plagued with short attention spans, which bodes poorly for traditional approaches to developing deep knowledge. Fortunately, this new generation is growing up knowing.

Section V includes the following Chapters: The Art of Knowing (Chapter 16); The New Decision-Makers (Chapter 17); and A Guess about the Future (Chapter 18).

Chapter 16
The Art of Knowing

Every decision and the actions that decision drives is a learning experience that builds on its predecessors by broadening the sources of knowledge creation and the capacity to create knowledge in different ways. For example, as an individual engages in more and more conversations across the Internet in search of meaning, thought connections occur that cause an expansion of shallow knowledge. As we are aware, *knowledge begets knowledge*. In a global interactive environment, the more that is understood, the more that can be created and understood. This is how our personal learning system works. As we tap into our internal resources, *knowledge enables knowing, and knowing inspires the creation of knowledge.*

We've alluded to the concept of "knowing" throughout this book, but have not defined it; nor is this easy to do, since the word and concept are used so many different ways. We consider Knowing as a *sense* that is supported by our tacit knowledge. It can be poetically described as *seeing beyond images, hearing beyond words, sensing beyond appearances, and feeling beyond emotions.*

In this chapter, we provide a Knowing Framework that focuses on methods to increase individual sensory capabilities. This Framework specifically refers to our five external senses and to the increase of the ability to consciously integrate these sensory inputs *with our tacit knowledge*, that knowledge created by past learning experiences that is *entangled with* the flow of spiritual tacit knowledge continuously available to each of us. In other words, knowing—**driven by the unconscious as an integrated unit**—is the *sense* gained from experience that resides in the *subconscious* part of the mind, *and* the energetic connection our mind enjoys with the *superconscious*. The subconscious and superconscious are both part of our unconscious resources, with the subconscious directly supporting the embodied mind/brain and the superconscious focused on tacit resources involving larger moral aspects, the emotional part of human nature and the higher development of our mental faculties. When engaged by an intelligent mind which has moved beyond logic into conscious processing based on trust and recognition of the connectedness and interdependence of humanity, these resources are immeasurable.

In Figure 13 below, the superconscious is described with the terms spiritual learning, higher guidance, values and morality, and love. It is also characterized as "pre-personality" to emphasize that there are no personal translators such as beliefs and mental models attached to this form of knowing. The flow of information from the superconscious is very much focused on the moment at hand and does not bring with it any awareness patterns that could cloud the decision-makers full field of perception.

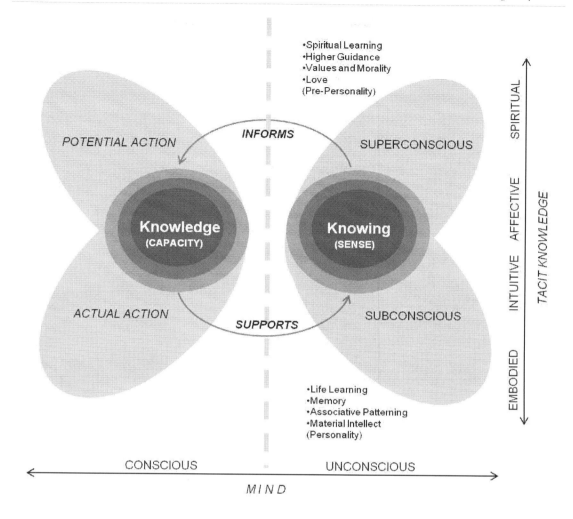

Figure 13: The Eternal Loop of Knowledge and Knowing

In contrast, the memories stored in the subconscious are very much a part of the personality of the decision-maker, and may be heavily influenced by an individual's perceptions and feelings at the time they were formed. Embodied tacit knowledge would be based on the physical preferences of personality expression while affective tacit knowledge would be based on the feelings connected with the personality of the decision-maker. For example, if there was a traumatic event that occurred in childhood that produced a feeling of "helplessness," later in life there might be neuronal patterns that are triggered that reproduce this feeling when the adult encounters a similar situation. While these feelings may have been appropriate for the child, they would rarely be of service to a seasoned, intelligent decision-maker.

Descriptive terms for the subconscious include life learning, memory, associative patterning, and material intellect. The subconscious in an autonomic system serving a life-support function. We all must realize that **the human *subconscious* is in service to the conscious mind**. It is not intended to dominate decision-making. The subconscious expands as it integrates and connects (complexes) all that we put into it through our five external senses. *It is at the conscious mind level that we develop our intellect and make choices that serve as the framework for our subconscious processing.*

Figure 13 is a nominal graphic showing the continuous feedback loops between knowledge and knowing. Thinking about (potential) and experiencing (actual) effective action (knowledge) supports development of embodied, intuitive and affective tacit knowledges. When we recognize and use our sense of knowing—regardless of its origin—we are tapping into our tacit knowledge to inform our decisions and actions. These decisions and actions, and the feedback from taking those actions, in turn expand our knowledge base, much of which over time will become future tacit resources. Since our internal sense of knowing draws collectively from all areas of our tacit knowledge, the more we open to this inner sense, respond accordingly, and observe and reflect on feedback, the more our inner resources move beyond limited perceptions which may be connected to embedded childhood memories.

Critical Areas of Knowing

The Knowing Framework encompasses three critical areas. The first is "knowing our self," learning to love and trust ourselves. This includes deep reflection on our self in terms of beliefs, values, dreams and purpose for being, and appreciation for the unique beings that we are. It includes understanding of our goals, objectives, strengths and weaknesses in thought and action, and internal defenses and limitations. By knowing ourselves we learn to work within and around our limitations and to support our strengths, thus ensuring that the data, information, and knowledge informing our system is properly identified and interpreted. Further, knowing our self means recognizing that we are a social being, part of the large ecosystem we call Gaia and inextricably connected to other social beings around the world, which brings us to the second critical element: knowing others.

We live in a connected world, spending most of our waking life with other people, and often continuing that interaction in our dreams! There is amazing diversity in the world, so much to learn and share with others. Whether in love or at war, people are always in relationships and must grapple with the sense of "other" in accordance with their beliefs, values and dreams.

> We live in a connected world, spending most of our waking life with other people, and often continuing that interaction in our dreams!

The third critical area is that of "knowing" the situation in as objective and realistic a manner as possible, understanding the situation, problem, or challenge in context (see Chapter 4, "The Complexity of Situations"). In the military this is called situational awareness and includes areas such as culture, goals and objectives, thinking patterns, internal inconsistencies, capabilities, strategies and tactics, and political motivations. The current dynamics of our environment, the multiple forces involved, the complexity of relationships, the many aspects of events that are governed by human emotion, and the unprecedented amount of available data and information make situational awareness a challenging but essential phenomenon in many aspects of our daily lives.

As we move away from predictable patterns susceptible to logic, decision-makers must become increasingly reliant on their "gut" instinct, an internal sense of knowing combined with high situational awareness. Knowing then becomes key to decision-making. The mental skills honed in knowing help decision-makers identify, interpret, make decisions, and take appropriate action in response to current situational assessments.

This construct of knowing can be elevated to the organizational level by using and combining the insights and experiences of individuals through dialogue and collaboration within teams, groups, and communities, both face-to-face and virtual. Such efforts significantly improve the quality of understanding and responsiveness of actions of the organization. They also greatly expand the scope of complex situations that can be handled through knowing because of the greater resources brought to bear—all of this significantly supported by technological interoperability.

Organizational knowing is an aspect of *organizational intelligence*, the capacity of an organization as a whole to gather information, generate knowledge, innovate, and to take effective action. This capacity is the foundation for effective response in a fast-changing and complex world. Increasing our sensory and mental processes contributes to the "positioning" understood by the great strategist Sun Tzu in the year 500 B.C. when he wrote his famous dictum for victory: *Position yourself so there is no battle* (Clavell, 1983). Today in our world of organizations and complex challenges we could say "Position ourselves so there is no confusion."

> Position ourselves so that there is no confusion.

By exploring our sense of knowing we expand our understanding of ourselves, improve our awareness of the external world, learn how to tap into internal resources, and increase our skills to affect internal and external change. The Knowing Framework provides ideas for developing deep knowledge within the self and sharing that knowledge with others to create new perceptions and levels of understanding. Since each situation and each individual is unique, this Framework does not provide specific answers. Rather, it suggests questions and paths to follow to find those answers.

Principles of Knowing

In response to a changing environment, the Knowing Framework presented below in its expanded form was first developed at the turn of the century for the U.S. Department of the Navy. There are a number of recognized basic truths that drove its development. These truths became the principles upon which the Knowing Framework is based.

(1) Making decisions in an increasingly complex environment requires new ways of thinking.

(2) All the information in the world is useless if the decision-maker who needs it cannot process it and connect it to their own internal values, knowledge, and wisdom.

(3) We don't know all that we know.

(4) Each of us has knowledge far beyond that which is in our conscious mind. Put another way, we know more than we know we know. (Much of our experience and knowledge resides in the unconscious mind.)

(5) By exercising our mental and sensory capabilities we can increase those capabilities.

(6) Support capabilities of organizational knowing include organizational learning, knowledge centricity, common values and language, coherent vision, whole-brain learning, openness of communications, effective collaboration, and the free flow of ideas.

The concept of knowing focuses on the cognitive capabilities of observing and perceiving a situation; the cognitive processing that must occur to understand the external world and make maximum use of our internal cognitive capabilities; and the mechanism for creating deep knowledge and acting on that knowledge via the self as an agent of change. Each of these core areas will be discussed below in more detail.

The Cognitive Capabilities

The cognitive capabilities include observing, collecting and interpreting data and information, and building knowledge relative to the situation. The six areas we will address are: listening, noticing, scanning, sensing, patterning, and integrating. These areas represent means by which we perceive the external world and begin to make sense of it.

Listening

The first area, listening, sets the stage for the other five cognitive capabilities. Listening involves more than hearing; it is a sensing greater than sound. It is a neurological cognitive process involving stimuli received by the auditory system. The linguist Roland Barthes distinguished the difference between hearing and listening when he says: "Hearing is a physiological phenomenon; listening is a psychological act." What this means is that there is a choice involved in listening in terms of the listener choosing to interpret sound waves to potentially create understanding and meaning (Barthes, 1985).There are three levels of listening: alerting, deciphering and understanding. Alerting is picking up on environmental sound cues. Deciphering is relating the sound cues to meaning. Understanding is focused on the impact of the sound on another person. Active listening is intentionally focusing on who is speaking in order to take full advantage of verbal and non-verbal cues.

In developing active listening, imagine how you can use all your senses to focus on what is being said. One way to do this is to role-play, imagining you are in their shoes and feeling the words. Active listening means fully participating, acknowledging the thoughts you are hearing with your body, encouraging the train of thought, actively asking questions when the timing is appropriate. The childhood game of pass the word is an example of a fun way to improve listening skills. A group sits in a circle and whispers a message one to the next until it comes back to the originator. A variation on this theme is Chinese Whispers where a group makes a line and starts a different message from each end, crossing somewhere in the middle and making it to the opposite end before sharing the messages back with the originators. Another good group exercise is a "your turn" exercise, where one individual begins speaking, and another person picks up the topic, and so forth. Not knowing whether you are next in line to speak develops some good listening skills.

The bottom line is that what we don't hear cannot trigger our knowing. Awareness of our environment is not enough. We must listen to the flow of sound and search out meaning, understanding and implications.

Noticing

The second area, noticing, represents the ability to observe around us and recognize, i.e., identify those things that are relevant to our immediate or future needs. We are all familiar with the phenomenon of buying a new car and for the next six months recognizing the large number of similar cars that are on the streets. This is an example of a cognitive process of which we are frequently unaware. We notice those things that are recently in our memory or of emotional or intellectual importance to us. We miss many aspects of our environment if we are not focusing directly on them. Thus the art of noticing can be considered the art of "knowing" which areas of the environment are important and relevant to us at the moment, and focusing in on those elements and the relationships among those elements. It is also embedding a recall capability of those things not necessarily of immediate importance but representing closely related context factors. *This noticing is a first step in building deep knowledge, developing a thorough understanding and a systems context awareness of those areas of anticipated interest.* This is the start of becoming an expert in a given field of endeavor, or situation.

A classic example of mental exercises aimed at developing latent noticing skills is repetitive observation and recall. For example, think about a room that you are often in, perhaps a colleague's office or a friend's living room. Try to write down everything you can remember about this room. You will discover that despite the fact you've been in this room often, you can't remember exactly where furniture is located, or what's in the corners or on the walls. When you've completed this exercise, visit the room and write down everything you see, everything you've missed. What pictures are on the walls? Do you like them? What personal things in the room tell you something about your colleague or friend? How does the layout of furniture help define the room? (These kinds of questions build relationships with feelings and other thinking patterns.) Write a detailed map and remember it. A few days later repeat this exercise from the beginning. If you make any mistakes, go back to the room again, and as many times as it takes to get it right. Don't let yourself off the hook. You're telling yourself that when details are important you know how to bring them into your memory. As your ability to recall improves, repeat this exercise focusing on a street, a building, or a city you visit often.

Scanning

The third area, scanning, represents the ability to review and survey a large amount of data and information and selectively identify those areas that may be relevant. Because of the exponential increase in data and information, this ability becomes more and more important as time progresses. In a very real sense, scanning represents the ability to reduce the complexity of a situation or environment by objectively filtering out the irrelevant aspects, or environmental noise. By developing your own system of environmental "speed reading," scanning can provide early indicators of change.

Scanning exercises push the mind to pick up details and, more importantly, patterns of data and information, *in a short timeframe*. This is an important skill that law enforcement officers and investigators nurture. For example, when you visit an office or room that you've never been in before, take a quick look around and record your first strong impressions. What feelings are you getting? Count stuff. Look at patterns, look at contrasts, look at colors. Try to pick up everything in one or two glances around the room. Make a mental snapshot of the room and spend a few minutes impressing it in your memory. As you leave, remember the mental picture you've made of the room, the way you feel. Impress upon yourself the importance of remembering this. This picture can last for days, or years, despite the shortness of your visit. Your memory can literally retain an integrated *gestalt* of the room. Realize that what you can recall is only a small part of what went into your mind.

Sensing

The fourth area, sensing, represents the ability to take inputs from the external world through our five external senses and ensure the translation of those inputs into our mind to represent as accurate a transduction process (the transfer of energy from one form to another) as possible. The human ability to collect information through our external sensors is limited because of our physiological limitations. For example, we only see a very small part of the electromagnetic spectrum in terms of light, yet with technology we can tremendously expand the sensing capability. As humans we often take our senses for granted, yet they are highly-sensitized complex detection systems that cause immediate response without conscious thought! An example most everyone has experienced or observed is a mother's sensitivity to any discomfort of her young child. The relevance to "knowing" is, recognizing the importance of our sensory inputs, to learn how to fine tune these inputs to the highest possible level, then use discernment and discretion to interpret them.

Exercise examples cited above to increase noticing, scanning, and patterning skills will also enhance the sense of sight, which is far more than just looking at things. It includes locating yourself in position to things. For example, when you're away from city lights look up on a starry night and explore your way around the heavens. Try to identify the main constellations. By knowing their relative position, you know where you are, what month it is, and can even approximate the time of day. The stars provide context for positioning yourself on the earth.

Here are a few exercise examples for other senses. Hearing relates to comprehension. Sit on a park bench, close your eyes and relax, quieting your mind. Start by listening to what is going on around you---conversations of passersby, cars on a nearby causeway, the birds chattering, the wind rustling leaves, water trickling down a nearby drain. Now stretch beyond these nearby sounds. Imagine you have the hearing of a panther, only multidirectional, because you can move your ears every direction and search for sounds. Focus on a faint sound in the distance, then ask your auditory systems to bring it closer. Drag that sound toward you mentally. It gets louder. If you cup one hand behind one ear and cup the other hand in front of the opposite ear, you can actually improve your hearing, focusing on noises from the back with one ear and noises from the front with the other. How does that change what you are hearing?

Next time you are in a conversation with someone, focus your eyes and concentrate on the tip of their nose or the point of their chin. Listen carefully to every word they say, to the pause between their words, to their breathing and sighs, the rise and fall of their voice. Search for the inflections and subtle feelings being communicated behind what is actually being said. When people are talking, much of the meaning behind the information they impart is in their feelings. The words they say are only a representation, a descriptive code that communicates thought, interacting electrical pulses and flows influenced by an emotion or subtle feeling. By listening in this way, with your visual focus not distracting your auditory focus, you can build greater understanding of the subtleties behind the words.

There are many games that accentuate the sense of touch. An old favorite is blind man's bluff; more current is the use of blindfolding and walking through the woods used in outdoor management programs. Try this at home by spending three or four hours blindfolded, going about your regular home activities. At first you'll stumble and bump, maybe even become frustrated. But as you continue, your ability to manage your movements and meet your needs using your sense of touch will quickly improve. You will be able to move about your home alone with relative little effort, and you'll know where things are, especially things that are alive, such as plants and pets. You will develop the ability to *feel* their energy. Such exercises as these force your unconscious mind to create, re-create, and surface the imagined physical world. It activates the mind to bring out into the open its sensitivity to the physical context in which we live.

Patterning

The fifth area, patterning, represents the ability to review, study, and interpret large amounts of data/events/information and identify causal or correlative connections that are relatively stable over time or space and may represent patterns driven by underlying phenomena. These hidden drivers can become crucial to understanding the situation or the enemy behavior. This would also include an understanding of rhythm and randomness, flows and trends. Recall the importance of structure, relationships, and culture in creating emergent phenomena (patterns) and in influencing complex systems.

A well-known example of the use of patterning is that of professional card players and successful gamblers, who have trained themselves to repeatedly recall complicated patterns found in randomly drawn cards. To learn this skill, and improve your patterning skills, take a deck of cards and quickly flip through the deck three or four at a time. During this process, make a mental picture of the cards that are in your hand, pause, then turn over three or four more. After doing this several times, recall the mental picture of the first set of cards. What were they? Then try to recall the second set, then the third.

The secret is not to try and remember the actual cards, but to close your eyes and recall the mental picture of the cards. Patterns will emerge. After practicing for awhile, you will discover your ability to recall the patterns---as well as your ability to recall larger numbers of patterns---will steadily increase. As you increase the number of groups of cards you can recall, and increase the number of cards within each group, you are increasing your ability to recall complex patterns.

Study many patterns found in nature, art, science, and other areas of human endeavor. These patterns will provide you with a "mental reference library" that your mind can use to detect patterns in new situations. Chess experts win games on pattern recognition and pattern creation, not on individual pieces.

Integrating

The last area in the cognitive capabilities is integration. This represents the top-level capacity to take large amounts of data and information and pull them together to create meaning; this is frequently called sense-making. This capability, to pull together the major aspects of a complex situation and create patterns, relationships, models, and meaning that represent reality is what enables us to make decisions. This capability also applies to the ability to integrate internal organization capabilities and systems.

While we have used the word "integrating" to describe this capability, recall that the human mind is an associative patterner that is continuously complexing (mixing) incoming information from the external environment with all that is stored in memory. Thus, while the decision-maker has an awareness of integrating, the unconscious is doing much of the work and providing nudges in terms of feelings and speculative thought. Our unconscious is forever our partner, working 24/7 for us.

These five ways of observing represent the front line of cognitive capabilities needed to assist all of us in creative and accurate situational awareness and building a valid understanding of situations. To support these cognitive capabilities, we then need processes that transform these observations and this first-level knowledge into a deeper level of comprehension and understanding.

The Cognitive Processes

Internal cognitive processes that support the capabilities discussed above include visualizing, intuiting, valuing, choosing, and setting intent. These five internal cognitive processes greatly improve our power to understand the external world and to make maximum use of our internal thinking capabilities, transforming our observations into understanding.

Visualizing

The first of these processes, visualizing, represents the methodology of focusing attention on a given area and through imagination and logic creating an internal vision and scenario for success. In developing a successful vision, one must frequently take several different perspectives of the situation, play with a number of assumptions underlying these perspectives, and through a playful trial-and-error, come up with potential visions. This process is more creative than logical, more intuitive than rational, and wherever possible should be challenged, filtered, and constructed in collaboration with other competent individuals. Often this is done between two trusting colleagues or perhaps with a small team. While there is never absolute assurance that visualizing accurately represents reality, there are probabilities or degrees of success that can be recognized and developed.

Intuiting

The second supporting area is that of intuiting. By this we mean the art of making maximum use of our own intuition developed through experience, trial-and-error (Chapter 5), and deliberate internal questioning and application. There are standard processes available for training oneself to surface intuition (see Chapter 14). Recognize that intuition is typically understood as being the ability to access our unconscious mind and thereby make effective use of its very large storeroom of observations, experiences, and information. In our framework, intuition is one of the four ways tacit knowledge expresses (Chapter 12).

Empathy represents another aspect of intuition. Empathy is interpreted as the ability to take oneself out of oneself and put oneself into another person's world. In other words, as the old Native American saying goes, "Until you walk a mile in his moccasins, you will never understand the person." The ability to empathize permits us to translate our personal perspective into that of another, thereby understanding their interpretation of the situation and intuiting their actions. A tool that can be used to trigger ideas and dig deeper into one's intuitive capability, bringing out additional insights, is "mind mapping." Mind mapping is a tool to visually display and recognize relationships from discrete and diverse pieces of information and data (Wycoff, 1991). Empathy is also one of the values addressed in Chapter 17.

Valuing

Valuing represents the capacity to observe situations and recognize the values that underly their various aspects and concomitantly be fully aware of your own values and beliefs. A major part of valuing is the ability to align your vision, mission, and goals to focus attention on the immediate situation at hand. A second aspect represents the ability to identify the relevant but unknown aspects of a situation or competitor's behavior. Of course, the problem of unknown unknowns always exists in a turbulent environment and, while logically they are impossible to identify because by definition they are unknown, there are techniques available that help one reduce the area of known unknowns and hence reduce the probability of them adversely affecting the organization.

A third aspect of valuing is that of meaning, that is, understanding the important aspects of the situation and being able to prioritize them to anticipate potential consequences. Meaning is contingent upon the goals and aspirations of the individual. It also relies on the history of both the individual's experience and the context of the situation. Determining the meaning of a situation allows us to understand its impact on our own objectives and those of our organization. Knowing the meaning of something lets us prioritize our actions and estimate the resources we may need to deal with it.

Choosing

The fourth supporting area is that of choosing. Choosing involves making judgments, that is, conclusions and interpretations developed through the use of rules-of-thumb, facts, knowledge, experiences, emotions and intuition. While not necessarily widely recognized, judgments are used far more than logic or rational thinking in making decisions. This is because all but the simplest decisions occur in a context in which there is insufficient, noisy, or perhaps too much information to make rational conclusions. Judgment makes maximum use of heuristics, meta-knowing, and verication.

Heuristics represent the rules-of-thumb developed over time and through experience in a given field. They are shortcuts to thinking that are applicable to specific situations. Their value is speed of conclusions and their usefulness rests on consistency of the environment and repeatability of situations. Thus, they are both powerful and dangerous. Dangerous because the situation or environment, when changing, may quickly invalidate former reliable heuristics and historically create the phenomenon of always solving the last problem; yet powerful because they represent efficient and rapid ways of making decisions where the situation is known and the heuristics apply.

Meta-knowing is knowing about knowing, that is, understanding how we know things and how we go about knowing things. With this knowledge, one can more effectively go about learning and knowing in new situations as they evolve over time. Such power and flexibility greatly improve the quality of our

> Meta-knowing is knowing about knowing, understanding how we know things and how we go about knowing things.

choices. Meta-knowing is closely tied to our natural internal processes of learning and behaving as well as knowing how to make the most effective use of available external data, information, and knowledge and intuit that which is not available. An interesting aspect of meta-knowing is the way that certain errors in judgment are common to many people. Just being aware of these mistakes can reduce their occurrence. For example, we tend to give much more weight to specific, concrete information than to conceptual or abstract information. (See Kahneman et al., 1982, for details.)

Verication is the process by which we can improve the probability of making good choices by working with trusted others and using *their* experience and knowing to validate and improve the level of our judgmental effectiveness. Again, this could be done via a trusted colleague or through effective team creativity and decision-making.

Setting Intent

Intent is a powerful internal process that can be harnessed by every human being. Intention is the source with which we are doing something, the act or instance of mentally setting some course of action or result, a determination to act in some specific way. It can take the form of a declaration (often in the form of action), an assertion, a prayer, a cry for help, a wish, visualization, a thought or an affirmation. Perhaps the most in-depth and focused experimentation on the effects of human intention on the properties of materials and what we call physical reality has been that pursued for the past 40 years by Dr. William Tiller of Stanford University. Tiller has proven through repeated experimentation that it is possible to significantly change the properties (ph) of water by holding a clear intention to do so. His mind-shifting and potentially world-changing results began with using intent to change the acid/alkaline balance in purified water. The ramifications of this experiment have the potential to impact every aspect of human life.

What Tiller has discovered is that there are two unique levels of physical reality. The "normal level" of substance is the electric/atom/molecule level, what most of us think of and perceive as the only physical reality. However, a second level of substance exists that is the magnetic information level. While these two levels always interpenetrate each other, under "normal" conditions they do not interact; they are "uncoupled." Intention changes this condition, causing these two levels to interact, or move into a "coupled" state. Where humans are concerned, Tiller says that what an individual intends for himself with a strong sustained desire is what that individual will eventually become (Tiller, 2007).

While informed by Spiritual, the Embodied, Intuitive and Affective tacit knowledges are *local expressions of knowledge*, that is, directly related to our expression in physical reality in a specific situation and context. Connecting Tiller's model of intention with our model of tacit knowledge, it begins to become clear that effective intent relates to an alignment of the conscious mind with the tacit components of the mind and body, that is Embodied, Intuitive, and Affective tacit knowledge. We have to *know* it, *feel* it, and *believe* it to achieve the coupling of the electric/atom/molecule level and magnetic information level of physical reality.

As we use our power of intent to co-create our future, it is necessary to move our focus from outcome to intention, not worrying about what gets done but staying focused on what you are doing and how you "feel" about what you are doing. Are we in alignment with the direction our decisions are taking us? If not, back to the drawing board—that's looking closer at you, the decision-maker, and ensuring that your vision is clear and your intent is aligned with that vision.

> As we use our power of intent to co-create our future, it is necessary to move our focus from outcome to intention.

In summary, the five internal cognitive processes—visualizing, intuiting, valuing, choosing and setting intent—work with the six cognitive capabilities—listening, noticing, scanning, patterning, sensing, and integrating—to process data and information and create knowledge within the context of the environment and the situation. However, this knowledge must always be suspect because of our own self-limitations, internal inconsistencies, historical biases, and emotional distortions, all of which are discussed in the third area of knowing: the Self as an Agent of Change.

The Self as an Agent of Change

The third area of the knowing framework—the self as an agent of change—is the mechanism for creating deep knowledge, a level of understanding consistent with the external world and our internal framework. As the unconscious continuously associates information, the self as an agent of change takes the emergent deep knowledge and uses it for the dual purpose of our personal learning and growth, and for making changes in the external world.

As introduced in Chapter 3, deep knowledge consists of beliefs, facts, truths, assumptions, and understanding of an area that is so thoroughly embedded in the mind that we are often not consciously aware of the knowledge. To create deep knowledge an individual has to "live" with it, continuously interacting, thinking, learning, and experiencing that part of the world until the knowledge truly becomes a natural part of the inner being. An example would be that a person who has a good knowledge of a foreign language can speak it fluently; a person with a deep knowledge would be able to think in the language without any internal translation and would not need their native language to understand that internal thinking.

In the discussion of self as an agent of change, there are ten elements that will be presented. Five of these elements are internal: know thyself, mental models, emotional intelligence, learning and forgetting, and mental defenses; and five of these elements are external: modeling behaviors, knowledge sharing, dialogue, storytelling, and the art of persuasion.

Internal Elements

Alexander Pope, in his essay on man (1732-3), noted that: "Know then thyself, presume not God to scan; the proper study of mankind is man." We often think we know ourselves, but we rarely do. To really understand our own biases, perceptions, capabilities, etc., each of us must look inside and, as objectively as possible, ask ourselves, who are we, what are our limitations, what are our strengths, and what jewels and baggage do we carry from our years of experience. Rarely do we *take ourselves out of ourselves and look at ourselves*. But without an objective understanding of our own values, beliefs, and biases, we are continually in danger of misunderstanding the interpretation we apply to the external world. Our motives, expectations, decisions, and beliefs are frequently driven by internal forces of which we are completely unaware. For example, our emotional state plays a strong role in determining how we make decisions and what we decide.

The first step in knowing ourselves is awareness of the fact that we cannot assume we are what our conscious mind thinks we are. Two examples that most of us have experienced come to mind. The first is that we frequently do not know what we think until we hear what we say. The second example is the recognition that every act of writing is an act of creativity. Our biases, prejudices, and even brilliant ideas frequently remain unknown to us until pointed out by others or through conversations. Consciousness is our window to the world, but it is clouded by an internal history, experiences, feelings, memories, and desires.

After awareness comes the need to constantly monitor ourselves for undesirable traits or biases in our thinking, feeling, and processing. Seeking observations from others and carefully analyzing our individual experiences are both useful in understanding ourselves. We all have limitations and strengths, and even agendas hidden from our conscious mind that we must be aware of and build upon or control.

Part of knowing ourselves is the understanding of what mental models we have formed in specific areas of the external world. Mental models are the models we use to represent our own picture of reality. They are built up over time and through experience and represent our beliefs, assumptions, and ways of interpreting the outside world. They are efficient in that they allow us to react quickly to changing conditions and make rapid decisions based upon our presupposed model. Concomitantly, they are dangerous if the model is inaccurate or misleading.

Because we exist in a rapidly changing environment, many of our models quickly become outdated. We then must recognize the importance of continuously reviewing our perceptions and assumptions of the external world and questioning our own mental models to ensure they are consistent with reality (Senge, 1990). Since this is done continuously in our subconscious, we must

> Because we exist in a rapidly changing environment, many of our models quickly become outdated.

continuously question ourselves as to our real, versus stated, motives, goals and feelings. *Only then can we know who we are, only then can we change who we will be.*

The art of knowing not only includes understanding our own mental models, but the ability to recognize and deal with the mental models of others. Mental models frequently serve as drivers for our actions as well as our interpretations. When creating deep knowledge or taking action, the use of small groups, dialogue, etc. to normalize mental models with respected colleagues provides somewhat of a safeguard against the use of incomplete or erroneous mental models.

A subtle but powerful factor underlying mental models is the role of emotions in influencing our perception of reality. This has been extensively explored by Daniel Goleman (1995) in his seminal book *Emotional Intelligence*. Emotional intelligence is the ability to sense, understand, and effectively apply the power and acumen of emotions as a source of human energy, information, connection, and influence. It includes self-control, zeal and persistence, and the ability to motivate oneself. To understand emotional intelligence, we study how emotions affect behavior, influence decisions, motivate people to action, and impact their ability to interrelate. Emotions play a much larger role in our lives than previously understood, including a strong role in decision-making. For years it was widely held that rationality was the way of the executive. Now it is becoming clear that the rational and the emotional parts of the mind must be used together to get the best performance in organizations.

Much of emotional life is unconscious. Awareness of emotions occurs when the emotions enter the frontal cortex. As affective tacit knowledge, emotions in the subconscious play a powerful role in how we perceive and act, and hence in our decision-making. Feelings come from the limbic part of the brain and often come forth before the related experiences occur. *They represent a signal* that a given potential action may be wrong, or right, or that an external event may be dangerous. Emotions assign values to options or alternatives, sometimes without our knowing it. There is growing evidence that fundamental ethical stances in life stem from underlying emotional capacities. These stances create the basic belief system, the values, and often the underlying assumptions that are used to see the world—our mental model. From this short treatment of the concept, it is clear that emotional intelligence is interwoven across the ten elements of the self as an agent of change. (See Goleman, 1995 and 1998.)

Creating the deep knowledge of knowing through the effective use of emotional intelligence opens the door to two other equally important factors: learning and forgetting. Learning and letting go—in terms of "filing" away or putting away on the bookshelf—are critical elements of the self as an agent of change because they are the primary processes through which we change and grow. They are also the prerequisite for continuous learning, so essential for developing competencies representing all of the processes and capabilities discussed previously. Because the environment is highly dynamic and will continue to become more complex, learning will be more and more essential and critical in keeping up with the world.

Since humans have limited processing capability and the mind is easily overloaded and tends to cling to its past experience and knowledge, "letting go" becomes as important as learning. Letting go is the art of being able to let go of what was known and true in the past. Being able to recognize the limitations and inappropriateness of past assumptions, beliefs, and knowledge is essential before creating new mental models and for understanding ourselves as we grow. It is *one of the hardest acts of the human mind* because it threatens our self-image and may shake even our core belief systems.

The biggest barrier to learning and letting go arises from our own individual ability to develop invisible defenses against changing our beliefs. These self-imposed mental defenses have been eloquently described by Chris Argyris (1990). The essence of his conclusion is that the mind creates built-in defense mechanisms to support belief systems and experience. These defense mechanisms are invisible to the individual and may be quite difficult to expose in a real-world situation. They are a widespread example of not knowing what we know, thus representing invisible barriers to change. Several authors have

> The biggest barrier to learning and letting go arises from our self-imposed ability to develop invisible defenses against changing our beliefs.

estimated that information and knowledge double approximately every nine months. If this estimate is even close, the problems of saturation will continue to make our ability to acquire deep knowledge even more challenging. We must learn how to filter data and information through vision, values, goals, and purposes using intuition and judgment as our tools. This discernment and discretion within the deepest level of our minds provides a proactive aspect of filtering, thereby setting up purposeful mental defenses that reduce complexity and provide conditional safeguards to an otherwise open system. This is a fundamental way in which the self can simplify a situation by eliminating extraneous and undesirable information and knowledge coming from the external world.

The above discussion has identified a number of factors that can help us achieve an appropriate balance between change and our resistance to change. This is an important attribute: not all change is for the best, yet rigidity begets antiquity. This balance is situational and comes only from experience, learning, and a deep sense of knowing when to change and when not to change the self.

This section has addressed the self as an agent of change through internal recognition of certain factors that can influence self-change. Another aspect of change is the ability of the self to influence or change the external world. This is the active part of knowing. Once the self has attained deep knowledge and understanding of the situation and external environment, this must be shared with others, accompanied by the right actions to achieve success. We live in a connected world.

External Elements

The challenge becomes that of translating knowledge into behavior, thus creating the ability to model that behavior and influence others toward taking requisite actions. Role-modeling has always been a prime responsibility of leadership in the government as well as the civilian world. Having deep knowledge of the situation the individual must then translate that into personal behavior that becomes a role model for others to follow and become motivated and knowledgeable about how to act. Effective role-modeling does not require the learner to have the same deep knowledge as the role model, yet the actions and behaviors that result may reflect the equivalent deep knowledge and over time creates deep knowledge in the learner—but only in specific situations. This is how you share the effectiveness from learning and thereby transfer implicit knowledge.

Wherever possible, of course, it is preferable to develop and share as much knowledge as possible so that others can act independently and develop their own internally and situation-driven behavior. This is the reason knowledge management and communities of practice and interest require management attention. Since most deep knowledge is tacit, knowledge sharing can become a real challenge.

A third technique for orchestrating external change is through the use of dialogue. Dialogue is a process described by David Bohm (1992) to create a situation in which a group participates as coequals in inquiring and learning about some specific topic. In essence, the group creates a common understanding and shared perception of a given situation or topic. Dialogue is frequently viewed as the collaborative sharing and development of understanding. It can include both inquiry and discussions, but all participants must suspend judgment and not seek specific outcomes and answers. The process stresses the examination of underlying assumptions and listening deeply to the self and others to develop a collective meaning. This collective meaning is perhaps the best way in which a common understanding of a situation may be developed as a group and understood by others.

Another way of creating change and sharing understanding is through the effective use of the time-honored process of storytelling. Storytelling is a valuable tool in helping to build a common understanding of our current situation in anticipating possible futures and preparing to act on those possible futures. Stories tap into a universal consciousness that is natural to all human communities. Repetition of common story forms carries a subliminal message, a subtext that can help convey a deep level of complex meaning. Since common values enable consistent action, Story in this sense provides a framework that aids decision-making under conditions of uncertainty.

Modeling behavior, knowledge sharing, dialogue, and storytelling are all forms of building understanding and knowledge. Persuasion, our fifth technique, serves to communicate and share understanding with others a specific conviction or belief and/or to get them to act upon it. To change the external environment we need to be persuasive and to communicate the importance and need for others to take appropriate action. The question arises: When you have deep knowledge, what aspects of this can be used to effectively influence other's behavior? Since deep knowledge is tacit knowledge, we must learn how to transfer this to explicit knowledge. Nonaka and Taguichi (1995) and Polyani (1958) have done seminal work in this area. Persuasion, as seen from the perspective of the self, gets us back to the importance of using all of our fundamental values, such as personal example, integrity, honesty, and openness to help transfer our knowing to others.

As can be seen in the discussion above, **all four forms of tacit knowledge inform knowing**. The Knowing Framework seeks to engage our senses and hone our internal processing mechanisms to take full advantage of our minds/brains/bodies. By bringing our focus on knowing, we have the opportunity to move through relational, experiential, and cultural barriers that somewhere along the course of our lives have been constructed, and sometimes self imposed. This, however, is not the case for many of the young decision-makers moving into the workplace.

We are Entering a New World

At the beginning of this book we introduced the current climate, one of increasing change, uncertainty and complexity. Through an in-depth discussion of complexity and decision-making, we have begun to realize that indeed every decision about the future is a guess—howbeit hopefully an informed guess—and part of a larger decision journey. Since we must co-evolve with our environment for our very survival, new characteristics and ways of thinking and being are emerging in our younger generations. They are open to the fullness of who they are, growing up unencumbered by the weights and barriers carried by generations attempting to control their environment. These young decision-makers are the subject of our next chapter.

Chapter 17
The New Decision-Makers

The young decision-makers moving up in today's organizations—members of what is generally referred to as the Net Generation or the Millennials—are Internet savvy, and engage heavily in social media. The term Net Generation as used here describes the group of decision-makers growing up with the Internet and who began to enter the workforce around the turn of the century. We live in unprecedented technologically-advanced times. "Yet new information technology merely reflects the field of intelligence that is growing upon the earth. It does not cause it." (Carey, 1996, p. 100) Let's not forget, there has been no breakthrough in technology that was not first a thought in the human mind, a thought that had to be made explicit, described in some communicable form. The creative thought occurred first, followed by its effective application (knowledge) to create the tangible innovation. Action follows thought; and action changes the world.

Of particular significance to a discussion of the new decision-makers are the characteristics of how the Net Generation engages the world, and *this is a generation that **does** engage*. "They organize themselves, publish themselves, inform themselves and share with their friends—without waiting for an authority to instruct them" (Tapscott, 2010), howbeit an underlying pattern of this need for immediacy is an impatience with business models and processes of the preceding generation (Boyd, 2013). Similarly, Hadar (2009) describes this generation as optimistic and determined, and notes that they like public activism and Elmore (2010) points out that they are both high-performance and *high maintenance*, more likely to "rock the boat" than any prior generation (Johns, 2003). Let's dig a bit deeper and explore the values that underlie these behaviors. The research project "The Net Generation: a Strategic Investigation," which involved interviewing 9,442 young people, resulting in the publication of *Grown Up Digital*, will be used as a foundational information resource (Tapscott, 2009).

Emerging Values

The personal values of a decision-maker, *which are also likely to represent generational values*, can exercise tremendous influence over his/her decisions regarding how to solve a problem and take the best action in a situation. Note that values are knowledge, and as such are situation dependent and context sensitive (Avedisian and Bennet, 2010). German sociologist Karl Mannheim forwards that a person's thoughts, feelings and behaviors, including their values, are shaped by the generation to which a person belongs (Mannheim, 1980). We agree.

Consistent with Knowledge (Informing) and Knowledge (Proceeding), there is both an *information* (or content) part of values, and a *process* or *action* part of values, that is, Values (Informing) and Values (Proceeding). Values (Informing) is that which is highly regarded, perceived as worthy or desirable, and Values (Proceeding) is the way values are put together and acted upon in a specific situation or context.

Values begin as principles, a rule or standard considered good behavior (American Heritage Dictionary, 2006). As these principles are repeatedly expressed (acted upon) by an individual or across an organization, they become embedded behaviors, both considered the norm and expected (Avedisian and Bennet, 2010). For example, the principles of freedom, equality, human dignity, tolerance, and the celebration of diversity have a long and storied history in the United States (Lakoff, 2006). Although today these are recognized as values core to a democracy, Knowledge (Informing), there is still disagreement among the political infrastructure when translating them into action, Knowledge (Proceeding). Knowledge (Informing) appears to be the higher-order pattern, that is, less susceptible to change.

Recognizing the new social knowledge paradigm—which supports the creation, leveraging and application of knowledge—the core and operational values linked to this generation of decision-makers include integrity, empathy, transparency, participation, collaboration, contribution, learning and creativity (Avedisian and Bennet, 2010).

The foundational value of **Integrity** is defined as "steadfast adherence to a strict moral or ethical code" (American Heritage Dictionary, 2006). An organization or person of integrity is "whole," aligns words and actions; keeps commitment, does the right thing, and engages in fair dealing. From the perspective of the Net Generation,

> *Integrity is the foundation of the new enterprise. In North America, Net Geners define integrity as being honest, considerate, and transparent. They expect employers to be this way, and live by their commitment. Young people respond well to management integrity and quickly become engaged.* (Tapscott, 2009, p.162)

Without integrity, ethical standards and excellence lack practical meaning. The sometimes-hidden idea underlying integrity is *consistency and steadfast adherence*, producing an authenticity that is in concert with accepted moral standards of an organization or a culture. Thus while integrity may be a fundamental value, the *way* it is understood and expressed, Knowledge (Proceeding), may be different across organizations, or around the world. Nonetheless, because of its consistency within the context in which it is expressed, integrity is a powerful conveyor of trust among decision makers, and between an organization and its stakeholders.

The second foundational value is **empathy.** Empathy is defined as the "identification with and understanding of another's situation, feelings, and motives" (American Heritage Dictionary, 2006). In *The Empathetic Civilization*, Rifkin explains that "empathy" is the act of identifying with another's struggle as if it were one's own, and is the ultimate expression of a sense of equality. "Empathy requires a porous boundary between I and thou that allows the identity of two beings to mingle in a shared mental space" (Rifkin, 2009, p.160). Empathy asserts the unconditional value of the human person and the meaning of his growth and the growth of his fellow man. When coupled with integrity, empathy can help create a credible relationship, company and product/service from the perspective of all key stakeholders. It builds the foundation not just for collaboration and participation, but for true fraternity, reciprocity, and integration.

Integrity and empathy provide the pre-conditions for the effectiveness of other more operational values by creating trust and mutual respect, and providing a non-judgmental environment, all of which form the basis of communication through shared understanding. Empathy and integrity are not mutually independent. First, empathy needs to be understood, confirmed and practiced in the light of integrity. Without integrity, empathy may degenerate into sentimentality. Second, integrity is softened by empathy. Without empathy, integrity may become judgmental, and even harsh and unforgiving. Together, empathy and integrity serve as a foundation for effective teamwork and facilitate new knowledge creation, sharing and leveraging, enabling new, quick, flexible, and effective responses.

> Integrity and empathy, which are not mutually independent, provide the pre-conditions for the effectiveness of other more operational values by creating trust and respect.

The concept of **transparency**, described as an operational value, is defined as: easily seen through or detected and free from guile; candid or open (The American Heritage Dictionary, 2006). Again, we see a level of interdependency emerging. Empathy and integrity facilitate transparency by fostering trust, while transparency, in turn, reinforces trust. Unless transparency is balanced by empathy and integrity, it could foster misunderstanding and break down trust and relationships rather than supporting them.

Tapscott agrees that transparency as a core value for Net Geners is critical to establishing trusting, long-term relationships (Tapscott, 2009, p. 267). He forwards that true transparency "must make the processes, underlying assumptions, and political presuppositions (including supporting research) of policy explicit and subject to criticism" (Tapscott, 2009, p. 266). Beyond sharing documents on websites, transparency extends to openly sharing ideas, feelings, personal view points, and different levels of knowledge (Bennet and Bennet, 2008d). Therefore, transparency moves beyond surface knowledge to a focus on shallow knowledge, with the responsibility to ensure some level of understanding and meaning that makes information actionable in a changing, uncertain and complex environment.

Participation as an operational value is a keystone for the Net Generation, who reach out and creatively engage ideas and people around the world. This participation extends to political engagement and community service. For example, in the 2004 U.S. Presidential elections more people under the age of 30 cast votes than people over 65, with the biggest increase in the 18-24 age group. As Leyden et al. describe, "Signs indicate that Millennials are civic-minded, politically engaged, and hold values long associated with progressives, such as concern about economic inequalities ... and a strong belief in government" (Leyden et al., 2007, p. 1). In the area of community service, according to a 2006 report for the Corporation for National and Community Service, teens 16 to 19 years of age are spending twice as much time volunteering as in 1989 (Grimm et al., 2007). In the area of the economy, Tapscott sums up, "There is a new age of participation emerging in the economy ... The Net Generation ... is driving the democratization of information content" (Tapscott, 2009, p. 258). This was exactly the intent of the Open Government directive issued in December 2009 by U.S. President Obama.

The Directive sets forth three principles for government: transparency, participation, and collaboration. Government organizations—and by extension the private, educational and nonprofit sectors that support those government organizations—are provided general and specific directions for achieving behavior changes in support of these principles. Per the Directive, a starting place is expanded access to information by making it available online in open formats, and developing a policy framework supporting the use of emerging technologies. Concurrent with this Directive, the U.S. Attorney General issued new guidelines under the Freedom of Information Act (FOIA) reinforcing the principle that openness is the Federal Government's default position. As these directives and guidelines ripple down through the U.S. Federal sector, each government organization develops and puts into action an implementation plan (including Departmental directives and guidelines) consistent with the higher-level direction, and so on down through the hierarchy that comprises government organizations. Dependent on the strength of these various directives, individual behaviors begin to change which, over time, become part of the way work is done. For those individuals in resonance with these principles, as actions consistent with these principles are repeated over and over, they not only become organizational values, but personal values (Avedisian and Bennet, 2010). An associated example of the democratization of information content is the launching of www.data.gov, the official U.S. government site providing increased public access to federal government datasets.

Collaboration means, "to work together, especially in a joint intellectual effort" (American Heritage Dictionary, 2000). In the current environment, the meaning of collaboration has extended from relatively intact internal groups at the team, unit, or company level to a fluid, changing interdependent network of diverse contributors across the internal and external environments. A decision-maker has a new type of peer network, one that moves from autonomy to interdependence, from deference to dialogue, and from a primary focus on doing a job well to a focus on contribution to collective purposes (Heckscher, 2007, p.108-109). In this peer network, alignment around such values as collaboration, transparency, and contribution make it possible for knowledge workers to work together in environments that are open, changing, and diverse. Collaboration is a core value embraced by the Net Geners, involving engagement and participation. "Collaboration as Net Geners know it, is achieving something *with* other people, experiencing power through other people, not by ordering a gaggle of followers to do your bidding." (Tapscott, 2009, p. 163). As noted by a student researcher, "Collaboration and communication are second nature for the Millennial generation." (Panetta, 2013, p. 51)

Closely linked to participation and collaboration, **contribution** measures success and performance in the context of helping peers and an organization move toward a common mission and strategy. *Participation is the act of engagement, collaboration is how to engage, and contribution is the result of that engagement.* The purpose-driven orientation of contribution is a motivating force in the lives of Net Generation knowledge workers. Through global connectivity, Net Geners share openly, engaging other's ideas and contributing their ideas freely.

As an operational value **learning** is integrally related to the ability to contribute. Learning in the CUCA environment means receiving, understanding, thinking critically, and learning how to adapt and apply knowledge quickly in new and unfamiliar situations. The learning of the Net Generation is unique. Learning in social settings locates learning "not in the head or outside it, but in the relationship between the person and the world, which for human beings is a social person in a social world." (Wenger, 2009, p. 1) The Net Generation is learning together, in groups and communities, through continuous interactions around the world. This new mode of learning is just-in-time, interactive, collaborative, fun, engaging, taps multiple senses (e.g., multi-media) and fosters discovery. Learning affects every other value, offering a way of practicing and applying each of the values in every aspect of work life including interactions with peers, customers, vendors, how work gets done, and how success is measured. This learning is collaborative. Demonstrating the interdependence between learning, empathy and collaboration, Tapscott says,

> *It goes without saying that collaborative learning, with its emphasis on mindfulness, attunement to others, nonjudgmental interactions, acknowledgement of each person's unique contributions, and recognition of the importance of deep participation and a shared sense of meaning coming out of embedded relationships, can't help but foster greater empathic engagement.* (Tapscott, 2009, p. 607)

As defined by Andreason (2005), **creativity** is emerging new or original ideas or seeing new patterns in some domain of knowledge. In other words, creativity can be considered as the *ability to perceive new relationships and new possibilities*, see things from a different frame of reference, or realize new ways of understanding/having insight or portraying something. Innovation means the creation of new ideas *and* the transformation of those ideas into useful applications; thus, the combination of creativity and contribution as operational values bring about innovation. A creative environment is fueled by the values of integrity, empathy, transparency, collaboration, learning, and contribution which foster trust and a spirit of collaborative success (Avedisian and Bennet, 2010).

The values and abilities characterizing the Net Generation help support sustainability in a changing, uncertain and increasingly complex environment (see Chapter 1), and no doubt *that environment is contributing to the development of those abilities*. Today there is access to unlimited information, and each of us intuitively knows that using that information effectively (knowledge) is the key to success. Flooded by new thoughts and ideas, this generation surfs information, rarely focusing on a specific domain of knowledge long enough to acquire deep knowledge, and *the extent of their awareness determines their range of mobility*. The Net Generation operates at the edge of human thought, a place where insights find their way into expression. In other words, there is already *a level of co-evolving that can be observed in the Net Generation.* As the environment continues to change, so do and are decision-maker capabilities and capacities to ensure flexibility, quick response, resilience, robustness and continuous learning, all of which contribute to sustainability in a CUCA environment (Bennet and Bennet, 2005).

We are Social Creatures

The idea of social networking has been around for centuries. We are social creatures. However, Cozolino believes that we are just waking up to the complexity of our own brains and how they are linked together, and that "all of our biologies are interwoven" (Cozolino, 2006, p. 3). As we achieve global connectivity it is our minds that are creating that interweaving of thought, which in turn is enabling the emergence of new ideas and innovations.

Studies in social neuroscience have affirmed that over the course of evolution physical mechanisms have developed in our brains to enable us to learn through social interactions. These physical mechanisms provide vehicles for us to get the knowledge we need for survival (Johnson, 2006). People are in continuous two-way interaction with those around them, and the brain is continuously changing in response. We are not always conscious of this since a great deal of this communication occurs in the unconscious (Bennet and Bennet, 2007c).

> Over the course of evolution, physical mechanisms have developed in our brains to enable us to learn through social interactions.

Global connectivity and the Internet have brought about new modes of social networking. Through studying historical interactions of teams and communities (Wenger, 2009), the need to develop—and build upon—trusted relationships to facilitate learning emerged. From a neuroscience perspective, trust in a relationship is very important in enhancing learning. When a secure, bonding relationship in which trust has been established occurs there is a cascade of biochemical processes that stimulates and enhances the growth and connectivity of neural networks throughout the brain (Schore, 1994). This process reduces fear, a significant impediment to learning (Johnson, 2006), and promotes neural growth and learning, that is, the creation of knowledge (*the capacity to take effective action*). Further, Cozolino has found that social interaction and affective attunement actually contribute to the evolution and sculpting of the brain, that is, they not only stimulate the brain to grow, but facilitate organization and integration (Cozolino, 2002). An example of affective attunement is eye contact as expressed by the adage "the eyes are the seat of the soul".

But what can we glean from the eyes from current perceptions of the Internet? The new concept of social networking—one that utilizes the Internet—demands a shift in our perceptions, and a further shift from relationship-based interactions to idea-based interactions, or a refocus of the balance between the two. On first reflection, a considerable loss of context must be acknowledged since, as users flit from connection to connection, a plethora of interactions bereft of physical face-to-face relationship building are created. We all learned the power of non-verbals in communication. A great deal is accomplished automatically through non-verbal means as people unknowingly and effortlessly express feelings, beliefs and desire as they navigate their social worlds (Choi et al., 2004).

Further, trust emerges again and again in the literature—whether in the field of Education, Sociology, Organizational Development, Knowledge Management or Neuroscience—as a factor required for the free flow of knowledge. De Furia (1997) proposes five behaviors that help build trust: sharing relevant information, reducing controls, allowing for mutual influence, clarifying mutual expectations, and meeting expectations. What kind of trust can be achieved through social media?

> Trust emerges again and again in the literature as a factor required for the free flow of knowledge.

Virtual networking primarily relies on the resonance of ideas to develop a level of trust (see Figure 14). This is quite different than the personal relationships or connections built up over time through personal and work interactions. However, those people who connect and exchange ideas continuously *do* build a level of trust based on *their feelings about the responses to their ideas by those with whom they interact*. Since the focus of exchange is on the creative interplay of ideas, generally in a specific domain of knowledge, *there is no expectation of outcomes*. This is much like the way communities of practice and interest operate with the focus on knowledge and the creation of new ideas (Wenger, 1998). Thus, "relevant" information is domain knowledge. Since social media offer a platform for the free flow of ideas, the behavior proposed by De Furia (1997) that would appear to have the greatest relevance to building trust in this new social reality is *allowing for mutual influence*.

An additional level of trust that must be present is the trust of self. Only by respecting our intellect and trusting our perceptions and ideas, building self-confidence in our ideas, can we continue to engage in this type of intellectual exchange and build trust of another's responses. This does not appear to be an area of difficulty for most of the Net Generation. As a generation, the new generation believes they are special; their parents have told them, their schools have told them and television has told them (Espinoza et al., 2010). Burke (2004) agrees, pointing out that they have unconventional ideas and aren't afraid to say so.

Note that building trust in another's responses does not mean agreement with those responses. Rather, this means that we *intellectually respect those responses and trust that they are being provided from an honest and intellectual framework*. As such, we choose to focus and reflect on those responses in resonance with our own intelligent frame of reference.

Further, there is the concept of six degrees of separation that comes into play. If I know someone that you know who was a close colleague of someone else who owns a company that another individual is a partner in, then we have a starting place for building a working level of trust. This phenomenon is particularly effective in the military. If individuals have served on the same ship at some point in their career, or experienced service in the same conflict area of the world, there is an immediate understanding, a common respect and relationship to begin an exchange.

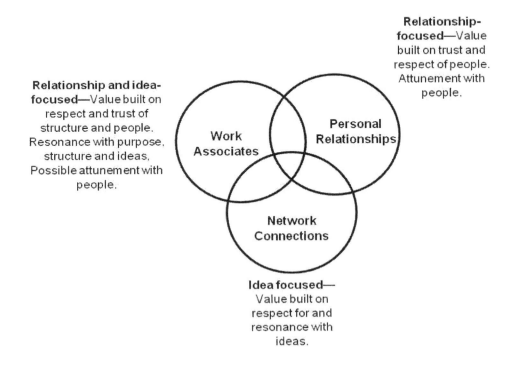

Figure 14: *New ways of thinking about relationships in our networked world.*

In this new environment of virtual networking—a cooperative association of interconnected informational beings, and all the subtext that comes with that distinction—there is an ever-increasing amount of information emerging. The individual decision-maker has greater responsibility in terms of discretion and discernment. This everyday social networking lays the groundwork for the decisions that socially engaged individuals will make in the future. (See the discussion of Relationship Network Management in Bennet and Bennet, 2004.) Thus, the continuous expansion of shallow knowledge is **an area of strength for the next generation of knowledge workers**. This knowledge (as a *potential or actual capacity*) prepares decision-makers for a changing and uncertain future by expanding areas of thought and conversation beyond a bounded functional and operational area of focus. New areas of interest are discovered, ideas expanded, and *judgments and decisions made from a more holistic framework*.

A nominal representation of this shift from a primary focus on surface knowledge in 2000 to a primary focus on shallow knowledge as we move toward 2020 is represented in Figure 15. The representation in Figure 14 is based on studies in education, organizations and complexity (Bennet and Bennet, 2008d, 2010; Chickering et al., 2005; Clausing, 1994; National Research Council, 2000; Oakes and Lipton, 1999). Figure 11 is speculative based on the anticipated social aspects of developing shallow knowledge. As future decision-makers communicate and learn via the Internet they expand their levels of shallow knowledge.

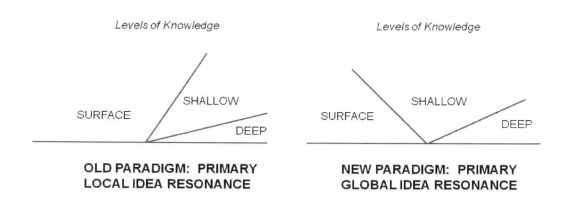

Figure 15: *(Left) A nominal graph illustrating the historic (2000) level of knowledge achieved by knowledge workers consistent with the level of decisions made in an organization (Bennet and Bennet, 2008d, 2010). (Right) A nominal graph illustrating the future (2020) level of knowledge achieved by knowledge workers. The increase in shallow knowledge is a result of consistent expanded interactions via social media (data from Tapscott, 2008).*

In Chapter 3 we drew parallels among the levels of knowledge and levels of learning, complexity of situations, complexity of decision-making, and complexity of actions; for example, the relationship between the levels of knowledge and simple, complicated and complex systems. Recognizing that the frame of reference and set of assumptions underlying the approach to a solution may significantly impact success, let's look at a complicated situation. Recall that "complicated" implies that causality can be identified and understood. However, while a complicated situation would have knowable and predictable patterns of behavior, the number of interrelated parts and connections among the parts may be so large that there will be some difficulty in identifying cause and effect relationships. Thus, this situation requires information (surface knowledge) *and* shallow knowledge to provide the context of the specific domain of causality related to the situation. Then, by logical analysis, systematic investigation, and deductive processes, the situation at hand can be corrected as desired (Bennet and Bennet, 2008a).

The implications of continuous social interactions (conversations, dialogues and multilogues) across an expanded global network (capacity) are staggering. When needed, decision-makers have the ability to develop context and generate ideas around a specific issue at hand (capability). Further, swimming around and diving up and down in the global shallows—which are filled with a diversity of views, perspectives, concepts and cultures—spurs uninhibited creativity and more significant innovation than surface swimming. Decision-makers in the connected, global world can be *mentally stimulated by interactions involving diverse views, perspectives, concepts and cultures* and are not bounded by local ideas.

Creativity and innovation thrive on different ideas and ways of looking at things, and flourish from connecting different streams of thought. From cross-domain stimulation of an open mind, new and often unsought patterns will emerge. A key phrase here is "open mind," that is, a mind not "limited" (whether purposefully or otherwise) to a specific direction or bounded domain of knowledge. Open mind describes a decision-maker co-evolving with a CUCA environment

> Creativity and innovation thrive on different ideas and ways of looking at things, and flourish from connecting different streams of thought.

and searching out relationships between the mission/vision/purpose/values of their organizational alliance and the potential offered within their environmental opportunity space (Bennet and Bennet, 2004). These are decision-makers seeking a window of opportunity in terms of space and time in a turbulent environment.

Because this new social way of being, thinking and acting taps into a huge diversity of experience, there is also an increased *appreciation of difference*, and with it comes a tolerance of diversity. "They are a true global generation; smarter and more tolerant to diversity than their predecessors." (Panetta, 2013) Immersion coupled with conversation and dialogue is quite the opposite of the Cold War isolation approach. *If they choose to do so*, the Net Generation may truly have the potential to create a global humanity.

Shallow knowledge requires context, whether that context applies to a specific domain, connects domains, or crosses domains. In contrast, recall that developing *deep knowledge* in a specific domain requires bounding an area of interest, and focusing on that domain over time to develop lived experience and expertise within both the conscious and unconscious mind. While one does not necessarily preclude the other, by definition deep knowledge requires a commitment of time and focus *around a specific domain* which will likely allow less time and focus for developing breadth of thought and following other interests.

As the environment continues to become more complex (and perhaps more fragile), the need for *deep knowledge to make the best decisions* and take effective action does not go away. Indeed, there will most likely be an increase in the amount of deep knowledge needed (and developed) to co-evolve with an increasingly CUCA environment. This is an assumption built on historic occurrences ... and the Net Generation is *creating their own history*!

The question becomes, while the Net Generation appears to be expanding their shallow knowledge, that is, developing understanding with context, how will these new decision-makers fare when they tackle higher-order complex issues that require deep knowledge? Will decision-makers of the future lose access to the deep knowledge historically deemed necessary for strategic decision-making?

The answer is simultaneously illusive and obvious. Recall our in-depth treatment on engaging tacit knowledge in Section IV and our presentation of the Knowing Framework in Chapter 16. This new generation of decision-makers appears to have greater openness and access to the workings of their unconscious, and the unconscious is the seat of our multidimensionality. This, of course, is not the entire answer. The mind/brain must be mentally and emotionally healthy to provide a platform for accessing the unconscious, recognizing the value of ideas in a specific domain of knowledge, and taking action on decisions.

Nonetheless, given enough exposure—perhaps the exposure provided by continuous interactions with diverse thinking and cultures—the unconscious *can and often does* come up with the best decisions for the situation at hand. Ironically, this intuitive approach to decision-making—tapping into the unconscious and providing greater access to tacit knowledge—**simplifies the decision-making process in the midst of increasing complexity**. Unhindered by the need to constantly tabulate mentally each and every detail, thoughts are able to flow freely, drawing from an expanded state of awareness and that which has been embodied, much like an athlete preparing for the Olympics. A generation down the road, the earlier sections of this book may well become a reference document for historic decision-making in a complex world!

Chapter 18
A Guess about the Future

Big Data is here. There is no doubt that most decisions made since the dawning of humanity have been based on incomplete information and knowledge of the situation at hand. We have yet to fully understand ourselves, and as the environment has become increasingly complex it has become more difficult to discern system boundaries and relationships among elements of the system, and the outcomes have become increasingly uncertain.

There is an excitement that comes with this trend. The human being is stimulated by uncertainty; it is part of the lived experience: the need to grow, try new things out, and find new ways of coping and excelling in our world. From this desire and intent emerge new ways of handling information and developing deeper knowledge, recognition of patterns from information stored in systems around the world, knowledge sharing through social networking media, and real-time visual data streaming from satellites and millions of sensors and GPS-enabled smartphones and cameras. This is the idea of big data, metaphorically referred to as the growing of a planetary nervous system with the human as one type of sensor (Smolan and Erwitt, 2013).

We *know* more! Our conscious processing is moving closer to the model of mind/brain functioning as introduced in Section III. We're gaining greater access to our unconscious, increasing our awareness of, and trust in, untapped information resources that are inherent in the biological and energetic functioning of what it is to be human. We're focusing more at the systems level, pulling out of our limited individual frames of reference to consider the *whole* and the interactions among the parts, recognizing the patterns of our activity and the importance of those patterns in our current and future work environments.

A Short Review

As we increasingly forge into complex environments, leaving the industrial age further behind, hopefully moving from an information and knowledge-based society toward that wisdom that has historically been so illusive, decision-makers must continue to create and apply the best knowledge they can. Understanding this decision process requires good definitions—a clear understanding of information and knowledge—and how the mind/brain/body through patterns (thoughts) and actions is able to learn, make decisions, take actions, and anticipate the outcome of those actions. So we have broken down the process, the elements of a decision, to study it one frame at a time from the viewpoints of knowledge, complexity and Neuroscience. As a result of the significant literature in these fields emerging over the past 15 years, we are beginning to understand just how decision-making occurs, providing us with a new starting place from which to develop insights and tap into our capacity to know.

The traditional language of decisions implies a causal and deterministic connection between the decision and the end goal, whereas with complex systems there may be no predictable end goal and no single direct causal connection that works. In Section II we forwarded that one *may be able* to construct a decision strategy that informs and guides problem resolution through a sequence of decisions and actions leading toward an acceptable solution. Such a plan might include (or anticipate) acts of seeding; boundary management; sense and response; identification of sources, sinks and regenerative loops; tipping points and butterfly effects; stability patterns; emergence flows; and miscellaneous external perturbations. While each of these has their own causal impact, the complexity of the system prohibits predicting their paths.

By studying specific complex systems, we seek to create an *intuitive and unconscious capacity* to understand their behavior and meaning. We know that systems are often combinations of simple, complicated and complex segments. This has both advantages and disadvantages. While the simple and complicated aspects can be dealt with via historical decision processes, with often visible cause-and-effect relationships, their success can lead decision-makers to

> By studying specific complex systems, we seek to create an intuitive and unconscious capacity to understand their behavior and meaning.

assume that the same approach applies to complex situations. And, of course, complexity and complicated parts of the system are frequently intermixed. Here, of course, as discussed earlier, is where educated intuition, insight, judgment and deep comprehension may prove invaluable.

Since rational decision-making can be developed and has a historic precedence, most individuals rely on logic with its supporting data and information to make and defend their decisions, even if problems are complex. In fact, it seems probable that most rational decisions that fail do so because they have not accounted for the complexity of the problem situation. And, of course, some rational decisions have turned out to be right not because they were logically accurate but because of the complexity of the problem.

It remains to be seen how—or if—it is possible to take a complex situation and identify these separate aspects of the system in such a way that one could choose the most effective decision strategy. We do know that each new gain in comprehension brings a corresponding reduction of complexity, and that you as the decision-maker at the point of action are in the best position to determine the way ahead. Knowledge is context-sensitive and situation-dependent. Those in the middle of the system with the deepest knowledge of the situation are in an excellent position to make the best decisions *if, and only if,* they can shift their frame of reference, taking a broad systems perspective and approach while engaging their deep knowledge of the elements of the system, their interrelations, and the boundary conditions.

In Section III we introduced the resonance between the current decision environment and the workings of the mind/brain. Theories, beliefs and ideas that are invariant forms at the highest hierarchal level of the prefrontal cortex significantly influence decision-making. These invariant concepts are continuously integrated across complementary sensing modes (visual, auditory, somatic, etc.) and through a downward feedback loops in the prefrontal cortex provide the decision-maker with some capacity to anticipate the outcome of actions. The larger the number of, and connections among, invariant forms developed through experience and learning, the more robust the spectrum of concepts available to the decision-maker which offer (1) a greater potential for adaptable decision-making, and (2) a higher probability of achieving the expected outcome. Thus, the workings of our mind/brain can provide a model for decision-making in a complex situation.

As introduced in Section IV, the way ahead is one of learning, adapting, taking risks, collaborating and creating organizations where employees are willing and able to deal with complexity and uncertainty, and to tap into their higher mental faculties. These are decision-makers who have the knowledge, freedom and fortitude to take responsibility and action.   This environment demands intelligent decision-makers equipped with knowledge, present-day situational awareness and the knowing which emerges from the tacit realms of the mind/brain. Recognizing that any model is an artificial construct, we introduced four aspects of tacit knowledge: embodied, intuitive, affective and spiritual, and the idea of *extraordinary consciousness*.

> This environment demands intelligent decision-makers equipped with knowledge, present-day situational awareness and knowing.

Extraordinary consciousness is developing a heightened sensitivity to, awareness of, and connectivity with our unconscious mind, purposefully acting to expand our conscious awareness through engaging tacit knowledge. Doing so gives each of us the ability to make better use of our tacit knowledge, and the capacity to focus on the art of knowing, the *sense* gained from experience that resides in the subconscious part of the mind *and* the energetic connection our mind enjoys with the superconscious. Finally, as we explored the Net Generation, the realization began to surface that perhaps this sense of knowing coupled with an expansion of shallow knowledge is how this generation is—and will be—able to simply and successfully navigate the complex decision environment.

A Guess about the Future

Almost every day we feel new energies erupting around the world: new thoughts, new feelings, new knowing, all contributing to new situations that require new decisions and actions from each and every one of us. Indeed, a global consciousness is emerging. As individuals and organizations, we are realizing that there are larger resources available to us, and that, as complex adaptive systems linked to a flowing fount of knowing, we can bring these resources to bear to achieve our ever-expanding vision of the future.

Are we as a race up to the challenge? We think yes. There is buoyancy in the human spirit that in the moment of challenge rises to the occasion.

A starting place is to engage ourselves fully in the decision-making journey and venture into exciting and unknown territory armed with our internal and external knowledge resources, realizing that we can create knowledge for the moment at hand. It is no surprise that thought leaders around the world have individually and collectively linked knowledge and action (Bennet, 2005). We must let go of many of our favored concepts, images and beliefs, releasing attachment to past knowledge in favor of our immediate experience and the learning that occurs as we tap into our internal and external senses, and then act.

As we learn to navigate our complex environment, the dynamic relationship between knowledge and knowing provides a key for decision-makers of all ages. Human beings learn from experiences, the flow of life that has the potential to equip us to make better choices in the future, only to be shifted and relearned in the moment of action, observation and reflection to flow into the next moment of action. For every moment of our lives we are deciding and acting, setting the very course for our future, choosing the thoughts that will manifest our desires. Every moment offers the opportunity to tap into this *awesome power of our human minds* and decide the direction of our lives, and perhaps even our race and our planet.

Appendix A
Moving from Knowledge to Wisdom, from Ordinary Consciousness to Extraordinary Consciousness

In a 2005 research study (Bennet, 2005), 27 of the 34 knowledge management thought leaders interviewed tied knowledge to action. Similarly, we define knowledge as *the capacity (potential or actual) to take effective action in varied and uncertain situations* (Bennet and Bennet, 2007a). As with knowledge so with wisdom; a rich diversity of definitions and descriptions abound, but there are common themes.

Focusing on work occurring around the turn of this century, Csikszentmihalyi and Nakamura (2005) described wisdom as referring to two distinct phenomena. The first was the *content* of wisdom (information) and the second an individual's *capacity to think or act* wisely. Focusing on the content of wisdom, Clayton and Birren (1980) said that individuals perceived wisdom differently when socio-demographic variables were changed, that is, as we now recognize about knowledge, they considered wisdom as context-sensitive and situation dependent. The works of Holliday and Changler (1986); Erikson (1998), Sternberg (1990), Jarvis (1992), Kramer and Bacelar (1994), Bennett-Woods (1997), Merriam and Caffarella (1999) all take the position that wisdom is grounded in life's rich experiences,

> *... [wisdom] therefore is developed through the process of aging ... wisdom seems to consist of the ability to move away from absolute truths, to be reflective to make sound judgments related to our daily existence, whatever our circumstances.* (Merriam and Caffarella, 1999, p. 165)

A number of researchers have considered wisdom as a part of intelligence (Smith, Dixon and Baltes, 1989; Dittmann-Kohli and Baltes, 1990). Baltes and Smith (1990) go on to say that wisdom is "a highly developed body of factual and procedural knowledge and judgment dealing with what we call the 'fundamental pragmatics of life'." In contrast, from qualitative research with Buddhist monks, Levitt (1999) said that the monks tended toward a spiritual definition and believed that all people were capable of wisdom, regardless of their intellect. From a similar persuasion, Trumpa (1991) sees wisdom as a state of consciousness with the qualities of spaciousness, friendliness, warmth, softness and joy. Similarly, Woodman and Dickinson (1996) see wisdom as the state of consciousness that allows the spiritual Self to be active. Wisdom also appears to have an affective component (Brown, 2000). The neurobiological roots of this were confirmed by Sherman (2000) who discovered that some brain-damaged patients who lacked wisdom also lacked the evaluative affects used to choose a course of action (make a decision).

In the early years of knowledge management (KM), thought leaders argued that wisdom was the end of a continuum made up of *data→information→ knowledge→wisdom*. But, as Peter Russell explains,

> *Various people have pointed to the progression of data to information to knowledge ... Continuing the progression suggests that something derived from knowledge leads to the emergence of a new level, what we call wisdom. But what is it that knowledge gives us that takes us beyond knowledge? Through knowledge we learn how to act in our own better interests. Will this decision lead to greater well-being, or greater suffering? What is the kindest way to respond in this situation? ... Wisdom reflects the values and criteria that we apply to our knowledge. Its essence is discernment. Discernment of right from wrong. Helpful from harmful. Truth from delusion.* (Russell, 2007)

Around the turn of the century, the U.S. Department of the Navy (DoN) placed knowledge at the beginning and wisdom near the end of their change model (Porter et al., 2003; Bennet and Bennet, 2004, 2008c). The change model consists of the following progression to facilitate increased connectedness and heightened consciousness: (1) closed structured concepts, (2) focused by limited sharing, (3) awareness and connectedness through sharing, (4) creating concepts and sharing these concepts with others, (5) advancement of new knowledge shared with humanity at large, (6) creating wisdom, teaching, and leading, and (7) creating (and sharing) new thought in a fully aware and conscious process. In this model, prior to reaching wisdom at level 6, there is the insertion of values (framed in the context of the greater good). Values was absent in the discussion of knowledge in support of the earlier levels of the model since the positive or negative value of knowledge is situation-dependent and context sensitive.

The change model described above follows the flow of the seven levels of consciousness. In order of growth toward wisdom and beyond, these seven levels focus on: (1) structured concepts: material, ideological, causative; (2) spiritual concepts: focused and limited love at the personal level; (3) spiritual concepts: soul as part of a larger structure, awareness and connectedness through giving; (4) senses other souls: giving what is needed by others so they can create virtue; balance, humility and hierarchy of thought and need in giving virtue; (5) spiritual awareness: planetary level, advancement of new knowledge communicated to humanity and re-communicated in mental framework; contribution to development of civilization to assist in creating virtue; (6) understanding soul as part of God (wisdom): creating virtue, teaching in soul capacity, leading; and (7) awareness of soul as a functional part of God: creating more of God in a fully aware and conscious method (MacFlouer, 1999).

Nussbaum (2000) forwards that all knowledge is in the service of wisdom. Nelson (2004) says that wisdom is the knowledge of the essential nature of reality. Further, similar to what was expressed in the Navy model, Sternberg defines wisdom as "the application of tacit knowledge as mediated by values toward the goal of achieving a common good" (Sternberg, 1998, p. 353), thus suggesting that tacit knowledge is a prerequisite for developing wisdom and wisdom is defined in a social rather than individual context. We agree. Using the levels of knowledge model introduced in Chapter 3, having deep knowledge (very often tacit) includes the ability to recognize patterns within a domain of knowledge, enabling a decision-maker to effectively apply learning from one situation to an entirely different situation in that same domain of knowledge. Wisdom takes this pattern-recognition and application ability the next step, enabling a decision-maker to *recognize and apply patterns across domains for the greater (or common) good.*

In a comparative study of two groups (one characterized as elderly and one characterized as creative), Orwell and Perlmutter (1990) discovered that wisdom was associated with advanced self-development and self-transcendence. Goldberg (a clinical professor of neurology) raises the question: if memory and mental focus decline with age, why is it that our wisdom and competence grow? After validating these two propositions, he answers the question by asserting that *tacit knowledge* does not suffer appreciable decline with age because it represents high-level patterns of procedural knowledge—knowledge of solving problems (Goldberg, 2005). These are patterns that represent chunks or groups of other patterns. If a mind has been active throughout life these high-level patterns represent competence, insight and deep (tacit) knowledge that may be considered wisdom. Thus while memory, specific facts and attention may decline with age, the knowledge of how to solve problems or what needs to be done in a specific situation does not appear to decline. Tacit knowledge and wisdom may remain strong and even continue to grow with age. What this also implies is that tacit knowledge—particularly as we age—is primarily process knowledge. See Section IV for an in-depth treatment of tacit knowledge.

Some core words associated with wisdom that appear throughout the literature include:

understanding (Clayton and Birren, 1980; Chandler and Holliday, 1990; Orwell and Perlmutter, 1990; Levitt, 1999; Stevens, 2000);

empathy (Clayton and Birren, 1980; Csikszentmihalyi and Rathunde, 1990; Chandler and Holliday, 1990; Levitt, 1999; Shedlock and Cornelius, 2000);

knowledge (Baltes and Smith, 1990; Clayton and Birren, 1980; Sternberg, 1998; Shedlock and Cornelius, 2000);

knows self (Chandler and Holiday, 1990; Levitt, 1999; Damon, 2000; Stevens, 2000; Shedlock and Cornelius, 2000);

living in balance (Birren and Fisher, 1990; Meacham, 1990); and

systemic thinking (Chandler and Holliday, 1990; Stevens, 2000; Shedlock and Cornelius, 2000).

Macdonald describes this systemic thinking as "acting with the well-being of the whole in mind" (Macdonald, 1996, p. 1). Further, Murphy (2000) points out that wisdom is at home in several levels of the hierarchy of complexity. As she observes, "understanding of a phenomenon at each level of the hierarchy can be enhanced by relating it to its neighboring levels" (Murphy, 2000, p. 7). Schloss explains that the levels of a hierarchy are interrelated via feedback loops; increased understanding results from following these feedback loops from one level to another and back again (Schloss, 2000). Similarly, Erikson says that a sense of the complexity of living is an attribute of wisdom. A wise person embraces the,

> ... *sense of the complexity of living, of relationships, of all negotiations. There is certainly no immediate, discernible, and absolute right and wrong, just as light and dark are separated by innumerable shadings ... [the] interweaving of time and space, light and dark, and the complexity of human nature suggests that ... this wholeness of perception to be given partially and realized, must of necessity be made up of a merging of the sensual, the logical, and the aesthetic perceptions of the individual.* (Erikson, 1988, p. 184)

As can be noted in this brief treatment, the concept of wisdom is clearly related to knowledge—and in particular to tacit knowledge—and has also been related to the phenomenon of consciousness. Wisdom is clearly connected with systemic, hierarchical thinking, and the complexity of human nature has been brought into the discussion. Wisdom appears to deal with the cognitive and emotional, personal and social, as well as the moral and religious aspects of life. As Costa sums up in *Working Wisdom*:

> *Wisdom is the combination of knowledge and experience, but it is more than just the sum of these parts. Wisdom involves the mind and the heart, logic and intuition, left brain and right brain, but it is more than either reason, or creativity, or both. Wisdom involves a sense of balance, an equilibrium derived from a strong, pervasive moral conviction ... the conviction and guidance provided by the obligations that flow from a profound sense of interdependence. In essence, wisdom grows through the learning of more knowledge, and the practiced experience of day-to-day life—both filtered through a code of moral conviction.* (Costa, 1995, p. 3)

From our viewpoint, we believe that wisdom comes from a love for humanity and all life, and a broad perspective of humanity and the long-term future. As introduced earlier, it is the ability to have deep knowledge in one domain (understanding the patterns of relationships and behaviors) and apply it in another domain of knowledge *for the greater good*. Thus, it *builds on* the *data → information → knowledge* continuum but defines a higher level in terms of value.

To quickly lay the groundwork for understanding our usage of consciousness, we provide representative viewpoints from several fields. The psychologist William James said that consciousness was the name of a non-entity in that it stands for the function of knowing (a process) (McDermott, 1977). The psychologist J. Allan Hobson considers consciousness as awareness of the world, the body and the self (Hobson, 1999). In neuroscience terms, this would be the sensitivity to outside stimuli as translated through the brain and neuron connections into patterns that to the mind represent thoughts. The Nobel Laureate physiologist Gerald Edelman considered consciousness as a process of the flow of thoughts, images, feelings and emotions

(Edelman and Tononi 2000). The spiritualist Ramon describes consciousness as the "energized pool of intent from which all human experience springs" (Ramon, 1997, p. 48).

We agree that consciousness is a process, and not a state. It is private, continuous, always-changing and felt to be a sequential set of ideas, thoughts, images, feelings and perceptions (Bennet, 2001). Another high-level property of consciousness is its unity. The mind is continually integrating the incoming signals from the environment as well as connecting many different processing areas within the brain and combining them into a coherent flow of conscious thinking or feeling. When we see a snapshot of the visible world, it almost always appears as a coherent, unified whole.

Ordinary consciousness represents the customary or typical state of consciousness, that which is common to everyday usage, or of the usual kind. Polanyi sees tacit knowledge as not part of one's ordinary consciousness (Polanyi, 1958); thus tacit knowledge resides in the unconscious. Expanding consciousness to purposefully access and apply tacit knowledge moves the decision-maker beyond ordinary consciousness to what we call *extraordinary consciousness*. Extraordinary consciousness is acquiring a greater awareness of and connectivity to information stored in the unconscious in order to facilitate the application of that information and knowledge. The expanded state of extraordinary consciousness may be achieved through such techniques as meditation, lucid dreaming, hemispheric synchronization, and other ways of quieting the conscious mind, and by doing so allowing/encouraging accessibility to information in the unconscious. Such techniques create a heightened sensitivity to, awareness of, and connection with our unconscious mind together with its memory and thought processes.

In our earlier discussion of wisdom, Csikszentmihalyi and Nakamura (1990) described wisdom as referring to two distinct phenomena: the content of wisdom and the capacity to think or act wisely. This parallels our understanding of knowledge as both Kn_I and Kn_P (described above). In other words, wisdom has an information component, W_I, and a process component, W_P. Knowledge and wisdom would then both deal with the *nature and structure of information*, with nature being (or representing) the quality or constitution of information and structure being (or representing) the process of building new information. Wisdom would represent higher discernment and achieving extraordinary consciousness to provide new, situation-dependent, context-sensitive knowledge—perhaps taking the form of intuition, which through pattern recognition can be applied across domains for the greater good. The tacit knowledge driving what is surfaced would be both Knowledge (Informing) and Knowledge (Proceeding), although as noted by Goldberg (2005), primarily Knowledge (Proceeding). On the other hand, consciousness appears to be a flow, with extraordinary consciousness representing increased sensitivity to, awareness of, and connectivity with our unconscious mind, purposefully acting to expand our conscious awareness through engaging tacit knowledge. As a process, consciousness represents a characteristic of the human mind to be *aware* of the nature and structure of information coming from either external or internal sources. *Moving beyond ordinary consciousness to extraordinary consciousness, also a process, increases this awareness to include more fully engaging our tacit knowledge.*

As another point of comparison, wisdom has been repeatedly related to systemic thinking and the recognition of a higher order of interdependence in the hierarchy of life, perhaps even the universe. Similarly, extraordinary consciousness goes beyond ordinary consciousness, increasing sensitivity to, and awareness of, that which is tacit (that which is in the unconscious) whether embodied, affective, intuitive or spiritual. See Section IV on "Engaging Tacit Knowledge." With this larger sensitivity and awareness of that which is tacit would come increased understanding of the interdependence associated with patterns of information, some of which would be patterns of patterns (possibly hierarchical in nature, although they might be represented by any three-dimensional patterns in space).

Figure 16 provides a visual representation of the relationships among knowledge, consciousness and extraordinary consciousness. The dotted lines represent a movement from ordinary consciousness into extraordinary consciousness, at whatever level that may occur. The wavy lines represent the fluctuating boundary between explicit and tacit knowledge, with implicit knowledge describing what was thought tacit but triggered into consciousness by incoming information.

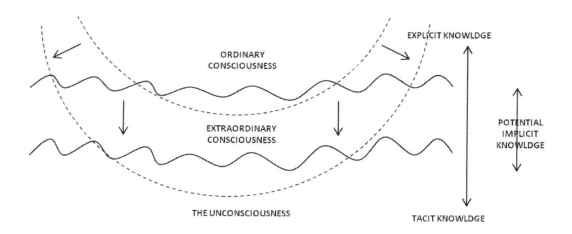

Figure 16: *Conceptual model relating knowledge and consciousness.*

While there is much thinking and experimentation needed to truly understand wisdom, it is increasingly clear that extraordinary consciousness—expanding our sensitivity and awareness of that which is tacit and the ability to apply it—has an important role to play in developing this understanding.

Appendix B
Parable of the Watchmakers

(Paraphrased from Herbert Simon)

There were two watchmakers, Hora and Tempus. They both manufactured very fine watches, were highly regarded, and had phone orders throughout the day. However, Hora prospered while Tempus became poorer and poorer (finally losing his shop). The watches both made had the same level of complexity, about 1,000 parts each. The difference was in their approach to creating the watches. Tempus constructed his watches such that his work fell to pieces every time he had to answer the phone. Hora designed his watches so that he could put together subassemblies of about ten elements each, so that when he had to put down a partly assembled watch to answer the phone, he lost only a small part of his effort. (Simon, 1969)

The implication for biological forms, and organizations as living systems, is that "the time required for the evolution of a complex form from simple elements depends critically on the numbers and distribution of potential intermediate stable forms." This is a hierarchy of potential stable "subassemblies," what Simon says is "nothing more than survival of the fittest—that is, of the stable." (Simon, 1969, p. 93)

References

Ackoff, R. L. (1978). *The Art of Problem Solving: Accompanied by Ackoff's Fables*. New York: John Wiley and Sons.

Ackoff, R. L. (1998). *Ackoff's Best: His Classic Writings on Management*. New York: John Wiley and Sons.

Adolfs, R. (2004). "Processing of emotional and social information by the human amygdala" in Gazzaniga, M.S. (Ed.), *The Cognitive Neurosciences III*. Cambridge: The Bradford Press.

Amann, T. (2003). "Creating space for somatic ways of knowing within transformative learning theory" in Wiessner, C.A., S.R. Meyer, N.L. Pfhal, and P.G. Neaman (Eds.), *Proceedings of the Fifth International Conference on Transformative Learning*. Columbia, MD: Teacher's College, Columbia University, pp. 26-32.

Amen, D.G. (2005). *Making a Good Brain Great*. New York: Harmony Books.

American Heritage Dictionary 4th Ed. (2006). Boston: Houghton Mifflin Co.

Anderson, J.R. (1983). *The Architecture of Cognition*. Cambridge: Harvard University Press.

Anderson, V. and L. Johnson, (1997). *Systems Thinking Basics: From Concepts to Causal Loops*. Cambridge: Pegasus Communications.

Andreason, N. (2005). *The Creating Brain: The Neuroscience of Genius*. New York: The Dana Foundation.

Anonymous. Appeared in numerous emails to authors and is available on dozens of Internet sites. Retrieved April 5, 2009, from http://www.gamedev.net/community/forums/topic.asp?topic_id=375056

Argyris, C. (1971). "Resistance to Rational Management Systems" in *Decision Making in a Changing World*. New York: Auerbach Publishers, pp. 13-26.

Argyris, C. (1990). *Overcoming Organizational Defenses: Facilitating Organizational Learning*. Englewood Cliffs, NJ: Prentice Hall.

Ashby, W. R. (1964). *An Introduction to Cybernetics*. London: Methuen.

Atwater, F.H. (2004), *The Hemi-Sync Process*. Faber, VA: The Monroe Institute.

Auyang, S.Y. (1998). *Foundations of Complex-System Theories in Economics, Evolutionary Biology, and Statistical Physics*. New York: Cambridge University Press.

Avedisian, J. and A. Bennet (2010). "Values as knowledge: A new frame of reference for a new generation of knowledge workers" in *The New Horizon (*July), Vol 18, No. 3, pp. 255-265.

Axelrod, R. and M. Cohen. (1999). *Harnessing Complexity: Organizational Implications of a Scientific Frontier*. New York: The Free Press.

Bak, P. (1996). *How Nature Works: The Science of Self-Organized Criticality*. New York: Capernicus.

Baltes, P.B. and J. Smith (1990). "Toward a psychology of wisdom and its ontogenesis" in Sternberg, R.J. (Ed.), *Wisdom: Its Nature, Origins, and Development*. Cambridge: Cambridge University Press.

Barthes, R. (1985). *In the Responsibility of Forms*. New York: Hill and Wang.

Battram, A. (1996). *Navigating Complexity: The Essential Guide to Complexity Theory in Business and Management*. London: The Industrial Society.

Begley, S. (1996). "Your Child's Brain" in *Newsweek*, 127(8), 19 February, pp. 54-59.

Begley, S. (2007). *Train Your Mind Change Your Brain: How a New Science Reveals our Extraordinary Potential to Transform Ourselves*. New York: Ballantine Books.

Bennet, A. (2005). *Exploring Aspects of Knowledge Management that Contribute to the Passion Expressed by its Thought Leaders*. Self-Published, Frost, WV. Available on www.mountainquestinstitute.com.

Bennet, D. (1997). *IPT Learning Campus*: *Gaining Acquisition Results through IPTs*. Alexandria, VA: Bellwether Learning Center.

Bennet, D. (2001), "Loosening the world knot", unpublished paper available at www.mountainquestinstitute.com.

Bennet, D. (2006). "Expanding the knowledge paradigm", in *VINE: The Journal of Information and Knowledge Management Systems*, Vol. 36, No. 2, pp. 175-181.

Bennet, D. (2009). *Exploring Recent Findings in Neuroscience that Can Enhance Adult Learning*. Self-Published, Frost, WV. Available at www.mountainquestinstitute.com.

Bennet, D. and A. Bennet (1996). Private Communication at MIT.

Bennet, A. and D. Bennet. (2003). "The partnership between organizational learning and knowledge management" in Holsapple, C. W. (ed.) *Handbook on Knowledge Management 1: Knowledge Matters*. Heidelberg, Germany: Springer Verlag, pp. 439-460.

Bennet, A. and D. Bennet (2004). *Organizational Survival in the New World: The Intelligent Complex Adaptive System*. New York: Elsevier.

Bennet, D. and A. Bennet (2005). "Facing and Embracing The New Reality", workshop and research framework for sustainability factors as part of the Senior Executive Service Forum Series held at the International Trade Center in Washington, D.C., unpublished.

Bennet, A. and D. Bennet (2006). "Learning as associative patterning" in *VINE: The Journal of Information and Knowledge Management Systems*, Vol. 36, No. 4, pp. 371-376.

Bennet, A. and D. Bennet (2007a). *Knowledge Mobilization in the Social Sciences and Humanities: Moving from Research to Action*. Frost, WV: MQIPress.

Bennet, A. and D. Bennet (2007b). "The knowledge and knowing of spiritual learning", in *VINE*, Vol. 37, No. 2, pp. 150-168.

Bennet, A. and D. Bennet (2007c). "CONTEXT: The shared knowledge enigma", in *VINE*, Vol. 37, No. 1, pp. 27-40.

Bennet, A. and D. Bennet (2008a). "The decision-making process for complex situations in a complex environment" in Burstein, F. and C.W. Holsapple (Eds.), *Handbook on decision support systems*. New York: Springer-Verlag, pp. 3-20.

Bennet, A. and D. Bennet (2008b). "A new change model: Factors for initiating and implementing personal action learning" in *VINE: The Journal of Information and Knowledge Management Systems*, Vol. 38, No. 4 (December), pp. 378-387.

Bennet, A. and D. Bennet (2008c). "Moving from knowledge to wisdom, from ordinary consciousness to extraordinary consciousness" in *VINE: The Journal of Information and Knowledge Management Systems,* Vol. 38, No. 1, pp. 7-15.

Bennet, D. and A. Bennet (2008d). "The depth of KNOWLEDGE: Surface, shallow and deep in *VINE*: *The Journal of Information and Knowledge Management Systems*, Vol. 38, No. 4 (December), pp. 405-420.

Bennet, D. and A. Bennet (2008e). "Engaging tacit knowledge in support of organizational learning" in *VINE: The Journal of Information and Knowledge Management Systems*, Vol. 38, No. 1, pp. 72-94.

Bennet, A. and D. Bennet (2008f). "Moving from knowledge to wisdom, from ordinary consciousness to extraordinary consciousness" in *VINE: The Journal of Information and Knowledge Management Systems,* Vol. 38, No. 1, pp. 7-15.

Bennet, A. and D. Bennet (2008g). "The human knowledge system: Music and brain coherence" in *VINE: The Journal of Information and Knowledge Management Systems,* Vol. 38, No. 3, pp. 277-295.

Bennet, D. and A. Bennet (2009), "Associative patterning: The unconscious life of an organization" in Girard, J.P. (Ed.), *Building organizational memories.* Hershey, PA: IGI Global, pp. 201-224.

Bennet, A. and D. Bennet (2010). "MULTIDIMENSIONALITY: Building the infrastructure for the next generation knowledge worker" in *On the Horizon*, Vol. 18, No. 3, pp. 249-254.

Bennett-Woods, D. (1997). "Reflections on wisdom", unpublished paper, University of Northern Colorado.

Birren, J.E. and Fisher, L.M. (1990). "The elements of wisdom: Overview and integration", in Sternberg, R.J. (Ed.), *Wisdom: Its Nature, Origins, and Development.* Cambridge: Cambridge University Press.

Blackmore, S. (1999). *The Meme Machine*. Oxford: Oxford University Press.

Bohm, D. (1992). *Thought as a System*. New York: Routledge.

Brown, W.S. (2000). "Wisdom and human neurocognitive systems: Perceiving and practicing the laws of life", in Brown, W.S. (Ed.), *Understanding Wisdom: Sources, Science and Society*. Philadelphia: Templeton Foundation Press.

Buchanan, M. (2001). *Ubiquity, the Science of History or Why the World is Simpler than We Think*, London: Phoenix.

Buchanan, M. (2004). "Power laws and the new science of complexity management" in *Strategy + Business*, Issue 34, Spring 2004, Canada, pp. 70-79.

Bullard, B. and A. Bennet (2013). *REMEMBRANCE: Pathways to Expanded Learning with Music and Metamusic®*, Frost, WV: MQI Press.

Burke, M. (2004). "Generational Differences Survey Report" in *Society for Human Resource Management*, August.

Byrnes, J.P. (2001). *Minds, Brains, and Learning: Understanding the Psychological and Education Relevance of Neuroscientific Research*. New York: The Guilford Press.

Callender, C. and N. Huggett (2001). *Physics Meets Philosophy at the Planck Scale: Contemporary Theories in Quantum Gravity*. Cambridge, UK: Cambridge University Press.

Capra, F. (1996). *The Web of Life: A New Scientific Understanding of Living Systems*. New York: Anchor Books, Doubleday.

Carey, K. (1996). *The Third Millennium: Living in the Posthistoric World*. New York: HarperCollins Publishers.

Chandler, M.J. and S. Holliday (1990). "Wisdom in a postapocalyptic age" in Sternberg, R.J. (Ed.), *Wisdom: Its Nature, Origins, and Development*. Cambridge: Cambridge University Press.

Checkland, P. and S. Holwell. (1998). *Information, Systems and Information Systems: Making Sense of the Field*. New York: John Wiley and Sons.

Chickering, A.W. (1977), *Experience and Learning: An Introduction to Experiential Learning*. New Rochelle, NY: Asme Press.

Chickering, A. W., Dalton, J. C., and Stamm, L. (2005). *Encouraging authenticity and spirituality in higher education*. San Francisco: Jossey-Bass.

Choi, Y.S., H.M. Gray and N. Ambady (2004). "The glimpsed world: Unintended communication and unintended perception" in Hassin, R.R., J.S. Uleman and J.A. Bargh (Eds.), *The New Unconscious*. New York: Oxford University Press, pp. 309-33.

Christos, G. (2003). *Memory and Dreams: The Creative Human Mind*. New Brunswick, NY: Rutgers University Press.

Church, D. (2006). *The Genie in Your Genes: Epigenetic Medicine and the New Biology of Intention*. Santa Rosa, CA: Elite Books.

Churchland, P. S. (2002). *Brain-Wise: Studies in Neurophilosophy*. Cambridge: The MIT Press.

Clausing, D. (1994). *Total Quality Development: A Step-By-Step Guide to World-Class Concurrent Engineering*. New York: Asme Press.

Clavell, J. (ed.) (1983). *The Art of War: Sun Tzu*. New York: Dell Publishing.

Clayton, V. and J.E. Birren. (1980). "The development of wisdom across the lifespan: a reexamination of an ancient topic" in Baltes, P.B. and Brim, O.G.J. (Eds), *Life Spa Development and Behavior*. Burlington, MA: Academic Press (Elsevier), pp. 104-135.

Costa, J.D. (1995). *Working Wisdom: The Ultimate Value in the New Economy*. Toronto: Stoddart.

Cozolino L. (2002). *The Neuroscience of Psychotherapy: Building and Rebuilding the Human Brain*. New York: Norton.

Cozolino, L. and S. Sprokay (2006). "Neuroscience and adult learning" in Johnson, S. and Taylor, T. (Eds.), *The Neuroscience of Adult Learning*. San Francisco: Jossey-Bass.

Csikszentmihalyi, M. (1990). *Flow: The Psychology of Optimal Experience*. New York: Harper and Row.

Csikszentmihalyi, M. (2003). *Good Business: Leadership, Flow, and the Making of Meaning*. New York: The Penguin Group.

Csikszentmihalyi, M. and K. Rathunde (1990). "The psychology of wisdom: An evolutionary interpretation", in Sternberg, R.J. (Ed.), *Wisdom: Its Nature, Origins, and Development*. Cambridge: Cambridge University Press.

Csikszentmihalyi, M. and J. Nakamura (2005). "The role of emotions in the development of wisdom", in Sternberg, R.J. and Jordan, J., A Handbook of Wisdom: Psychological Perspectives. New York: Cambridge University Press.

Damasio, A. (2007). "How the brain creates the mind" in Bloom, F.E. (Ed.), *Best of the Brain from Scientific American: Mind, Matter, and Tomorrow's Brain*. New York, NY: Dana Press, pp. 58-67.

Damasio, A. R. (1994), *Descartes' Error: Emotion, Reason, and the Human Brain*. New York: G.P. Putman's Sons.

Damon, W. (2000). "Setting the stage for the development of wisdom: Self-understanding and moral identity during adolescence" in Brown, W.S. (Ed.), *Understanding Wisdom: Sources, Science and Society*. Philadelphia: Templeton Foundation Press.

Davis, S. and C. Meyer. (1998). *Blur: The Speed of Change in the Connected Economy*. Reading, MA: Addison-Wesley.

De Furia (1997). Interpersonal Trust Survey, Hoboken, NJ: Pfeiffer Pubishers (Wiley).

Delmonte, M.M. (1984). "Electrocortical activity and related phenomena associated with meditation practice: A literature review", in *International Journal of Neuroscience*, 24, pp. 217-231.

Dittmann-Kohli, F. and P.B. Baltes (1990). Toward a neofunctionalist conception of adult intellectual development: wisdom as a prototypical case of intellectual growth", in Alexander, C. and Langer, E. (Eds.), *Beyond Formal Operations: Alternative Endpoints to Human Development*. New York: Oxford University Press.

Dobbs, D. (2007). "Turning off depression", in Bloom, F.E. (Ed.), *Best of the Brain from Scientific American: Mind, Matter and Tomorrow's Brain*, New York: Dana Press.

Dvir, R. (2006). "Knowledge city, seen as a collage of human knowledge moments" in Carrillo, F.J. (Ed.), *Knowledge Cities: Approaches, Experiences, and Perspectives*. Oxford: Butterworth Heinemann Elsevier.

Edelman, G. and G. Tononi. (2000). *A Universe of Consciousness: How Matter Becomes Imagination*. New York: Basic Books.

Edwards, W. (1971). "Don't waste an executive's time on decision making" in *Decision Making in a Changing World*. New York: Auerbach Publishers, pp. 63-78.

Eich, E., Kihlstrom, J. F., Bower, G. H., Forgas, J. P., and Niedenthal, P. M. (2000). *Cognition and Emotion*. New York: Oxford University Press.

Ellinor, L. and Gerard, G. (1998). *Creating and Sustaining Collaborative Partnerships at Work*. Dialogue: Rediscover the Transforming Power of Conversation. New York: John Wiley and Sons.

Elmore, T. (2010). *More predictions for Generation iY in the workplace*. Retrieved September 2013 from: www.savetheirfutuenow.com/predictions

Ericsson, K.A., Charness, N., Feltovich, P.J. and Hoffman, R.R. (Eds.) (2006). *The Cambridge Handbook of Expertise and Expert Performance*. New York: Cambridge University Press.

Erikson, J.M. (1988). *Wisdom and the Senses: The Way of Creativity*. New York: Norton.

Espejo R., W. Schuhmann, M. Schwaninger, and U. Bilello (1996). *Organizational Transformation and Learning: A Cybernetic Approach to Management*. New York: John Wiley and Sons.

Espinoza, C., C. Rusch and M. Ukleja (2010). *Managing the Millennials: Discover the Core Competencies for Managing Today's Workforce*. Hoboken, NJ: Wiley and Sons.

Fischer, R. (1971). "A cartography of ecstatic and meditative states", *Science*, 174 (4012), pp. 897-904.

Forrester, J. W. (1961). *Industrial Dynamics*. Portland, OR: Productivity Press.

Gardner, J. N. (2003). *Biocosm: The New Scientific Theory of Evolution: Intelligent Life is the Architect of the Universe*. Maui, HI: Inner Ocean Publishing, Inc.

Gazzaniga, M.S. (Ed.) (2004). *The Cognitive Neurosciences III*. Cambridge: The MIT Press.

Gell-Mann, M. (1995). *The Quark and the Jaguar: Adventures in the Simple and the Complex*. New York: Abacus.

Gladwell, M. (2000). *The Tipping Point: How Little Things Can Make a Big Difference*. Boston: Little, Brown and Company.

Goldberg, E. (2005). *The Wisdom Paradox: How Your Mind Can Grow Stronger as Your Brain Grows Older*. New York, NY.

Goleman, G.M. (1988). *Meditative Mind: The Varieties of Meditative Experience*. New York: G.P. Putnam.

Goleman, D. (1995). *Emotional Intelligence*. New York: Bantam Books.

Goleman, D. (1998). *Working with Emotional Intelligence*. New York: Bantam Books.

Grimm, R., N. Dietz, J. Foster-Bey, D. Reingold and R. Nesbit (2006). "Volunteer Growth in America: A Review of Trends Since 1974", Research Report, Corporation for National and Community Service, December 2006.

Haberlandt, K. (1998). *Human memory: Exploration and application.* Boston: Allyn and Bacon.

Hadar, G. (2009). "Reaching across Generational Lines" in *ei: Managing the Enterprise Information Network*.

Hannon, B. and M. Ruth. (1997). *Modeling Dynamic Biological Systems*. New York: Springer-Verlag.

Harrison, E. (2003). *Masks of the Universe: Changing Ideas on the Nature of the Cosmos*. Cambridge, UK: University Press.

Hawkins, J. (2004), *ON Intelligence: How a New Understanding of the Brain will Lead to the Creation of Truly Intelligent Machines*. New York: Henry Hold and Company.

Heckscher, C. (2007). *The Collaborative Enterprise*. New Haven, CT: Yale University Press.

Hobson, J.A. (1999). *Consciousness*. New York: Scientific American Library.

Hodgkin, R. (1991), "Michael Polanyi—Profit of life, the universe, and everything", *Times Higher Educational Supplement*, September 27, p. 15.

Holland, J. H. (1998). *Emergence: From Chaos to Order.* Reading, MA: Addison-Wesley Publishing Company.

Holliday, S.G. and M.J. Chandler (1986). *Wisdom: Explorations in Adult Competence: Contributions to Human Development*. Vol. 17, Karger, Basel.

Jarvis, P. (1992). *Paradoxes of Learning: On Becoming an Individual in Society*, San Francisco: Jossey-Bass.

Jevning, R., Wallace, R.K. and Beidenbach, M. (1992), "The physiology of meditation: A review", *Neuroscience and Behavioral Reviews*, 16, pp. 415-424.

Johns, K. (2003). *Managing generational diversity in the workforce*. Trends and Tidbits. Retrieved September 2013 from www.workindex.com

Johnson, S. (2001). *Emergence: The Connected Lives of Ants, Brains, Cities, and Software*. New York: Scribner.

Johnson, S. (2006). The neuroscience of the mentor-learner relationship. In S. Johnson and K. Taylor (Eds.), *The Neuroscience of Adult Learning*: *New Directions for Adult and Continuing Education*. San Francisco, CA: Jossey-Bass.

Kahneman, D., P. Slovic and A. Tversky (1982). *Judgment Under Uncertainty: Heuristics and Biases*. New York: Cambridge University Press.

Kandel, E.R. (2006a). *In Search of Memory: The Emergence of a New Science of Mind*. New York: W.W. Norton and Company.

Kandel, E.R. (2006b). *The Neuroscience of Adult Learning: New Directions for Adult and Continuing Education*. San Francisco, CA: Jossey-Bass.

Kauffman, S. (1995). *At Home in the Universe: The Search for the Laws of Self-Organization and Complexity*. New York: Oxford University Press.

Kelly, K. (1994). *Out of Control: The Rise of Neo-Biological Civilization*. New York: Addison-Wesley Publishing Company.

Kelly, S. and M. A. Allison (1999). *The Complexity Advantage: How the Science of Complexity Can Help Your Business Achieve Peak Performance*. New York: McGraw-Hill.

Kelzer, K. (1987). *The Sun and the Shadow: My Experiment with Lucid Dreaming*. Virginia Beach, VA: ARE Press.

Kim, D. H. (1995). *Systems Thinking Tools: A User's Reference Guide*. Cambridge, MA: Pegasus.

Kirsner, K., Speelman, C., Maybery, M., O'Brien-Malone, A., Anderson, M. and MacLeod, C. (Eds.). (1998), *Implicit and Explicit Mental Processes*, Mahwah, NJ: Lawrence Erlbaum Associates, Publishers.

Klein, G. (2003). *Intuition at Work: Why Developing Your Gut Instincts Will Make You Better at What You Do*. New York: Doubleday.

Koestler, A. and J.R. Smythies (1969). Beyond Reductionism: New Perspectives in the Life Sciences. Proceedings of the Alpbach Symposium, Conference Publication.

Kolb, D.A. (1984), *Experiential Learning: Experience as the Source of Learning and Development*. Englewood Cliffs, NJ: Prentice Hall.

Kramer, D.A. and W.T. Bacelar (1994). "The educated adult in today's world: Wisdom and the mature learner", in Sinnott, J.D. (Ed.), *Interdisciplinary Handbook of Adult Lifespan Learning*. Westport, Conn: Greenwood Press.

Kuntz, P.G. (1968). *The Concept of Order*. Seattle, WA: University of Washington Press.

Laszlo, E. (1999). *The Systems View of the World: A Holistic Vision for Our Time*. Cresskill, NJ: Hampton Press, Inc.

Laszlo, E. (1983). Systems Science and World Order: Selected Studies. Oxford: Pergamon Press.

Laszlo, E. and D. Keys, Eds. (1981). *Disarmament: the Human Factor*, Proceedings of a Colloquium on the Societal context for Disarmament, sponsored by Unitar and Planetary Citizens and Ervin Laszlo and Donald Keys. Oxford: Pergamon Press.

Laszlo, E. (Ed.). (1973). *The World System: Models, Norms, Variations*. New York: George Braziller.

Leslie, J. (Ed.) (1998). *Modern Cosmology and Philosophy*. Amherst, NY: Prometheus Books.

Levitt, H.M. (1999). "The development of wisdom: An analysis of Tibetan Buddhist experience", in *Journal of Humanistic Psychology*, 39(2), pp. 86-105.

Leyden, P., R. Teixeria and E. Greenberg (2007). "The Progressive Politics of the Millennial Generation", Generational Study, New politics Institute, June 20, 2007, www.newpolitics.net (accessed April 26, 2010).

Luhmann, N. (1995). *Social Systems*. Stanford, CA: Stanford University Press.

Macdonald, C. (1996). *Toward Wisdom: Finding Our Way to Inner Peace, Love, and Happiness*. Charlottesville, VA: Hampton Roads.

Mannheim, K. (1980). *Structure of Thinking*. London: Routledge and Kegan Paul.

Marchese, T.J. (1998). "The new conversations about learning: Insights from neuroscience and anthropology, Cognitive Science and Workplace Studies" in *New Horizons for Learning*. Retrieved January 19, 2008, from www.newhorizons.org/lifelong/higher_ed/marchese.htm

Marton F. and Booth, S. (1997). *Learning and Awareness*. Mahwah, NJ: Erlbaum.

Matthews, R.C. (1991). "The forgetting algorithm: How fragmentary knowledge of exemplars can yield abstract knowledge" in *Journal of Experimental Psychology: General*, 120, pp. 117-119.

Maturana, H. R. and Varela, F. J. (1987). *The Tree of Knowledge: The Biological Roots of Human Understanding*. Boston: New Science Library, Shambhala.

Mavromatis, A. (1991), *Hypnagogia*. New York: Routledge.

McDermott, J.J. (1977). *The Writings of William James*. Chicago, IL: University of Chicago Press.

McMaster, M. D. (1996). *The Intelligent Advantage: Organizing for Complexity*. Newton, MA: Butterworth-Henemann.

Meacham, J.A. (1990). "The loss of wisdom", in Sternberg, R.J. (Ed.), *Wisdom: Its Nature, Origins, and Development*. Cambridge: Cambridge University Press.

Merriam, S. B., Caffarella, R.S. and Baumgartner, L. M. (2007). *Learning in Adulthood: A Comprehensive Guide*. San Francisco, CA: John Wiley and Sons, Inc.

Merriam, S.B., Caffarella, R.S. and Baumgartner, L.M. (2006). *Learning in Adulthood: A Comprehensive Guide*. San Francisco, CA: John Wiley and Sons, Inc.

Merriam, S.B. and R.S. Caffarella, R.S. (1999). *Learning in Adulthood: A Comprehensive Guide* (2nd Ed.). San Francisco, CA: Jossey-Bass.

Meyer, C. and S. Davis. (2003). *It's Alive: The Coming Convergence of Information, Biology, and Business*. New York: Crown Business.

Mezirow, J. (1991). *Transformative Dimensions of Adult Learning*, San Francisco, CA: Jossey-Bass.

Miller, J. G. (1978). *Living Systems*. New York: McGraw-Hill.

Moon, J.A. (2004). *A Handbook of Reflective and Experiential Learning: Theory and Practice*. New York: Routledge-Falmer.

Morecroft, J. D. W. and J. D. Sterman (Eds) (1994). *Modeling for Learning Organizations*. Portland, OR: Productivity Press.

Morowitz, H. J. (2002). *The Emergence of Everything: How The World Became Complex*. New York: Oxford University Press.

Morrison, F. (1991). *The Art of Modeling Dynamic Systems*: *Forecasting for Chaos, Randomness, and Determinism*. New York: John Wiley and Sons. Inc.

Mulvihill, M.K. (2003). "The Catholic Church in crisis: Will transformative learning lead to social change through the uncovering of emotion?" in Weissner, C.A., S.R. Meyers, N.L. Pfhal, and P.J. Neaman (Eds.), *Proceedings of the 5th International Conference on Transformative Learning*. New York: Teachers College, Columbia University, pp. 320-325.

Murphy, N. (2000). "Introduction: A hierarchical framework for understanding wisdom" in Brown, W.S. (Ed.), *Understanding Wisdom: Sources, Science and Society*. Philadelphia, PA: Templeton Foundation Press.

Myers, N. (1984). *GAIA: An Atlas of Planet Management*. Garden City, NY: Anchor.

National Research Council (2000). *How People Learn*: *Brain, Mind, Experience, and School*. Washington, D.C.: National Academy Press.

Nelson, A. (2004). "Sophia: Transformation of human consciousness to wisdom", unpublished paper, Fielding Graduate University, Santa Barbara, CA.

Nelson, C.A., M. de Haan and K.M. Thomas (2006), *Neuroscience of Cognitive Development: The Role of Experience and the Developing Brain*. Hoboken, NJ: John Wiley and Sons.

Nonaka, I. and H. Takeuchi (1995). *The Knowledge-Creating Company: How Japanese Companies Create the Dynamics of Innovation*. New York: Oxford University Press.

Nouwen, H.J.M. (1975). *Reaching Out: The Three Movements of the Spiritual Life*. New York: Doubleday.

Nussbaum, S.W. (2000). "Profundity with panache: the unappreciated proverbial wisdom of sub-Saharan Africa", in Brown, W.S. (Ed.), *Understanding Wisdom: Sources, Science and Society*. Philadelphia, PA: Templeton Foundation Press.

O'Connor, J. and I. McDermott. (1997). *The Art of Systems Thinking*. San Francisco, CA: HarperCollins Publishers.

Oakes, J. and Lipton, M. (1999). *Teaching to Change the World*. Boston, MA: McGraw-Hill College.

Omnes, R. (2001). *Quantum Philosophy: Understanding and Interpreting Contemporary Science*. Princeton, NJ: Princeton University Press.

Orwell, L. and M. Perlmutter (1990). "The study of a wise person: Integrating a personality perspective" in Sternberg, R.J. (Ed.), *Wisdom: Its Nature, Origins and Development*. Cambridge: Cambridge University Press.

Panetta, S. (2013). "How to Lead the Millennial Generation in the Workforce", Thesis Report, City University of Seattle.

Pattee, H. H. (1973). *Hierarchy Theory: The Challenge of Complex Systems*. New York: George Braziller.

Pert, C.B. (1997). *Molecules of Emotion: A Science behind Mind-Body Medicine*. New York: Touchstone.

Pinker, S. (2007). *The Stuff of Thought: Language as a Window into Human Nature*. New York: Viking Press.

Polanyi, M. (1958). *Personal Knowledge: Towards a Post-Critical Philosophy*. Chicago, IL: The University of Chicago.

Polanyi, M. (1967). *The Tacit Dimension*. New York: Anchor Books.

Porter, D., Bennet, A., Turner, R. and Wennergren, D. (2003). *The Power of Team: The Making of a CIO*. Alexandria, VA: Department of the Navy.

Potts, Paul (2007). *Paul Potts One Chance* music CD. Paul Potts was the winner of the *Britain's Got Talent* competition. SYCOmusic.

Ramon, S. (1997). *Earthly Cycles. How Past Lives and Soul Patterns Shape Your Life*. Ojai, CA: Pepperwood Press.

Ratey, J.J. (2001). *A User's Guide to the Brain: Perceptions, Attention, and the Four Theaters of the Brain*. New York: Pantheon Books.

Reber, A.S. (1993). *Implicit Learning and Tacit Knowledge: An Essay on the Cognitive Unconscious*. New York: Oxford University Press.

Reber, A.S. (1993). *Implicit Learning and Tacit Knowledge: An Essay on the Cognitive Unconscious*. New York: Oxford University Press.

Ricard, M. and T. X. Thuan. (2001). *The Quantum and the Lotus: A Journey to the Frontiers where Science and Buddhism Meet*. New York: Crown Publishers.

Ritchey, D. (2003). *The H.I.S.S. of the A.S.P.: Understanding the Anomalously Sensitive Person*. Terra Alta, WV: Headline Books, Inc.

Rifkin, J. (2009). *The Empathic Civilization: The Race to Global Consciousness in a World in Crisis*. New York: Penguin Group.

Rock, A. (2004). *The Mind at Night: The New Science of How and Why We Dream*. New York: Basic Books.

Ross, J. (2000). "Art education in the information age: A new place for somatic wisdom" in *Arts Education Policy Review*, 101(6), pp. 27-32.

Ross, P.E. (2006). "The expert mind" in *Scientific American*, August, pp. 64-71.

Russell, P. (2007). *What is Wisdom?*, downloaded 1/14/2008 from www.peterrussell.com/SP/Wisdom.php

Ryle, G. (1949). *The Concept of Mind*. London: Hutchinson, London.

Saaty, T. L. (1988). *Decision Making for Leaders: The Analytical Hierarchy Process for Decisions in a Complex World*. Belmont, CA: Wadsworth Publishing Co.

Sashkin, M. (1990). *Tough Choices: The Managerial Decision-Making Assessment Inventory*. King of Prussia, PA: Organization Design and Development, Inc.

Schloss, J.P. (2000). "Wisdom traditions as mechanisms for organismal integration: Evolutionary perspectives on homeostatic 'laws of life'," in Brown, W.S. (Ed.), *Understanding Wisdom: Sources, Science and Society*. Philadelphia, PA: Templeton Foundation Press.

Schon, D. A. (1983). *The Reflective Practitioner: How Professionals Think in Action*. New York: Basic Books.

Schore, A. N. (1994). *Affect regulation and the origin of the self: The neurobiology of emotional development*. Hillsdale, NJ: Erlbaum.

Senge, P. M. (1990). *The Fifth Discipline: The Art and Practice of the Learning Organization*. New York: Currency/Doubleday.

Shedlock, D.J. and S.W. Cornelius (2000). "Wisdom: perceptions and performance", paper presented at the Cognitive Aging Conference, Atlanta, GA.

Sherman, N. (2000). "Wise emotions" in Brown, W.S. (Ed.), *Understanding Wisdom: Sources, Science and Society*. Philadelphia, PA: Templeton Foundation Press.

Shorter Oxford English Dictionary (5th Ed.) (2002), Oxford: Oxford University Press.

Simon, H. A. (1969). *The Sciences of the Artificial*. Cambridge, MA: The MIT Press.

Skoyles, J.R. and Sagan, D. (2002). *Up From Dragons: The Evolution of Human Intelligence*. New York: McGraw-Hill.

Smith, B. (2013). Personal conversation with Dr. Boyd Smith, Principal Faculty, School of Management, City University of Seattle. Also, founder of www.Everyoneslifestory.com

Smith, J., Dixon, R.A. and Baltes, P.B. (1987). Age differences in response to life planning problems: A research analog for the study of wisdom, related knowledge, unpublished manuscript.

Smith, M.K. (2003). "Michael Polanyi and tacit knowledge" in *The Encyclopedia of Informal Education*, p. 2, www.infed.org/thinkers/Polanyi.htm

Smolan, R. and J. Erwitt (2013). *The Human Face of Big Data*. Winsted, CT: Against All Odds Productions.

Smolin, L. (1997). *The Life of the Cosmos*. London: Oxford University Press.

Sousa, D. A. (2006). *How the Brain Learns*. Thousand Oaks, CA: Corwin Press.

Stacey, R. D. (1992). *Managing the Unknowable: Strategic Boundaries Between Order and Chaos in Organizations*. San Francisco: Jossey-Bass, Inc.

Stacey, R. D. (1996). *Complexity and Creativity in Organizations*. San Francisco: Berrett-Hoehler Publishers.

Stacey, R. D., D. Griffin and P. Shaw. (2000). *Complexity and Management: Fad or Radical Challenge to Systems Thinking?* New York: Routledge.

Sterman, J. D. (1994). "Learning in and about complex systems" in *System Dynamics Review*, Vol. 10, nos. 2-3 (Summer-Fall), pp. 291-330.

Sternberg, R.J. (2003). *Wisdom, Intelligence, and Creativity Synthesized.* Cambridge, MA: Cambridge University Press.

Stevens, K. (2000). "Wisdom as an organizational construct: Reality or rhetoric?", unpublished dissertation, Fielding Institute, Santa Barbara, CA.

Stonier, T. (1990). *Information and the Internal Structure of the Universe: An Introduction into Information Physics.* New York: Springer-Verlag.

Stonier, T. (1992). *Beyond information: The natural history of intelligence.* London: Springer-Verlag.

Stonier, T. (1997). *Information and Meaning: An Evolutionary Perspective.* London: Springer-Verlag.

Sutherland, J. W. (1975). *Systems Analysis, Administration, and Architecture.* New York: Van Nostrand Reinhold Company.

Tallis, F. (2002). *Hidden Minds: A History of the Unconscious.* New York: Arcade Publishing.

Tapscott, D. (2010), *Grown Up Digital.* New York: McGraw Hill.

Tiller, W. (2007). *Psychoenergetic Science: A Second Copernican-Scale Revolution.* Walnut Creek, CA: Pavior.

Trumpa, C. (1991). *The Heart of the Buddha.* Boston, MA: Shambhala.

Van Gigch, J.P. (1978). *Applied General Systems Theory.* New York: Harper and Row, Publishers.

Vennix, J. A. M. (1996). *Group Model Building: Facilitating Team Learning Using System Dynamics.* New York: John Wiley and Sons.

Volk, T. (1998). *Gaia's Body: Toward a Physiology of Earth.* New York: Springer-Verlag.

von Bertalanffy, L. and A Rapoport (Eds.) (1964). *General Systems: Yearbook of the Society for General Systems Research*, VOL IX, The Society for General Systems Research, Bedford, MA.

von Bertalanffy, L. (1968). *General Systems Theory: Foundations, Development, Applications.* New York: George Braziller.

von Bertalanffy, L. (1981). *A Systems View of Man.* Boulder, CO: Westview Press.

von Krogh, G. and J. Roos (1995). "Managing Knowledge: Perspectives on Cooperation and Competition" in von Krogh, G. and J. Roos, *Organizational Epistemology.* London: MacMillan Press LTD.

Weick, K.E. (1995). *Sensemaking in Organizations.* Thousand Oaks, CA: Sage Publications.

Weinberg, G. M. (1975). *An Introduction to General Systems Thinking.* New York: John Wiley and Sons.

Wenger, E. (1998). *Communities of Practice: Learning, Meaning, and Identity.* Cambridge: Cambridge University Press.

Wenger, E. (2009). "Communities of practice and social learning systems: The career of a concept" in Blackmore, C. (Ed.) *Social Learning Systems and Communities of Practice.* Springer Verlag and the Open University.

West, M.A. (1980). "Meditation and the EEG", *Psychological Medicine*, 10, pp. 369-375.

Wheatley, M. J. (1994). *Leadership and the New Science: Learning about Organization from an Orderly Universe.* San Francisco: Berrett-Koehler Publishers.

White, R.W. (1959). "Motivation reconsidered: The concept of competence" in *Psychological Review*, Vol. 66, pp. 297-333.

Woodman, M. and E. Dickson (1996). *Dancing in the Flames: The Dark Goddess in the Transformation of Consciousness.* Boston: Shambhala.

Wycoff, J. (1991). *Mindmapping: Your Personal Guide to Exploring Creativity and Problem-Solving.* New York: The Berkley Publishing Group.

Zohar, D. and Marshall, I. (2000). *Connecting with Our Spiritual Intelligence.* Harrisonburg, VA: R.R. Donnelley and Sons Company.

Subject Index

associative patterning vii, 80, 81, 117
big data 13, 45, 145
change 12-17, 24, 31, 67
   actions 18
   (see knowing: agent of change)
   awareness 16
   belief 17
   empowerment 18
   feelings 18
   nurturing 75
   ownership 18
   patterns of 20, 60
   personal model 16-18
   (see self as an agent of change)
   understanding 17
complex adaptive mess (CAM) ix, 41,
   43-46, 49, 51, 53-54, 58-59,
   61-62, 65-72, 80
   examples of 42
complex adaptive organization ix,
   23-24, 26, 55, 69, 73-78
   intelligent 18
   steps for dealing with 73-78
complex adaptive systems vi, 17, 22,
   23-24, 32, 42, 63-65, 67, 68, 73,
   75, 77-78, 147
   behaviors of 44-46
   butterfly effect 45-46, 52, 65, 146
   correlations 45, 65
   description of vi-vii
   emergence 15, 45, 46, 52, 54, 61,
   110, 139, 146, 150
   feedback loops 12, 14, 19, 22,
   25, 30, 42-47, 51, 62, 64, 66,
   69, 75, 81, 86-88, 114, 117, 146,
   151
   human factor 55-58
   influencing 67-70
   mechanisms for influencing 51-55
     absorption 51, 65
     amplification 51-52, 65, 109

     boundary management 50, 51, 52,
     65, 145
     ontology 43, 51, 52
     optimum complexity 51, 52
     seeding 46, 50, 51, 53, 65, 145
     sense and respond 50, 51-52, 53,
     61
     simplification 13, 52, 54, 59, 77,
     82
     structural adaptation 52, 55
     trial and error 52, 55, 95
   nonlinearities 23, 27, 45, 47, 52,
   65, 67
   power laws 45, 47, 52, 65, 69-70
   process, sample 70
   solution team 71
   survival of 30
   time delays 13, 20, 43, 45, 47, 65,
   67
   tipping point 45, 47, 48, 52, 65,
   146
   unpredictability vii, 22, 33, 44, 47,
   51, 64, 66, 74
complexity 13-14
   (see complex adaptive systems)
   actions, of 59-63
     decide and act 60-61
     guiding principles 61-63
   decisions, of 48-58
   situations, of 41-47
     problem setting 43-44
     simple to complex 41-42
   systems in terms of 21-24
consciousness 152-154
   extraordinary ix, 103-110, 114,
   147, 153-154
     models 104, 154
   ordinary 91, 103, 114, 153-154
context 26, 28, 34, 36, 37, 56, 57, 73,
   88, 96, 106, 117, 120, 122, 125,
   126, 127, 139, 141, 142, 150

content 33, 82
    definition 32-33
    "king", is 72
    sensitivity vi, viii, 56, 57, 61, 69,
        73, 86, 95, 110, 133-134, 145,
        148, 149, 152
creativity v, 14, 23, 28, 62, 113, 126,
        128, 142, 151
    definition 137
    knowledge, as 15, 32, 36, 37
    value, as 134, 138-139
CUCA vii, 11-17, 18, 59, 90, 114,
        137-138, 142
decision-making
    barriers to 55-57
    cone of acceptable outcome model
        33
    complex adaptive systems, in
        (see complex adaptive systems)
    context, in vii
        (see context)
    expected outcome 32-34, 81-82
    group decision-making 57-58
    human factors 54-57
    information
        strategy 40, 64-67
        model 64
    preparation for 65-66
    tacit knowledge, and 110-113
idea resonance 140-143
    models 140, 141
knowing 114, 115-132
    cognitive capabilities 119-123
        integrating 123
        noticing 120-121
        listening 119-120
        patterning 122-123
        scanning 121
        sensing 121-122
    cognitive processes 124-127
        choosing 125-126
        intuiting 124
        setting intent 126-127
        valuing 126
        visualizing 124

critical areas of 117-118
    model 117
    principles of 118-119
    self as agent of change 127-132
        external elements 130-132
        internal elements 128-130
knowledge
    context sensitivity vii
        (see context)
    definition vi, 33
    era of 15-16
    explicit 48, 91-94, 95, 97, 100,
        102, 108-109, 110, 131, 133, 135,
        153
    implicit 41, 48, 91-94, 95, 100, 102,
        104, 109, 131, 153
    informing 34-35, 39, 57, 78, 83, 92,
        94, 96, 98, 100, 107, 117, 133-
        134, 152
    levels of 35-38, 48-50, 91, 135,
        141, 150
        deep 35, 36-38, 42, 48-50, 51, 54,
            59, 72, 76, 77, 88, 90, 109, 111,
            114, 118, 119, 120, 127, 129-
            131, 138, 142-143, 145, 150, 151
        models 40, 51
        shallow 36-38, 41, 48, 114, 115,
            135, 140-142, 146
        surface 35-36, 48, 49, 135, 140,
            141
    model 93
    proceeding 34-37, 39, 57, 40, 78,
        83, 92, 94, 96, 100, 107, 133-134,
        152
    tacit 34, 38, 59, 90-94, 95-101, 102-
        109, 110-113, 114-117, 124, 126,
        131-132, 143, 146, 149-153
        affective 98-99, 108-109, 117-
            118, 127, 130
        aspects 96-102
        embedding tacit kn 104, 105, 107-
            109, 112-114
        embodied 96-97, 107, 110, 117
        engaging 91-114
        inducing resonance 104, 110, 114

intuitive 97-98, 108
sensory vii, 96-97, 101, 103, 116, 119, 120, 122
spiritual 99-101, 109, 110, 116
sharing tacit kn viii, 103-104, 109, 112
surfacing tacit kn 103-106, 112-114
truth of vi, 33-34
learning 24, 34, 38, 54, 59, 61, 63, 70, 72, 73, 76-78, 88-89, 103, 104, 106-109, 113, 116, 126-127, 128, 130, 132, 139, 147, 148
barriers to 131
embodied 96
experiential 35, 88, 96, 97, 113
levels of 38-39, 49, 142
deep 60
model 40
surface 36-37
lifelong 15, 105, 117
mind/brain, in 81-82, 85
organizational 35, 46, 76, 120
shifting frame of reference 38-39
spiritual 100-102
tools 52, 58
value, as 135, 138-139
wisdom, in relationship to 151, 152
mind/brain 79
cortex 87-89
hierarchal patterns 84-86, 87
invariant form 83, 89
model for decision-making 80-89
Net Generation x, 134-139, 140, 143-144, 147
social creatures 139-144
systems
adaptation 15, 16, 22, 24, 26, 29, 52, 63, 71
structural 55
agents 22, 23, 24, 26, 28, 46, 54, 63, 68
background 20-21
boundaries 19, 28-29, 30, 33, 43, 45, 53, 145

chaotic 22, 24-25, 27, 42, 78
complex adaptive
(see complex adaptive systems)
complicated 23, 34, 40, 42
definition 19
environment 23-24, 26-31, 34-35, 39, 41, 43-45, 46, 48, 52-55, 57-59
equifinality 26
feedback loops 26, 44-47, 52, 63, 65, 67, 70, 73, 76-78, 82, 87-89, 97-98, 115, 118, 147, 152
information, as 33
inputs 26-27, 46, 85, 113, 116, 122
internal complexity 27, 63, 78
nonlinearity 23, 27, 45, 52
outputs 26, 27
patterns vii, ix, 19, 20, 22, 27, 29, 30, 33-34, 37-38, 42-43, 44, 45, 49, 51-52, 56, 58, 60, 61-64, 66, 73, 74, 76, 79, 80-83, 84-86, 90-92, 96, 97, 111-114, 116, 118-119, 121-124, 138, 142-143, 145-146, 151-154
mind/brain 87-89, 106, 107-109, 117
principles 29-31
purpose 29
self-organization 28, 63, 64, 66, 71
sinks 28, 44, 61, 65, 89, 146
sources 28, 44, 61, 65, 73, 75, 89, 146, 153
information 88
knowledge creation, of 38, 49, 96, 112, 116
structural 61, 73
structure 28, 29-30, 31, 64
system dynamics 20, 44, 76
systems space model 25
systems thinking 11, 20-21, 26, 29, 31, 76
terms and definitions 26-29
watchmakers parable 155

theory
  chaos 27
  competence 100
  complexity 51, 67
  definition 51-52, 79
  personal ix, 38, 79
  systems 20-21, 27, 29
uncertainty 12-15, 18, 24, 26, 54, 57,
    64, 66, 73, 77, 91, 132, 133, 145,
    147
unconscious vii-viii, ix, 14, 18, 35,
    37-40, 49, 56, 59, 62, 68, 70, 79,
    83, 84, 86, 93, 115, 116, 120, 123,
    124, 125, 128, 130, 139, 143-144,
    145, 146, 147, 153-154
  multidimensional vii, 53, 85, 100,
    144
  tacit kn, as 93, 97, 102, 103-109
    112-114

(see also knowledge, tacit)
values ix, 13, 18, 56, 58, 59, 70, 74,
    88, 89, 100, 109, 114, 116, 118,
    120, 125, 129-132, 134-139, 143,
    150
  collaboration 137
  contribution 138
  creativity 138-139
  emerging 134-139
  empathy 135-136
  integrity 135
  learning 138
  participation 136-137
  transparency 136
  valuing 126
wisdom 18, 69, 89, 100-101, 108, 119,
    145, 149-154
  knowledge spectrum, in 100

About Mountain Quest Institute

MQI is a research, retreat and learning center dedicated to helping individuals achieve personal and professional growth and organizations create and sustain high performance in a rapidly changing, uncertain, and increasingly complex world.

Current research is focused on Human and Organizational Development, Knowledge, Knowledge Capacities, Adult Learning, Values, Complexity, Consciousness and Spirituality. MQI has three questions: The Quest for Knowledge, The Quest for Consciousness, and The Quest for Meaning. **MQI is scientific, humanistic and spiritual and finds no contradiction in this combination**. See www.mountainquestinstitute.com

MQI is the birthplace of Organizational Survival in the New World: The Intelligent Complex Adaptive System (Elsevier, 2004), a new theory of the firm that turns the living system metaphor into a reality for organizations. Based on research in complexity and neuroscience—and incorporating networking theory and knowledge management—this book is filled with new ideas married to practical advice, all embedded within a thorough description of the new organization in terms of structure, culture, strategy, leadership, knowledge workers and integrative competencies.

Mountain Quest Institute, situated four hours from Washington, D.C. in the Monongahela Forest of the Allegheny Mountains, is part of the Mountain Quest complex which includes a Retreat Center, Inn, and the old Farm House, Outbuildings and mountain trails and farmland. See www.mountainquestinn.com The Retreat Center is designed to provide full learning experiences, including hosting training, workshops, retreats and business meetings for professional and executive groups of

25 people or less. The Center includes a 26,000 volume research library, a conference room, community center, computer room, 12 themed bedrooms, a workout and hot tub area, and a four-story tower with a glass ceiling for enjoying the magnificent view of the valley during the day and the stars at night. Situated on a 430 acres farm, there is a labyrinth, creeks, four miles of mountain trails, and horses, Longhorn cattle, Llamas and a myriad of wild neighbors. Other neighbors include the Snowshoe Ski Resort, the National Radio Astronomy Observatory and the CASS Railroad.

About the Authors

Drs. Alex and David Bennet, co-founders of the Mountain Quest Institute and co-authors of *Organizational Survival in the New World: The Intelligent Complex Adaptive System* (Elsevier, 2004) and *Knowledge Mobilization in the Social Sciences and Humanities: Moving from Research to Action* (MQIPress, 2007). They may be contacted at alex@mountainquestinstitute.com

Alex Bennet, a Professor at the Bangkok University Institute for Knowledge and Innovation Management, is internationally recognized as an expert in knowledge management and an agent for organizational change. Prior to founding the Mountain Quest Institute, she served as the Chief Knowledge Officer and Deputy Chief Information Officer for Enterprise Integration for the U.S. Department of the Navy, and was co-chair of the Federal Knowledge Management Working Group. Dr. Bennet is the recipient of the Distinguished and Superior Public Service Awards from the U.S. government for her work in the Federal Sector. Alex is a Delta Epsilon Sigma and Golden Key National Honor Society graduate with a Ph.D. in Human and Organizational Systems; degrees in Management for Organizational Effectiveness, Human Development, English and Marketing; and certificates in Total Quality Management, System Dynamics and Defense Acquisition Management.

David Bennet's experience spans many years of service in the Military, Civil Service and Private Industry, including fundamental research in underwater acoustics and nuclear physics, frequent design and facilitation of organizational interventions, and serving as technical director of two major DoD Acquisition programs. Prior to founding the Mountain Quest Institute, Dr. Bennet was CEO, then Chairman of the Board and Chief Knowledge Officer of a professional services firm located in Alexandria, Virginia. He is a Phi Beta Kappa, Sigma Pi Sigma, and Suma Cum Laude graduate of the University of Texas, and holds degrees in Mathematics, Physics, Nuclear Physics, Liberal Arts, Human and Organizational Development, and a Ph.D. in Human Development focused on Neuroscience and adult learning. He is currently researching the nexus of Science, the Humanities and Spirituality.

We hope you have enjoyed this book.

MQIPress is a wholly-owned subsidary of Mountain Quest Institute, LLC, located at 303 Mountain Quest Lane, Marlinton, West Virginia 24954, USA.

Possibilities that are YOU!

These little **Conscious Look Books** are focused on sharing 22 large concepts from *The Profundity and Bifurcation of Change*. Conversational in nature, each with seven ideas offered for the graduate of life experience. Available in soft cover from Amazon.

eBooks available in PDF format from MQIPress (US 304-799-7267 or alex@mountainquestinstitute.com) and Kindle format from Amazon. (Softback copies available mid-2019)

Five in-depth eBooks, *The Profundity and Bifurcation of Change*, heavily referenced and resourced. These books lay the groundwork for the **Intelligent Social Change Journey** (ISCJ), a developmental journey of the body, mind and heart, moving from the heaviness of cause-and-effect linear extrapolations, to the fluidity of co-evolving with our environment, to the lightness of breathing our thought and feelings into reality. Grounded in development of our mental faculties, these are phase changes, each building on and expanding previous learning in our movement toward intelligent activity. Available as eBooks from Amazon. (Available 2019 in soft cover.)

eBooks and soft-back copies available from Amazon.com

The Course of Knowledge: A 21st Century Theory

by Alex Bennet and David Bennet with Joyce Avedisian (2015)

Knowledge is at the core of what it is to be human, the substance which informs our thoughts and determines the course of our actions. Our growing focus on, and understanding of, knowledge and its consequent actions is changing our relationship with the world. Because **knowledge determines the quality of every single decision we make**, it is critical to learn about and understand what knowledge is. **From a 21st century viewpoint,** we explore a theory of knowledge that is both pragmatic and biological. Pragmatic in that it is based on taking effective action, and biological because it is created by humans via patterns of neuronal connections in the mind/brain.

In this book we explore *the course of knowledge.* Just as a winding stream in the bowls of the mountains curves and dips through ravines and high valleys, so, too, with knowledge. In a continuous journey towards intelligent activity, context sensitive and situation dependent knowledge, imperfect and incomplete, experientially engages a changing landscape in a continuous cycle of learning and expanding. *We are in a continuous cycle of knowledge creation such that every moment offers the opportunity for the emergence of new and exciting ideas, all waiting to be put in service to an interconnected world.* Learn more about this **exciting human capacity**!

Expanding the Self: The Intelligent Complex Adaptive Learning System

by David Bennet, Alex Bennet and Robert Turner (2015)

We live in unprecedented times; indeed, turbulent times that can arguably be defined as ushering humanity into a new Golden Age, offering the opportunity to embrace new ways of learning and living in a globally and collaboratively entangled connectedness (Bennet & Bennet, 2007). In this shifting and dynamic environment, life demands accelerated cycles of learning experiences. Fortunately, we as a humanity have begun to look within ourselves to better understand the way our mind/brain operates, the amazing qualities of the body that power our thoughts and feelings, and the reciprocal loops as those thoughts and feelings change our physical structure. This emerging knowledge begs us to relook and rethink what we know about learning, providing a new starting point to expand toward the future.

This book is a treasure for those interested in how recent findings in neuroscience impact learning. The result of this work is an expanding experiential learning model call the Intelligent Complex Adaptive Learning System, adding the fifth mode of social engagement to Kolb's concrete experience, reflective observation, abstract conceptualization and active experimentation, with the five modes undergirded by the power of Self. A significant conclusion is that should they desire, adults have much more control over their learning than they may realize.

Leading with the Future in Mind: Knowledge and Emergent Leadership

by David Bennet and Alex Bennet with John Lewis (2015)

We exist in a new reality, a global world where the individuated power of the mind/brain offers possibilities beyond our imagination. It is within this framework that thought leading emerges, and when married to our collaborative nature, makes the impossible an everyday occurrence. Leading with the Future in Mind, building on profound insights unleashed by recent findings in neuroscience, provides a new view that converges leadership, knowledge and learning for individual and organizational advancement.

This book provides a research-based tour de force for the future of leadership. Moving from the leadership of the past, for the few at the top, using authority as the explanation, we now find leadership emerging from all levels of the organization, with knowledge as the explanation. The future will be owned by the organizations that understand and can master the relationships between knowledge and leadership. Being familiar with the role of a knowledge worker is not the same as understanding the role of a knowledge leader. As the key ingredient, collaboration is much more than "getting along"; it embraces and engages.

The nature of the organization has moved beyond the factory and process metaphor, and is now understood as an intelligent complex adaptive system (ICAS). Leading with the Future in Mind covers the essentials of working, learning, and leading in an ICAS, covering knowledge and complexity, but also passion and spiritual energy. As social creatures living in an entangled world, our brains are linked together. We are in continuous interaction with those around us, and the brain is continuously changing in response. Wrapped in the mantle of collaborative leadership and engaging our full resources—physical, mental, emotional and spiritual—we open the door to possibilities. We are dreaming the future together.

Other books by the authors and available on Amazon...

Organizational Survival in the New World: The Intelligent Complex Adaptive System

by Alex and David Bennet (Elsevier, 2004), available in hard and soft formats from Amazon.

In this book David and Alex Bennet propose a new model for organizations that enables them to react more quickly and fluidly to today's fast-changing, dynamic business environment: the Intelligent Complex Adaptive System (ICAS). ICAS is a new organic model of the firm based on recent research in complexity and neuroscience, and incorporating networking theory and knowledge management, and turns the living system metaphor into a reality for organizations. This book synthesizes new thinking about organizational structure from the fields listed above into ICAS, a new systems model for the successful organization of the future designed to help leaders and managers of knowledge organizations succeed in a non-linear, complex, fast-changing and turbulent environment. Technology enables connectivity, and the ICAS model takes advantage of that connectivity by fostering the development of dynamic, effective and trusting relationships in a new organizational structure. AVAILABLE as a hardback and as an eBook FROM AMAZON.

Knowledge Mobilization in the Social Sciences and Humanities: Moving from Research to Action

by Alex Bennet and David Bennet (2007), available in hard and soft formats from Amazon.

This book takes the reader from the University lab to the playgrounds of communities. It shows how to integrate, move and use knowledge, an action journey within an identified action space that is called knowledge mobilization. Whether knowledge is mobilized through an individual, organization, community or nation, it becomes a powerful asset creating a synergy and focus that brings forth the best of action and values. Individuals and teams who can envision, feel, create and apply this power are the true leaders of tomorrow. When we can mobilize knowledge for the greater good humanity will have left the information age and entered the age of knowledge, ultimately leading to compassion and—hopefully—wisdom. AVAILABLE as an eBook FROM AMAZON

Also available in PDF format from MQIPress (US 304-799-7267 or alex@mountainquestinstitute.com) and Kindle format from Amazon.

REMEMBRANCE: Pathways to Expanded Learning with Music and Metamusic®

by Barbara Bullard and Alex Bennet (2013)

Take a journey of discovery into the last great frontier—the human mind/brain, an instrument of amazing flexibility and plasticity. This eBook is written for brain users who are intent on mining more of the golden possibilities that lie inherent in each of our unique brains. Begin by discovering the role positive attitudes play in learning, and the power of self-affirmations and visualizations. Then explore the use of brain wave entrainment mixed with designer music called Metamusic® to achieve enhanced learning states. Join students of all ages who are creating magical learning outcomes using music and Metamusic.® AVAILABLE as an eBook FROM AMAZON

The Journey into the Myst (Vol 1 of The Myst Series)

by Alex Bennet and David Bennet (2012)

What we are about to tell you would have been quite unbelievable to me before this journey began. It is not a story of the reality either of us has known for well over our 60 and 70 years of age, but rather, the reality of dreams and fairytales." This is the true story of a sequence of events that happened at Mountain Quest Institute, situated in a high valley of the Allegheny Mountains of West Virginia. The story begins with a miracle, expanding into the capture and cataloging of thousands of pictures of electromagnetic spheres widely known as "orbs." This joyous experience became an exploration into the unknown with the emergence of what the authors fondly call the *Myst*, the forming and shaping of non-random patterns such as human faces, angels and animals. As this phenomenon unfolds, you will discover how Drs. Alex and David Bennet began to observe and interact with the *Myst*. This book shares the beginning of an extraordinary *Journey into the Myst*.

Patterns in the Myst (Vol 2 of The *Myst* Series)

by Alex Bennet and David Bennet (2013)

The Journey into the Myst was just the beginning for Drs. Alex and David Bennet. Volume II of the *Myst* Series brings Science into the Spiritual experience, bringing to bear what the Bennets have learned through their research and educational experiences in physics, neuroscience, human systems, knowledge management and human development. Embracing the paralogical, patterns in the Myst are observed, felt, interpreted, analyzed and compared in terms of their physical make-up, non-randomness, intelligent sources and potential implications. Along the way, the Bennets were provided amazing pictures reflecting the forming of the *Myst*. The Bennets shift to introspection in the third volume of the series to explore the continuing impact of the *Myst* experience on the human psyche.

Made in the USA
Middletown, DE
03 June 2023